A Tapestry for the Soul

Psalm 67
Lamnatzeach!

A Tapestry for the Soul—
The Introduction to the Zohar
by Rabbi Yehudah Lev Ashlag

Explained using excerpts collated from his other writings,
including suggestions for inner work

Compiled by Yedidah Cohen

Nehora Press

Publisher:
Nehora Press:
P.O.Box 2586, Har Canaan, Safed 13410 Israel
tel: 972-4-6923254
email: nehora@actcom.co.il
www.nehorapress.com

©Yedidah Cohen 2010
First edition
Printed in USA
(Translated from *Ma'arag l'Neshamah—Hakdamah leSefer haZohar me'et haRav Yehudah Lev Ashlag*)

ISBN 9789657222041
Printed on acid-free paper from sustainably managed forests.

Library CIP data:
Ashlag, Yehudah.
  A tapestry for the soul-- the introduction to the Zohar : explained using excerpts collated from his other writings, including suggestions for inner work / by Rabbi Yehudah Lev Ashlag ; [trans. and] compiled by Yedidah Cohen. -- 1st ed.
       p. : ill. ; cm.
   Includes a translation of: Ma'arag leNeshamah: Hakdamah leSefer haZohar. Includes bibliographical references and index.
   ISBN: 978–965–7222–04–1

1. Ashlag, Yehudah. Hakdamah le-Sefer ha-Zohar. 2. Zohar--Criticism, interpretation, etc. 3. Cabala. I. Cohen, Yedidah. II. Title. III. Title: Hakdamah le-Sefer ha-Zohar. English.

BM525.A59 A7735 2009
296.1/62

For the reader: There are holy Names of God printed in this book. Please be mindful to treat the book respectfully, not taking it into the bathroom or leaving it on the floor.

for Mark
and for
Shahar
May their holy memories inspire us
and be for us a blessing

Contents

Preface and acknowledgements   ix

Introduction to *A Tapestry for the Soul*   13

Lesson One
Questions on the nature of God   17

Lesson Two
Inquiries into the nature of creation   27

Lesson Three
The ultimate aim and purpose of creation   37

Lesson Four
The substance of creation; the essence of the souls; affinity and difference of form   47

Lesson Five
The nature of evil; the different routes that body and soul travel; the purpose of the *mitzvot* in the healing of the will to receive for oneself alone; the means by which the higher levels of the soul are drawn to the person   57

Lesson Six
The states in which the souls exist simultaneously; free will   83

Lesson Seven
The true nature of the body and its purpose; the end of suffering; where am I acting from?   101

Lesson Eight
The essence of the soul; how desire begets needs and needs give birth to thoughts as to how to satisfy those needs; the differences between people   111

Lesson Nine
The language of the branches; the revival of the dead; the true goal and fulfillment of the will to receive   137

Lesson Ten
The work of our lives; further concerning the framework of uncleanness   147

Lesson Eleven
The purpose of the higher worlds; the final state of the souls; the development of the wills to receive   171

Contents

Lesson Twelve
The perception of the person who splits the shell of the will to receive for oneself alone   185

Lesson Thirteen
The relationship of the soul with the higher worlds; the *mitzvot*   205

Lesson Fourteen
The lights of the *Sephirot*, the vessels and the worlds; the ascension of the soul through the worlds   217

Lesson Fifteen
The ascension of the soul (*continued*)   225

Lesson Sixteen
The holographic nature of reality and its relationship to Torah; the nature of the book of the *Zohar* and its authorship   249

Lesson Seventeen
The revelation of the Kabbalah in our generation and the nature of our generation compared to previous generations   255

Lesson Eighteen
The innermost aspect of the Torah and its relationship to Israel and the world   261

Rabbi Yehudah Lev Ashlag
    Biography   268
    The Revelation of the Hidden   269

Original Kabbalah Art by Avraham Loewenthal   272

Glossary   274

Bibliography and Resources   283

Index   285

Index of Excerpts   295

Yedidah Cohen   296

Preface

When you pick up a book your questions are: What is this book? Who is it for?

This book is a study guide to a key text in Kabbalah, *the Introduction to the Zohar* by Rabbi Yehudah Lev Ashlag, as published in English in *In the Shadow of the Ladder*. It is for the student of Kabbalah who wants to learn directly from Rabbi Ashlag himself, without any intermediary. It is for the student who wants to use Kabbalah as it is meant to be used; as a tool to explore who we are, what are our souls' deepest desires, and what we are here in this life for.

You may ask, "Do I need any prior knowledge to use this book?" Not really. In principle it is self-contained. That said, I have to confess it is a book you are going to have to ponder over, discuss with your friends, read several passages more than once, argue with, consider, reconsider, write in your journal, and dialogue with. You may need to send me email questions, if and when you get stuck. You may wish to join or form a study group on this book—several have already formed prior to the book's publication in English—or you may wish to read it on your own.

A Tapestry for the Soul is a compilation of Rabbi Ashlag's work taken from a wide variety of his writings, arranged to accompany the on-going text of the *Introduction to the Zohar*, such that Rabbi Ashlag *himself* is teaching the *Introduction*. I would like to point out that this work is **compiled** but not edited; it really is Rabbi Ashlag who is the teacher. Here is authentic Kabbalah.

Most of the book consists of texts by Rabbi Ashlag, the twentieth century Kabbalist successor to both Rabbi Shimon Bar Yochai, the author of the *Zohar*, and to the Ari, Rabbi Isaac Luria, the author of the *Etz Chayim* (Tree of Life). However, I have included suggestions for journal work as an aid to seeing connections between the writings and our individual lives.

Should you read *In the Shadow of the Ladder* first? Both books have their place and are not similar to each other. *In the Shadow of the Ladder* may be compared to an overall view of a wood, *A Tapestry for the Soul* may be likened to focusing on some of the trees. The books may therefore be read or studied in any order. Hopefully, by the time you have finished *A Tapestry for the Soul* you will be well equipped for any further reading in the field of Jewish Kabbalah. Material you may find useful, including material that deals with how to apply the wisdom of the Kabbalah in our lives, may be found on our web-site, www.nehorapress.com. Equally, your insights, questions, and sharing of experiences, are all welcome. For those wanting to start a study group, there is special guidance available through the web-site.

Having myself been privileged to study the work of Rabbi Ashlag, it is my greatest pleasure to try and convey to you something of my own experience and excitement as I explore the different threads that make up the vast tapestry of his work.

With all my blessings that our learning should bring benefit to all humanity,
Yedidah Cohen

Acknowledgements

My husband Mark lived to read the first draft of the completed book in the original Hebrew, *Ma'arag l'Neshamah*, and I felt his presence throughout the book's writing.

I would like to thank my mother, Chaya Goodman, whose never-failing support has been crucial for this project. I would also like to thank Larry Loewenthal, Sary Manor, and Reuven Goldfarb for their editorial suggestions, Avraham Loewenthal for the generous donation of his art work and his ongoing enthusiasm, and Professor Michael Dickel for his thoughtful input on the journal work.

I would especially like to thank my English-speaking *chevrutas* and groups who show me how much they need authentic translations of Rabbi Ashlag in English.

Finally I would like to thank my sons Yigal and Asaph and my daughters Binah and Brachah who, day in and day out, show their support for this work by their patience, love, and understanding.

There are no words at all to express the debt of love and appreciation we all owe to the Masters Rabbi Yehudah Lev Ashlag and Rabbi Baruch Shalom haLevi Ashlag, may their holy memory be for a blessing. Working on this material brings me again and again back to the beginning, back to the question, Who am I? I give thanks to the Almighty for the incredible privilege and grace He has bestowed upon me of allowing me this precious task of bringing this holy wisdom to others.

A Tapestry for the Soul

Note to the Reader: I have done my best to deal with the gender issue relating to him and her. I respect the feelings this issue arouses. However the original texts were mostly written using the masculine gender only, and continually translating "he" as "he or she" proved to be either cumbersome or ungrammatical. I have had to come to a compromise: I have used "he or she" occasionally where possible, to remind us all that the work applies to both genders, but otherwise I have used "he" as referring to both genders. It is clear from the below quotations that the creation of the human being, his and her spiritual development and complete rectification, depend upon us all, male and female alike.

> *This is the book of the generations of Adam. On the day that God created Adam He created him in the image of God. Male and female He created them and He blessed them and He called their name "Adam" on the day of their creation. (Genesis 5:1-2)*

> *Adam (Man) is both male and female and is not called "Adam" except with the inclusion of both. (Zohar)*

> *He created them male and female and He called their name "Adam." Each one alone is only half a body and is not called "Adam." (Perush haSulam on above Zohar)*

> *The use of "he" as a pronoun for nouns embracing both genders is a simple practical convention rooted in the beginnings of the English language. (Strunk and White, The Elements of Style, fourth edition)*

Introduction to a Tapestry for the Soul

The *Zohar* is one of the central texts of the Kabbalah, the esoteric wisdom of Judaism. For centuries it was locked away, inaccessible to the understanding of ordinary men and women due to its very specific language. Rabbi Yehudah Lev Ashlag (1886-1955), may his memory be for a blessing, unlocked the code in which it was written in his great commentary on the *Zohar* called the *Perush haSulam* (The Ladder).

Rabbi Ashlag wrote several introductions to the *Zohar*, each one looking at its main ideas from different perspectives. Each of these "introductions" are, in fact, works of great complexity; nevertheless, they are often the first encounter a person has with the teaching of Rabbi Ashlag or even with the wisdom of the Kabbalah at all. In *A Tapestry for the Soul* we shall be studying the *Introduction to the Zohar (Hakdamah l'Sefer haZohar)* from its beginning to its end in a way that will uncover layers of meaning, look into its depths, and enable us to become acquainted with some of Rabbi Ashlag's other works.

Rabbi Ashlag opens the *Introduction to the Zohar* with questions we all ask at one time or another. What am I? What is God? What is the purpose of creation? What is the purpose of my life? Is there meaning in suffering? He continues by considering the origin of the soul, its evolution down through the higher worlds into the reality of this physical world, and the unique association it creates with the body. Rabbi Ashlag goes on to examine the true purpose of our lives and the help we can gain in fulfilling our potential through the esoteric wisdom of the Torah. He emphasizes the practical work of unconditional service, both in the traditional role of the commandments (*mitzvot*) and as opportunities that present themselves in the course of our daily interactions. This learning, as it brings light to our soul's path, illuminates our lives and allows us to see our true role as human beings more clearly.

Rabbi Ashlag addresses all of us, Jew and non-Jew, religious and secular. His concern is universal, being the establishment of the world of love for all humankind. In his lifetime he wrote extensively on the need for economic and social justice for society as a whole, but here in his *Introduction to the Zohar* it is the individual he is addressing, as it is at this level that change begins.

Introduction to a Tapestry for the Soul

The difficulties readers experience when they first approach Rabbi Ashlag's work stem from the fact that his works as a whole form a tapestry. Slowly, the reader begins to gather threads that weave an inner picture, incredible in its beauty. My role in collating, translating, and organizing this material is to help in the task of gathering the threads, but the relationship the reader develops is with Rabbi Ashlag alone. There is a tremendous importance in the direct encounter between the *Tzaddik*, the enlightened Master, and the student. No one can stand in Rabbi Ashlag's place as the teacher. As we shall learn in this work, the way in which the *Tzaddik* perceives the processes of both the higher spiritual worlds and those of this world, is totally different from that of the ordinary person. As we study the work of the *Tzaddik* we become imbued with the light of the *Tzaddik* himself.

Rabbi Ashlag, in all his writings, emphasizes the true purpose of learning this wisdom. The connection between ourselves and our Creator is through the holy soul that resides uniquely in each one of us. Yet it is largely unknown to us, and we are unaware of its importance, its actions, and its desires. Through studying the innermost part of Judaism, the Kabbalah, the soul of Judaism, we awaken the surrounding light that illuminates our soul. This rouses us to connect with our Creator, each in his or her own way. Therefore, throughout this work I have drawn the reader's attention to the possibilities of inner work inherent in the study. This is done in several ways: 1) by asking questions for the reader to look at in his or her own life, 2) through suggestions for journal work, and 3) through the inner work as explored in essays by Rabbi Baruch Shalom haLevi Ashlag, Rabbi Ashlag's firstborn son. Through these aids we can take our study personally and make it our own. Although the learning of the material itself, in which we try to discover Rabbi Ashlag's meaning, is best done in a group or with a friend, the inner work, being subtle and intimate, is largely conducted by oneself alone. I, personally, very much recommend the reader to dialogue with the material, with himself or herself, and suggest the use of a journal to record feelings, intuitions, and thoughts as they arise. The essays written by Rabbi Baruch Shalom haLevi Ashlag, based on oral discourses he heard from his father, were composed by him in the last years of his life in order to give practical guidance to his students on the spiritual path invoked by the Kabbalah.

In this *Introduction* Rabbi Ashlag discusses issues on which each one of us holds preconceived ideas. These are liable to interfere with our ability to hear what Rabbi Ashlag is really saying. A good approach to this material is to lay one's own opinions down for the duration of the study session in order to listen to Rabbi Ashlag with an open mind and an open heart. Only in this way can we avoid projecting our own ideas onto the material and distorting its message.

The way that Rabbi Ashlag teaches is different from the way that you and I have learned in the West. Western culture demands that we master the material we are learning, but in the study of the Kabbalah our approach is more humble. Any contact that we have with this material is seen as a very great privilege. Even when we read it without managing to understand it, we still need to be grateful for even the slightest contact with this wisdom. If questions arise for which we have yet to receive answers, we wait patiently, with an inner attitude of respect, valuing the question as the vessel for the answer, its light. As opposed to other fields of thought, wherein we progress in a straight line from A to B, the learning of Kabbalah is spiral in nature. Similar to life itself, it has patterns that repeat in varied forms. We find the same questions arising again and again, the answers coming at their own pace, naturally and when we are ready for them.

It is clear that we have merited a light that no previous generation was privileged to receive. The Kabbalah is accessible to us without pre-conditions of spiritual attainment. Until recently, a person had to be of the stature of a *Tzaddik* in order to have the Kabbalah opened to him; it was not available to women at all. Rabbi Ashlag, in his great love, did that which no other Sage did; he opened this great treasure for everyone. It is incumbent on all of us to treat this wisdom with the respect it deserves.

A note on the translation: Many people have negative associations with respect to the term "God." This is the accepted translation for the Hebrew term *haShem* (literally 'the Name'). As we shall learn in the context of the *Introduction* itself, there is no created intelligence that can know God as the One really is. This knowledge is in itself freeing, as it releases us from any inner imagery we may have. So, if you find a term being used that is not comfortable for you, feel free to change it. You may find "The Power of Love" or "The Root of all" as being more appropriate.

Terms used in the texts: Very often we find that Rabbi Ashlag introduces a new term but only explains its meaning further on in the material. I have tried to help the reader by inserting very short explanations of unfamiliar terms and of including a comprehensive glossary. Patience helps. Again, the process of the learning mirrors life!

Introduction to a Tapestry for the Soul

A Tapestry for the Soul comprises eighteen lessons in which we learn the entire *Introduction to the Zohar*, from beginning to end. Excerpts are taken from Rabbi Ashlag's other writings to illustrate the concepts discussed. These excerpts actually constitute the main writing of this book, as I have tried to keep my voice limited to pointing out issues under discussion, raising questions and clarifying sources. The excerpts are listed in the end of the book under "Bibliography and Resources," and there is also an Index of Excerpts.

Original artwork: Avraham Loewenthal, a student of Rabbi Ashlag and a gifted artist, whose work is inspired by his learning of the Kabbalah, has very kindly donated the artwork for the front cover, the frontispiece and a piece for reflection between chapters. The purpose of the art in Kabbalah is to provide an aid for inner reflection and meditation. Each piece is a unique artistic expression of a specific aspect of the wisdom of the Kabbalah.

For more complete details of the artwork see the section "Original Kabbalah Artwork by Avraham Loewenthal," on page 272.

Lesson One

Questions on the nature of God
Paragraph 1 from the Introduction to the Zohar

Rabbi Ashlag opens the *Introduction to the Zohar* with questions that touch us all. These are questions that concern the nature of reality and the purpose of our lives. The answers to these questions form the rest of this work.

In this first lesson we shall try and understand the questions that Rabbi Ashlag asks, just as they are. Although we may already have ideas concerning these issues, it is important to refrain from giving our own answers, as this interferes with our ability to relate to what Rabbi Ashlag is saying. A good approach to adopt is one of an open heart and an open mind, enabling us to truly hear what Rabbi Ashlag has to teach.

When we consider the questions Rabbi Ashlag is asking we first of all need to understand them in Rabbi Ashlag's own terms, only then can we look and see how they apply to ourselves. We begin with the first paragraph:

Introduction to the Zohar

> 1. In this *Introduction* I would like to clarify some seemingly simple matters. These are issues with which everyone is, to some extent, involved, and much ink has been spilled in the effort to clarify them. Despite this, we have not arrived at a sufficiently clear understanding of them.
>
> The first question we would like to ask is, "What is our essence?"

What does Rabbi Ashlag mean by the word 'essence' (Hebrew: *mahut*)? Rabbi Ashlag defines the term 'essence' in his essay *Mavo l'Zohar* (Prologue to the Zohar):

> We need to study now the four different ways we use to think about things. These are: *a)* matter, *b)* form that is clothed in matter, *c)* abstract form, and *d)* essence.
>
> I shall first explain them in connection with things that appear to the senses in this world. For example, when we talk about a warrior or a sincere person or a liar, we have: *a)* his matter, which is his body, *b)* the form that is clothed in his matter, which is his bravery, his truth, or his falsehood, *c)* abstract form—that is, it is possible to abstract the idea of being brave, or of being true, or of being

false from the matter of the man, and understand these three forms, as they are in themselves, as abstract virtues, not clothed in any matter or body. That is, we may conceive of the qualities of bravery, of veracity, or of falsehood, and be able to discern in them positive or negative values when they are abstracted from any matter.

   d) The essence of the man.

From this we can see that Rabbi Ashlag rules out the possibility that a person's essence is the body (matter); neither is it the personality (which would be the form, or combinations of form, that are enclothed within the body), nor does a person's essence consist of abstract qualities. So what is the essence of a person?

> And you should know that as regards the fourth characteristic, which is the essence of the man as he is in himself without matter, we have no conception of it whatsoever. Our five senses and our imagination can only show us the **actions** of the essence, but cannot reveal to us anything of the essence as it is in itself.
> … Our own essence itself, or what it consists of, is completely unknown to us. I feel and know that I take up a place in the world. I am solid, I am hot, and I think, which are some manifestations of the actions of my essence, but if you were to ask me, "What is my essence, my Self from which all these manifestations come?" I would not know what to answer you. Behold! The Divine Providence has withheld from us the ability of conceiving of **any** essence. We are able to grasp only overt manifestations or images of actions, which come forth from essences.[1]

So when Rabbi Ashlag asks, "What is our essence?" he means: What is that aspect of ourselves that is completely unknown to ourselves, which we cannot sense directly, imagine or grasp intellectually, yet which causes outward manifestations of its presence?

  At this stage Rabbi Ashlag is simply asking the question; his answers will emerge as we learn.

We proceed to his second question:

Introduction to the Zohar   1. *(continued)* Our second question is, "What is our role as part of the long chain of reality of which we are such little links?"

We need to consider two aspects to this question, 1) What is this long chain of reality? and 2) How are we links in it?

Lesson one

Rabbi Ashlag writes in his work *Hakdamah l'Panim Meirot u'Masbirot* (Introduction to the Welcoming and Illuminating Revelations) that consequent to Adam and Eve eating from the Tree of Knowledge, the one eternal soul that was theirs in the Garden of Eden left them. Instead, this soul split up, becoming all the souls that make up the human community—past, present, and future—such that each of us forms a part of the one original eternal soul that God created and gave to Adam and Eve.

To understand the following excerpt from the *Hakdamah l'Panim Meirot u'Masbirot*, we need to know that receiving for oneself alone separates us from the Creator. This type of receiving originates from the very beginning of creation, at the stage known as the *Tzimtzum*. Concerning this we shall learn subsequently:

> From this you may understand the severity of the consequence that followed the eating from the Tree of Knowledge, wherein all human beings became destined for mortality. This is the death, resulting from the eating, of which God forewarned Adam, "on the day that you eat from it you will surely die" (Gen. 2:17). The matter is, there was drawn into Adam's and Eve's limbs a huge form of receiving for oneself alone. This form of receiving came from the *Challal Panui* (empty space), which is the primal vessel of receiving.
>
> This *Challal Panui* is the uncorrected vessel—it receives for itself alone—that came into being following the *Tzimtzum* ('contraction', an initial event in the evolution of the spiritual worlds). Subsequent to the *Tzimtzum* the highest light cannot abide together with such a vessel, therefore, the eternal soul, which is described explicitly in the Scripture as, "and God blew into his nostrils the soul of life" (Gen. 2:7), had to leave Adam. Thus the life of the human became temporal, dependent on a piece of bread.
>
> This life is not eternal life. Unlike Adam's former life that was intended to be in the form of one soul, human life became, in comparison, like little sweat drops of life. That is to say, Adam's former life split into myriad droplets, such that every single drop is one part of his former life.
>
> Thus comes about the matter of the sparks of souls that are shared out among the generations of the entire human community. All the generations of the human community until the last generation, which completes the purpose of creation, form an array of one great chain. In this way, the work of God, may the One be blessed, is not changed at all by the sin of the Tree of Knowledge, but that light of life, that existed in its entirety in the first human, is now drawn out to form a great continuous chain.

Lesson one

> This great chain revolves unceasingly on the wheel of myriad forms until the end of the *tikkun* (the rectification of creation) because the works of God are, of necessity, living and enduring. And we go up in holiness and not down. Understand this very well. [2]

How does the knowledge that you are a part of the one eternal soul touch you personally? How does this knowledge affect the quality of your relationships with those who are close to you? How could it change your attitude towards those with whom you have difficulties? How does the knowledge that we are all part of the one eternal soul apply to the way we see our generation? To the way we see the Jewish people? To our relationship with the whole of humanity?

This is an opportunity for you to consider yourself as a unique part of an ongoing chain. Take the time to write in your journal your thoughts or ideas on each of these questions.

Now consider what Rabbi Ashlag is implying when he states, "And we go up in holiness and not down."

The next three questions that Rabbi Ashlag asks in the *Introduction to the Zohar* relate to the disparity that exists between the Creator, as being perfect and eternal, and our experience as imperfect created beings in this world.

Introduction to the Zohar

1. *(continued)* The third question concerns the paradox that when we look at ourselves we feel that we are defective or fallen to the extent that there can be none as despicable as ourselves. But when we look at the Creator who made us, then we find that we must really be creations of such high degree that there are none more praiseworthy than ourselves, since it has to be the case that from a perfect Creator only perfect works can issue.

This question contains a paradox in which there are two elements; one relates to our nature, the second relates to God's nature.

If we look at ourselves we see our own imperfections, our negative tendencies both of body and emotions. We are not always in good health, we often feel depressed, we do things we feel ashamed of afterwards. Yet if we consider the Creator, who made us, as the ultimate of perfection, then since He made us it follows that we really are perfect beings—despite appearances and despite our own experience—because from a perfect Creator only perfect works could issue.

However, one could infer that God is not a perfect Creator as His works seem to be so imperfect. Although this is a logical possibility, it is not compatible with the perception of our Sages.

At this point we need to consider the fact that the *Tzaddik* (the Sage who has reached enlightenment) perceives the works of God, that is to say God's Providence, in a way that is totally different from the way the ordinary person perceives the world and its events. You may find the following discussion taken from *In the Shadow of the Ladder* (Mark and Yedidah Cohen) to be of help.

> The Purpose of Creation
>
> "God created the world in order to give pleasure to the created beings," states Rabbi Ashlag in the *Introduction to the Zohar*. This, he says, is the purpose of the creation. It is what we shall experience when the world is based on love.
>
> We all have moments when we experience these words as having a ring of truth to them, but they do not resonate within us in our ordinary consciousness. We have only to look at our own suffering and the suffering of others to know that we are not receiving much pleasure. What can Rabbi Ashlag mean? How does he know that this is the Creator's purpose? He explains in his work *haHakdamah l'Talmud Eser haSephirot* (The Introduction to the Ten *Sephirot*) that our perception of how the One relates to us changes as we grow in our ability to give and to serve. The study of Kabbalah and its practice teach us how to give unconditionally. As we learn how to give, our perception of how God gives to us refines, grows, and changes.
>
> The ultimate perception of Divine Providence is that of the *Tzaddik*, the enlightened master, who knows and experiences that God is Good and does good to all, unconditionally. It is through the perception of the *Tzaddik* that Rabbi Ashlag knows the purpose of creation. Despite the fact that God as the One is, in essence, unknowable, the *Tzaddik* experiences the light that emanates from God as being totally good, totally giving, and totally benevolent to all that is created.[3]

From this we see that it is our perception as ordinary people that is liable to mislead us, as we do not have a true apprehension of the light of God.

Concerning our inability to comprehend the nature of God, the Ari (Rabbi Isaac Luria), the great Kabbalist, teaches in his work the *Etz Chayim* (Tree of Life):

> Before the creation of the four worlds there is the *Ein Sof* (the Infinite). He and His Name are One, in a unity both wondrous and concealed, may the One be

blessed. Even the angels that are closest to Him have no conception of the *Ein Sof*, may the One be blessed, since there is no created intelligence that can conceive of the One as He is, as He has no place, no limit, and no name. [4]

If it is impossible for any created being to conceive of the Creator, how can even the *Tzaddik* comprehend Him? Even more so, how can he apprehend the One as being good and perfect?

That which the *Tzaddik* perceives is actually of the light that emanates from the One, which is the manifestation of His actions, **but of the essence of God none of us have any conception.**

The knowledge that no one knows what the essence of God is, can actually be freeing. Nowadays many people have distorted conceptions of God. These arise from poor previous teaching, cultural conditioning, and factors such as unconscious projections that we put on God that stem from our childhood. The passages below, taken from the book *In the Shadow of the Ladder*, may be helpful in considering these issues:

The Term 'God'

Rabbi Ashlag usually uses the Hebrew word *haShem* (the Name) as referring to God. This is the colloquial term used, both in Hebrew writings and in spoken Hebrew, as a substitute for the holy four-letter Name of God, which is not pronounced. We have translated the term *haShem* as 'God', and this is its accepted translation in the English language. But this carries its own problems. Everyone comes to this work with previous ideas and conceptions carried over from their life-experiences and cultural conditioning, and these can influence our ideas of what God is and color what Rabbi Ashlag is actually saying.

The Ari states, "No thought can grasp the One." The One, in essence, is completely unknowable. No term, name, or attribute that we may ascribe to God can capture the essence of God in any way at all. In this sense, the term 'God' does not have any meaning as such. So, if you have negative connotations or feelings associated with the term 'God', as many of us may have, we suggest that you simply substitute a different term every time you come across the word 'God' in this book. You may find 'The Power of Love' or 'The Source of All', for example, to be more comfortable. [5]

Does God have a Gender?

Modern day sensitivity regarding not specifying a gender for God has helped us look closer at the language used in these texts which seem to be implying that God is a 'He'. Is Rabbi Ashlag simply using language from an older era or is a deeper meaning intended?

Lesson one

Male/female polarity is clearly expressed throughout the Kabbalah. The male, according to the language of the Kabbalah represents the attribute of giving. This stems from the simple biological fact that male-ness is expressed in nature through the capacity of giving seed to the female. Female-ness is expressed by the ability to receive seed from the male. This is as true of the plant and animal kingdoms as it is of the human.

God, referred to as 'He', is thus the Kabbalists' way of expressing that aspect of the light of God which has the attribute of Giver. God referred to as 'She' is commonly termed the *Shechinah* and implies the light of God when displaying the attribute of Receiver.

Since most of the texts relate to the One as acting according to the attribute of Giver, Rabbi Ashlag usually refers to God as 'He'. Rabbi Ashlag uses the term *Shechinah* when God is displaying the attribute of Receiver, and then uses the female form 'She'. It is clear that Rabbi Ashlag is not implying that God has a gender. He states more than once that the essence of the One is unknowable. God as 'He', in the language of the Kabbalah, does not mean that God is a male. It refers to the One when exhibiting the quality of giving benefit. [6]

The fourth question in our text concerns the goodness of God. As the question points out, this is not at all obvious!

Introduction to the Zohar

1. *(continued)* Our fourth question is, "According to our intellect, God must be good and do good, there being no higher good than that which God does. How, then, could the One create so many created beings who, right from the start, suffer and feel pain throughout all the days of their lives? Surely it is in the nature of the Good to do good or, at any rate, not to do so much harm!"

A question from the heart. A question we all ask.

Let yourself feel the pain within this question, identify with the pain in your own way, then write your feelings and your response to them in your notebook.

Introduction to the Zohar

1. *(continued)* Our fifth question is, "How is it possible that an eternal Being, without a beginning or an end, could bring into existence created beings which are finite, die, and have an end?"

Since God created us, shouldn't we be eternal like the One?
Are we like Him?

Lesson one

1. *Mavo l'Zohar, paragraphs 11–12*
2. *Hakdamah l'Panim Meirot uMasbirot, paragraph 18*
3. *In the Shadow of the Ladder, page 7*
4. *Talmud Eser haSephirot, part one, chapter two*
5. *In the Shadow of the Ladder, page 5*
6. *In the Shadow of the Ladder, page 6*

Ein Od Milvado!

"There is nothing other than the One!"

Lesson Two

Inquiries into the nature of creation
Paragraphs 2–3 from the Introduction to the Zohar

In this lesson Rabbi Ashlag continues his research by inquiring into the nature of creation. Once more, Rabbi Ashlag places his focus on the questions that he raises.

The answers to these preliminary questions and inquiries comprise the rest of the *Introduction to the Zohar*.

Introduction to the Zohar

2. In order to completely clarify all these matters, we first have to make some preliminary inquiries. We cannot investigate the essence of God as the One is in Himself, because thought cannot conceive of God's essence in any way at all. We have no notion of God as He is in Himself. However, we can and should investigate God in a way that is positive and fruitful, namely by looking at His acts, may the One be blessed. As the Torah recommends, "Know the God of your father and worship Him" (1 Chron. 28:9). It is also written in the Song of Unity, "From Your works, we know You."

We may ask, What are God's acts through which we may know the One? The Ari writes in the *Etz Chayim* (Tree of Life):

> And then it arose in His undifferentiated will to create the worlds and to bring forth the created beings; bringing to light the perfection of His works, His Names, and His attributes, for this was the reason for the creation of the worlds.

Rabbi Ashlag writes in his work *Matan Torah* (The Gift of the Torah):

> It is as our Sages have explained: From the moment God created the creation, His purpose has been to make His Godliness known to humankind. [2]

Thus we may say it is the creation that constitutes God's acts. And it is through His acts of creation that we may know the One.

Lesson two

Rabbi Ashlag continues by inquiring into the source of creation.

Introduction to the Zohar

2. *(continued)* So our first inquiry is, "How can we conceive of creation as being an innovation; something entirely new that was not included in God before He created it?" After all, it must be clear, if one thinks about it, that there cannot be anything that is not included within God, as commonsense tells us that one cannot give something if one does not have it within oneself to give.

The definition of the Hebrew word *barah* (to create) is, "to give rise to something entirely new." That being so, Rabbi Ashlag questions whether the creation is really a "creation," inasmuch as it cannot be considered as "new," seeing that it is inconceivable that it does not exist within God in some form, before He brought it forth from the potential to the actual.

Concerning this Rabbi Ashlag writes in his work *haPetichah l'Chochmat haKabbalah* (The Gateway to the Wisdom of the Kabbalah):

> For the four letters, Y-H-V-H, which constitute the Name of the Blessed One, encompass all of reality without any exception at all. [3]

This implies that the creation *is* included in the One.

Likewise, it is written in the *Zohar*:

> The Creator is the core principle and root of all the worlds. [4]

Is *everything* included in God? Everything!

Take time to feel and contemplate the depth and profundity of these statements. Write your response to them in your journal before you continue.

Introduction to the Zohar

2. *(continued)* Second inquiry: You may argue that since God is omnipotent, He must be able to create something that is entirely new and which He does not have within Himself! Then the question may be asked, "What may this reality be, concerning which, one may determine that it does not exist within God, but is a completely new reality?"

Here Rabbi Ashlag raises a different possibility: It is, generally speaking, impossible for anyone to give something that he does not have to give. However, since the Creator is omnipotent, we could think that ordinary rules need not apply.

Lesson two

Could it be possible for the One to give that which He does not have within Himself at all?

This question appears to contradict the statements we studied above from the *Petichah l'Chochmat haKabbalah* and the *Zohar*. We need to know that the words "within Himself" refer to God's essence (*the Atzmut*), of which even the *Tzaddik* knows nothing. We only know of the **acts** of the Creator; of the One's **essence** we know nothing at all. The highest level that the *Tzaddik* can contemplate is termed the *Ein Sof* (Infinite), which consists of God's light that has come forth from the essence of God, the *Atzmut*. The Ari explains that it is at this level, the level of the light of the *Ein Sof*, that the source of creation lies. Here are his words from his work, the *Etz Chayim*:

> Know that before the beings came forth, and the created beings were created, there was the simple highest Light filling all of reality. [5]

In order to understand this paragraph we need to know something of the language of the Kabbalah. The Kabbalah was written in a specific language called "the language of the branches." This derives from our spoken language and uses the same words, but in a very particular way, which we shall learn about later on in this book. In the meantime, we may translate this sentence of the *Etz Chayim* from the language of the branches to our spoken language as:

> "The prime cause of all creation is the highest, undifferentiated Light."

This settles Rabbi Ashlag's difficulty. The source of the creation is not the *Atzmut* (God's essence), but the light of the *Ein Sof*, (also considered as the Creator). It is this light, emanating from God's essence, that causes the creation. Thus the creation may indeed be considered both as new *and* as included within the Creator, may the One be Blessed. It is the light of the *Ein Sof* that is the cause and origin of creation.

What is the nature of the light that emanates from the Creator's essence? What did/does it create?

Rabbi Ashlag considers these questions subsequently.

Introduction to the Zohar

2. (continued) Third inquiry: The Kabbalists have said that the soul of the human is part of God in the sense that there is no difference between God and the soul, except that God is the whole and the soul, a part.

Lesson two

A very profound and beautiful statement. Take time to take it in, reflect on it. What does it mean to you to know that your essence is the same as that of the One? How does this make you feel about yourself? Write your response in your journal.

As we begin our day we say:

> Oh my God, the soul that you have given me is pure. You created it, You formed it, You breathed it into me, and You keep it within me … .(Prayer book) [6]

Introduction to the Zohar

2. *(continued)* The Kabbalists have said that the soul of the human is part of God in the sense that there is no difference between God and the soul, except that God is the whole and the soul, a part. The Kabbalists compare this to a stone quarried from a mountain. There is no difference between the stone and the mountain, except that the mountain is the whole and the stone is a part. If we look at this example, we can see that the stone is split off from the mountain by a blade that is specific for this purpose, and which separates the part from the whole. But how can we conceive this as pertaining to God—that He could separate off a part of His essence to the extent that it would leave His essence and become a part which is separated from Him? How can we conceive of the soul as being only a part of God's essence?

Here Rabbi Ashlag is asking: 1) How is it possible for God to separate off a piece of His essence? 2) What is the equivalent, in spiritual terms, of the physical blade which splits the stone from the mountain?

Again Rabbi Ashlag is asking questions but does not yet answer them. Instead he continues his inquiries by looking at the experiences of the created beings in creation.

Introduction to the Zohar

3. Fourth inquiry: The framework of evil in the world—that is to say, the *sitra achra* (the 'other side'), and the *klipot* (the 'shells', the lights that sustain the evil)—is so entirely estranged from God's holiness that one cannot even imagine such an extreme divergence. How is it possible for evil to issue forth and emerge from the Holy One? Not only that, but it is God, who is Holy, who sustains the framework of evil.

Everyone's question. It comes from the fact that **everything** is included in the *Ein Sof*. From the Creator issues *all* of creation, not just the nice part of it.

Now follows an inquiry into the nature of creation which many find somewhat surprising. It is an inquiry into the nature of the body, its purpose during our life-time, and its ultimate purpose in the scheme of creation. The term 'body' in the Kabbalah always refers to the mental, emotional, and spiritual body as well as to the physical. We shall be investigating the nature of the body later on in this *Introduction*.

Introduction to the Zohar

3. (continued) Fifth inquiry: This investigation concerns the revival of the dead. The body is so abject, that from the moment it is born it is destined for death and burial. Not only this, but the *Zohar* tells us that until the body is completely decomposed, the soul cannot ascend to its place in the Garden of Eden as long as any measure of the body still remains. If this is so, why do the dead need to be revived? Couldn't God have just given delight to the souls without the body? What is even more surprising is the statement of the Sages that when the revival of the dead will take place, the bodies will be resurrected together with their blemishes, so that no one can say that this is someone else! Only subsequently will God heal their blemishes. We need to understand why it would matter to God that people might say, "This is someone else," to the extent that He would re-create these blemishes which would then require healing.

Take some time to consider your own thoughts and feelings in connection with your physical body. What do you feel about having an imperfect body? What do you feel about the fact that this body is temporary and destined to die?

Introduction to the Zohar

3. (continued) The sixth inquiry: This concerns the statement of the Sages that the human (*Adam*) is at the center of reality. All the higher worlds, together with this physical world and all that is in them, were only created for the sake of the human (*Adam*).

Rabbi Ashlag in his text uses the Hebrew word *Adam*, which is often translated in English translations as the generic terms 'humankind' or 'Man'. This is distinct from other Hebrew terms for 'man' such as *ish*, or *gever*. This use of the term *Adam* has a greater connotation than we usually realize. Let's read the following excerpt taken from *In the Shadow of the Ladder*:

Adam, the Complete Human Being
The word *Adam* really means the human being who has the potential for exhibiting the highest consciousness and thus becoming one with God. *Adam* represents the archetypal human being, male and female; the one made in God's

Lesson two

image. The first soul that was created was called "Adam," half of which was female and half, male.

So Rabbi Ashlag's usage of the term *Adam* embraces all human beings who work to fulfill their own inner consciousness and potential. Male and female, we are all called upon to do the work of Torah and *mitzvot* (commandments, or good deeds) with full consciousness. Rabbi Ashlag taught that as regards the inner work, there is no difference between a man and a woman. [7]

Read the following passages from the *Zohar* which illustrate this:

We have learned that there are several spiritual levels by which human beings are designated: *Adam, Gever, Enosh, Ish*. The greatest of them all is *Adam*, as it is written in the Scripture, "And God created Adam in His image" (Gen. 1:27), and it is written, "… for in the image of God, He made Adam" (Gen. 9:6), and it is not written *Gever, Enosh*, or *Ish*. [8]

Rabbi Yehudah said to Rabbi Abba, "See, it is written, '… and Adam was not [present] to work the ground' (Gen. 2:5). What is the importance here that the Scripture mentions the name 'Adam'?"

Rabbi Abba said to him, "Come and see; all that exists in the world was only created for Adam, and everything exists for his sake. Therefore, nothing appeared in actuality in the world, and everything got delayed, until the one who was called 'Adam' came.

"And this is what is written, 'And every bush of the field had not yet appeared in the earth, and every grass of the field had not yet sprung up, because God had not caused the rain to fall on the ground and Adam was not [present] to work the ground.' (ibid.)

"'Not yet': [The creation had not yet become manifest] until the higher form that is called 'Adam' appeared. This is what the Scripture means when it says, 'and Adam was not present to work the ground,' that is to say, everything got held up for the sake of this form until it appeared.

"Therefore this form, Adam, was only created in the form that was fitting for him, and this is what is then written, 'then the Lord God created Adam,' with the full Name of God, such that the name 'Adam' implies the perfection of everything and the inclusivity of everything." [9]

Introduction to the Zohar

3. *(continued)* They (the Sages) also required that a person should believe that the whole world was created just for them.

Lesson two

Read the following passage from the Talmud:

> This is to tell of the greatness of the Holy Blessed One: When a person stamps several coins with one imprint, all the coins look alike. But the King of Kings, the Holy Blessed One, stamps each person with the imprint of the first human (Adam), and all of them are his/her offspring, yet each one looks different from every other one. Therefore, since the whole world was created from one human, Adam, every single person needs to say, "It is for my sake that the world was created!" [10]

We are all the offspring of Adam and thus individually unique. Therefore, we need to believe and say that the whole world was created for me, just as it was created for Adam.

This is an important aspect of inner work. When we truly do believe and say that the whole world was created uniquely for ourselves, we begin to see that every person we meet, every situation we come into or up against, has been created specifically for us. Write in your journal about a recent uncomfortable encounter, from the perspective that it was created just for you. Then write in your journal about a recent joyous event that happened to you, again from the perspective that it was created uniquely for you.

Introduction to the Zohar

3. *(continued)* It seems difficult to understand that God troubled to create all these worlds just for the sake of this little person, who, compared with the reality of this world, has only the value of a hair—and even much less if one compares him or her with the reality of the higher worlds, which are without number or limit. Furthermore, why would humankind need all of this?

Just feel the vast dimensions implied in this statement. See how it includes both the incredible vastness of the physical and spiritual creation, and, at the same time, the unique preciousness of each human life.

1. *Talmud Eser haSephirot, part one, chapter one, paragraph 2*
2. *Matan Torah, paragraph 6*
3. *haPetichah l'Chochmat haKabbalah, paragraph 3*
4. *Perush haSulam, volume one, paragraph 191*
5. *Talmud Eser haSephirot, beginning part one, chapter one*
6. *Siddur, beginning, Birkhot haShachar*

A page from the *Zohar*, Perush HaSulam

לח   תזריע

בְּמַר, דְּלָא יָדַע אֵינָשׁ טַעֲמָא דְּמַתִּיקָא, עַד דְּטָעִים מְרִירָא, מַאן עָבֵיד לְהַאי מְתִיקָא. הֲוֵי אוֹמֵר הַאי מְרִירָא. וְהַיְינוּ דִּכְתִיב גַּם אֶת זֶה לְעוּמַת זֶה עָשָׂה הָאֱלֹהִים. וּכְתִיב טוֹב אֲשֶׁר תֶּאֱחֹז בָּזֶה וְגַם מִזֶּה אַל תַּנַּח יָדֶךָ.

קז תָּאנָא בְּכַמָּה דַרְגִּין אִתְקְרֵי ב"נ: אָדָם, גֶּבֶר, אֱנוֹשׁ, אִישׁ. גָּדוֹל שֶׁבְּכֻלָּם אָדָם. דִּכְתִיב, וַיִּבְרָא אֱלֹהִים אֶת הָאָדָם בְּצַלְמוֹ. וּכְתִיב כִּי בְּצֶלֶם אֱלֹהִים עָשָׂה אֶת הָאָדָם. וְלָא כְּתִיב, גֶּבֶר, אֱנוֹשׁ, אִישׁ. א"ר יְהוּדָה, אִי הָכִי, וְהָא כְּתִיב אָדָם כִּי יַקְרִיב מִכֶּם קָרְבָּן לַיְיָ. מַאן בָּעֵי לְמִקְרַב קָרְבָּנָא. מַאן דְּאִיהוּ חַטָּאָה וּכְתִיב אָדָם.

קח אָמַר ר' יִצְחָק ת"ח, קִיּוּמָא דְּעָלְמָא וְתַתָּאִין, הוּא קָרְבָּנָא. נַיְיחָא דְּקוּבְּ"ה. וּמַאן אִתְחֲזֵי לְמִקְרַב קַמֵּיהּ הַאי נַיְיחָא, הֱוֵי אוֹמֵר הַאי אָדָם, דְּיַקִּירָא מִכֹּלָּא. א"ל אִי הָכִי, הָא כְּתִיב, אָדָם כִּי יִהְיֶה בְעוֹר בְּשָׂרוֹ וְגוֹ', וְהָיָה בְעוֹר בְּשָׂרוֹ לְנֶגַע צָרָעַת. אָמַר לֵיהּ, לְהַאי בָּעֵי קוּבְּ"ה לְדַכָּאָה יַתִּיר מִכֹּלָּא, דְּמַאן דְּאִיהוּ בְּדַרְגָּא עִלָּאָה דְּכֻלְּהוּ, לָא לֵיתִיב הָכִי.

מסורת הזהר
ז) (קהלת ז) שמות פה צ"ל. ה) (שם). ו) (בראשית א) הקסה"ז קפא צ"א. ז) (שם ט) שמות קיד צ"מ. ח) (ויקרא א) יתרו קד צ"ח.

חלופי גרסאות
ג מוסיף משום דכתיב. ד מוסיף ולא גבר אנוש איש, מאן. ה ל"ג וכתיב אדם. ו יתחזי. ז ל"ג האי. ח יקירא. ט יתיב.

הסולם

מאמר

ואע"פ שמתגלה סכלות במקום חסרון החכמה, הנה כנגד זה, נמצא לומד החכמה מן הסכלות הזאת, כלומר שהחכמה שמשיג הוא מכח הסכלות הזה שאינו נוגע בו, כנ"ל, וע"כ אינו נחשב לסכלות ממש, אלא **לְזעיר מן שטותא**, המספיק ללמוד ולדעת החכמה המאירה. וז"ש, והיינו דרב המנונא סבא, **כד הוו ילפין מניה חבריא רזי דחכמתא**, דהיינו שהיו לומדים ממנו איך להמשיך החכמה המאירה, הוה מסדר קמייהו פרקא דמלי דשטותא, בגין דיית תועלתא לחכמתא בגיניה, שהיה מסדר להם, שלא ימשיכו החכמה בפרקי ג"ר דחכמה, אשר הסכלות מתגלה אז בפרקים ההם, ולימד אותו שמסכלות הזה יבא תועלת לחכמה המאירה. כנ"ל. הה"ד יקר מחכמה ומכבוד סכלות מעט. כי כל עוד שהאירו הג"ר דחכמה, ולא היתה סכלות מעט, הרי היתה החכמה בבחי' הבל ורעות רוח, בלי חכמה ובלי כבוד, ועתה אחר שנתיחד השמאל עם הימין, אע"פ שיש סכלות מעט מחמת חסרון הג"ר דחכמה, הנה בשביל זה היא מאירה ברוב פאר והדר, שהמשיגה זוכה לחכמה וכבוד. וע"ד כתיב, ולבי נוהג בחכמה, היינו בו"ק דחכמה. ולאחוז בסכלות, היינו שלא להמשיך הג"ר דחכמה. וז"ש, טוב

(דפו"י דף מ"ז ע"ב *) דף מ"ח ע"א)

אדם איש

אשר תאחז בזה, דהיינו בחכמה, וגם מזה אל תנח ידך, שתאחוז גם בסכלות של חסרון הג"ר דחכמה.

קז תאנא בכמה דרגין וכו': למדנו, בכמה מדרגות נקרא בן אדם, שנקרא, אדם, גבר, אנוש, איש. הגדול שבכולם הוא אדם. שכתוב, ויברא אלקים את האדם בצלמו. וכתוב, כי בצלם אלקים עשה את האדם, ולא כתוב, גבר, אנוש, איש. אר"י, אם כן, הרי כתוב, אדם כי יקריב מכם קרבן לה'. מי צריך להקריב קרבן, היינו רק מי שהוא חוטא, שהוא מדרגה גרועה, וע"ז כתוב אדם.

קח **אמר ר' יצחק** וכו': אר"י, בוא וראה, הקיום של העולם, של העליונים ושל התחתונים הוא קרבן, שהוא נחת של הקב"ה, ומי ראוי להקריב לפניו נחת הזה, הוי אומר, שהוא האדם, היקר מכל, דהיינו שהוא יקר מגבר, אנוש, איש. אמר לו, אם כן, הרי כתוב, אדם כי יהיה בעור בשרו וגו' והיה בעור בשרו לנגע צרעת, ועכ"ז נקרא אדם. אמר לו, לזה, צריך הקב"ה לטהר אותו יותר מכל אחר, כי מי שהוא במדרגה עליונה על הכל, דהיינו אותו שנקרא אדם, לא ישב כך בלי טהרה.

ובגין

7. Translator's Introduction
8. Zohar, Tazria, paragraph 106
9. Zohar, Tazria, Perush haSulam, paragraph 113
10. Sanhedrin 37a

Ein Od Milvado!

"There is nothing other than the One!"

Lesson Three

The ultimate aim and purpose of creation
Paragraphs 4–6 of the Introduction to the Zohar

Introduction to the Zohar 4. In order to understand all these questions and investigations, one strategy is to look at the creation as a process and to examine its end state, which is the ultimate aim of creation. After all, it is not possible to understand any process by examining it while it is still developing. Only by looking at its final outcome can one understand it.

This is a very important point. A tailor takes a perfect piece of cloth and then cuts it up! If you did not know the ultimate aim of the tailor you would be quite justified in considering the tailor as being either mad or a vandal. It is not possible to know the ultimate aim of the tailor if all you see are the separate bits of fabric. To understand any process you have to know its ultimate aim; in this case, it is to make a garment.

Rabbi Ashlag is drawing our attention to the fact that we, like the pieces of cloth, are in the **process** of creation and we have not yet reached its completion. Therefore, in order to understand the process that we are in, we need to consider creation's ultimate purpose.

Introduction to the Zohar 4. (*continued*) It is clear that we are not dealing with a Creator who created the world without purpose. Only someone who had taken leave of their senses could conceive of a Creator who had no purpose in His creation.

From the fact that we ourselves work and create with a purpose, we can extrapolate that our Creator, who is our source and our root, certainly does.

Introduction to the Zohar 4. (*continued*) I know that there are certain self-styled wise men who do not follow the path of Torah, who say that God created the whole of reality but left it to its own devices, seeing that the created beings, being so worthless, were not fitting for such an exalted Creator to oversee their petty and despicable ways. But what they say is nonsense, for it would not be reasonable to assert that we are petty and worthless unless we had already concluded that we had created ourselves with all our defective and despicable tendencies.

Lesson three

We do often consider ourselves as being worthless or feel that we are petty, but Rabbi Ashlag is questioning this. Are we really petty and worthless? Who decides this? Only an incompetent creator would or could create worthless objects. If we decide we are worthless, then maybe the Creator is incompetent. But there is another possibility … .

Introduction to the Zohar

4. *(continued)* But from the moment we decide that the Creator, who is Perfect beyond all perfection, is the craftsman who created and planned our bodies with all their positive and negative tendencies, then we also have to say that from a perfect worker an imperfect or defective work can never issue.

This implies that we actually are perfect created beings, and certainly not defective as we so often seem … .

Introduction to the Zohar

4. *(continued)* Every work testifies to the quality of its maker. What blame may be attached to a shoddily made garment if an incompetent tailor sewed it? The story is told in the Talmud of Rabbi Elazar, the son of Rabbi Shimon, who chanced to meet an extremely ugly man. He said to the man, "How ugly you are!" "Tell the Craftsman who made me, 'How ugly is the vessel you have made!'" replied the man.

Here follows the full excerpt from the Talmud:

> It happened that Rabbi Elazar the son of Rabbi Shimon was coming from the study house of his teacher at Migdal Gedud. He was riding on his donkey, wandering by the side of the river, and feeling a great happiness. He was feeling pleased with himself because he had learned a lot of Torah. He happened to meet an extremely ugly man who addressed him, "Greetings, Rabbi!" But Rabbi Elazar did not reply.
>
> Rabbi Elazar said, "Ignorant man! How ugly you are. Maybe all the citizens of your town are as ugly as you?"
>
> The man replied, "I do not know; but go and tell the Craftsman who made me how ugly the vessel is that He made."
>
> Since he knew for himself that he had sinned, Rabbi Elazar got down from his donkey and prostrated himself before the man and said, "I apologize, please forgive me."
>
> The man said to him, "I shall not forgive you until you go to the Craftsman who made me and say to Him, 'How ugly is the vessel that You made!'"[1]

Lesson three

In telling this story from the Talmud, Rabbi Ashlag is emphasizing that the responsibility for the product rests on the creator who made it. Therefore, the responsibility for the outcome of the creation and the quality of the created beings rests entirely on the Creator.

Introduction to the Zohar

4. *(continued)* Philosophers who claim that it is due to our own lack of worth and insignificance that it was not fitting for God to watch over us, and so the One abandoned us, only publicize their own ignorance. If you were to meet a person who could invent new created beings just so that they should suffer and experience pain throughout their lives as we do, and, not only that, but who would then discard them as worthless without even wanting to supervise them in order to help them a little, wouldn't you despise such a person? Is it possible even to consider such a thing about God?

If it is inconceivable that we ourselves would act in this way, then how can we consider such a thing about the Creator who made us? From where do we know that behavior such as this is wrong? Our very judgment that it is unethical and despicable to create created beings who suffer all the days of their lives **also stems from the Creator who made us.**

Introduction to the Zohar

5. So common sense dictates that we understand the opposite of what appears, superficially, to be the case. **We are actually extremely good and supremely high beings, to the extent that there is no limit to our importance. We are entirely fitting creations for the Craftsman who made us.** Any lack that you might like to raise concerning our bodies, after all the excuses one might make, must fall squarely on the Creator who created us. He created us together with all our tendencies. It is clear that God made us and we did not make ourselves. He also knows all the processes that are consequent on our nature and on the evil tendencies He planted within us.

This paragraph contains two very important points: The first testifies to our real self-worth. The second relates to the Creator as a perfect Creator, who knows all the tendencies that He planted within us, and all their consequences.

> "We are actually extremely good and supremely high beings, to the extent that there is no limit to our importance. We are entirely fitting creations for the Craftsman who made us."

Lesson three

This above statement is a statement of heart-stopping wonder. It is at such variance with our upbringing, our experience, and our feelings of shame and guilt that so often come upon us. Take some time to ponder it. Meditate on it, breathe it in to your being. Write your feelings in your journal.

The second point that Rabbi Ashlag indicates above is that God knows all the processes and consequences of our nature that He, as our Creator, planted within us. This places the responsibility for our basic nature, and all that is consequent on it, on our Creator. It also implies that our evil tendencies are not there by accident, or because something went wrong, but because they have a purpose.

Introduction to the Zohar

5. *(continued)* But, as we have said, we must look to the end of the process of creation, and then we shall be able to understand it all. There is a proverb that says, "Do not show your work to a fool while you are still in the middle of it."

We have seen that considering something that is in process without knowing its ultimate aim is problematic, to say the least. Unless we know the purpose of the creation we can (and do) quite easily misunderstand God's intentions and actions towards us and towards the rest of the creation. We also do not understand ourselves correctly and misjudge our own qualities.

Our defective tendencies belong to the *process* of creation rather than to its ultimate aim. So therefore we *can* infer that God really is the perfect Craftsman and we *are* His perfect created beings. It is just that we are within the *process* of creation and not yet (at least in our everyday consciousness) at its superb finish.

Introduction to the Zohar

6. **Our Sages have taught us that God's only purpose in creating the world was in order to give pleasure to His created beings. It is here that we need to put our eyes and focus our thoughts because it is the ultimate aim and purpose of the creation of the world.** [2]

Consider these words carefully: "God's purpose in creation is to give pleasure to the created beings." Everything follows from this. Yet this is not our experience. Our lives do not appear to reflect the purpose of creation. We do not experience pleasure in the way the Creator wants us to. We only have to look at the reality of the world, to see and feel the suffering of our brothers and sisters, the destitution that afflicts millions, in order to know that our experience does not match the purpose of creation. As Rabbi Ashlag explains, this discrepancy stems from the fact that we are in the process of creation and have not yet reached its ultimate aim.

Introduction to the Zohar

6. *(continued)* We need to consider that since the purpose of creation was in order to give His created beings pleasure, it was therefore necessary for God to create within the souls an exceedingly large desire to receive all that He planned to give them. After all, the measure of any joy or of any pleasure is proportionate to the measure of our will to receive it, to the extent that as the will to receive grows larger, in like measure the pleasure received is the greater. Similarly, if the will to receive pleasure is lessened, then, in like measure, the pleasure in its receiving is correspondingly reduced.

The very purpose of creation itself necessitates the creation within the souls of a will to receive, that is of the most prodigious measure, compatible with the great amount of joy with which God intends to give delight, for great pleasure and a great will to receive it go together.

Rabbi Ashlag writes on this at the beginning of his book *haPetichah l'Chochmat haKabbalah* (The Gateway to the Wisdom of the Kabbalah):

(Note: The terms "purpose of creation" and "thought of creation" are synonymous.)

The purpose of creation is that God wants to give pleasure to the created beings, according to the gift of His ample hand, may the One be blessed. As a consequence, there was imprinted in the souls a will and great desire to receive God's plenty; for the will to receive is the vessel for the measure of delight that is to be had in the bounty. For, according to the size and urgency of the will to receive that bounty, so corresponds the measure of delight and pleasure to be had in the bounty—no less and no more. The will to receive the bounty, and the bounty itself, are so intimately connected together that they can only be separated in the sense that the pleasure is associated with the flow of giving benefit, and the will to receive it is associated with the created being who receives. Both the bounty itself and the will to receive it come from the Creator and stem necessarily from the thought of creation. However, we distinguish between them, as we mentioned above, in that the bounty stems from God's essence, may the One be blessed, which is to say that the bounty is light, *yesh m'yesh* ('is-ness'), which emanates from God's essence, whereas the will to receive, which is included within the bounty, is the root of all created beings. That is to say, the will to

Lesson three

receive is the root of new creation, *yesh m'ayin*, which implies something that did not have prior existence.

It is certain that there is no aspect of the will to receive in the essence of the Blessed One. Therefore it follows that the said will to receive is the sole material of creation from its beginning to its end. All the myriad variety of created beings, all their happenings, of which there is no measure, and their behaviors—those that have already come into being and those that will manifest in the future—are only different measures and arrays of the will to receive.

Everything that exists within these created beings, that is to say, all that is received within the will to receive, stamped as it is within the created beings, is drawn from God's essence, *yesh m'yesh*, may the One be blessed. This light does not have any aspect of new creation, *yesh m'ayin*, as it is not created at all but is drawn from God's eternity, *yesh m'yesh*.[3]

Rabbi Baruch Shalom haLevi Ashlag explains this above piece in his commentary *Or Shalom* that he taught on the *Petichah l'Chochmat haKabbalah*. The *Or Shalom* is an oral commentary that he taught on his father's works, which was subsequently written down by his students. His teaching on the above excerpt follows below. The words quoted from the *Petichah* itself are emphasized in bold:

> **The purpose of creation is that God wants to give pleasure to the created beings, according to the gift of His ample hand, may the One be blessed. As a consequence, there was imprinted in the souls a great will and desire to receive God's plenty.** Since it was the will of the One to give benefit to created beings, it was necessary to create those who would receive His Goodness. Therefore, He created in the created beings a will and desire to receive. Why? [Seemingly, the question is, Was it not possible to fulfill this purpose without this will to receive?] There is a general rule: Everything that we have in our nature is created by God. To ask, Why did the One do it this way? is to ask a question concerning matters prior to creation. But prior to creation we have no way of apprehending! We may only grasp what is in creation.[4]
>
> When we consider such a nature as is ours, we understand that it is impossible to enjoy anything unless we have a will to receive it or a desire for it. For example: If a person is hungry, he enjoys his meal. But if we were to provide even a banquet for someone who is not hungry he could not enjoy it. And so it is with everything; there is a lack and its gratification, which accords with the measure of the desire for the lack to be satisfied. And the measure of enjoyment is according to the measure of desire.

> In summary: We research only into the nature of creation as it is, and this is called, "By Your deeds we know You."[5] That is to say, all that we know of the Creator are through the One's deeds, which are revealed to us in the creation.
>
> This is what Rabbi Ashlag says: **For the will to receive is the vessel for the measure of delight that is to be had in the bounty. For, according to the size and urgency of the will to receive that bounty, so corresponds the measure of delight and pleasure to be had in the bounty—no less and no more. They are so intimately connected together;** in other words, they are equal. For example: If I have a meal, which aspect causes me the most pleasure? The meal itself or the will to receive it, that is to say my appetite? We have seen that if I have a meal but no appetite, or if I have an appetite but no meal, I have no pleasure. Since that is the case, when I have both the meal and the appetite I cannot separate between them in the sense of deciding which aspect contributes more to my pleasure. So how do we distinguish them? By negative and by positive. **The pleasure is associated with the flow of giving benefit, and the will to receive it is associated with the created being who receives.** We associate the negative with the created being, and the positive, that is the meal itself, we relate to the Creator. **Both of these come from the Creator and stem necessarily from the thought of creation.** In the will of the One, which is to give goodness to the created beings, there are thus two elements: the will to give them pleasure and the will to receive this pleasure, which the One created in them.[6]

Consider this in simple terms. The pleasure we receive in anything is proportionate to the amount we yearn for it and desire it. Thus lack and its gratification is what constitutes pleasure. As Rabbi Ashlag shows above, a banquet is enjoyed when we are hungry. It is not enjoyed if we arrive already satisfied. So the degree with which we feel lack for something is intimately related to the pleasure we receive on satisfying that lack. If we have no desire for something, even if it is good, it becomes a burden. What do you do with a gift a guest brings you but which you do not desire? It's hard even to find somewhere to put it.

But take someone who has been wandering in the desert without water for three days. Finally he comes across an oasis. The pleasure felt on quenching his thirst is immense.

We, together with the rest of humanity, have been wandering in a dreadful desert of the lack of the knowledge of God. Can we even conceive of the pleasure we shall receive when this, the ultimate lack, will be supplied?

Lesson three

List in your journal things you really want. What thoughts or actions do the items on your list lead to? Now consider how desire or lack is the prime motivating force in the Universe.

Can a person desire something he has neither concept of nor has ever experienced? Does a person desire something when they have it already?

What are the essential conditions for desire?

Since it is God's purpose to give the created beings pleasure, can you see how it is of necessity that the One implants within them a desire to receive all that the One wants to give?

Here we can see what our nature consists of and in what sense we are created beings. We are created, in that we have stamped within us the will to receive God's goodness. This will to receive is the nature of creation itself. It is the characteristic of all creation. What is received within this creation is God's light.

I feel this to be the most amazing statement I have ever read concerning the fundamental nature of the created world. I trained in medicine in University College, London. Subsequently I spent some years in research in physiology. I often pondered then on the nature of creation, wondering if there was some grand underlying unifying principle. I know of no statement in any scientific or other literature that so clearly explains the nature of the created world than that we have just learned.

1. *Taanit 20a*
2. *Etz Chayim, Sha'ar haClalim,* chapter one
3. *Petichah l'Chochmat ha Kabbalah,* paragraph 1
4. *Hagigah 11b*
5. *Song of Unity*
6. *Or Shalom on the Petichah l'Chochmat haKabbalah,* paragraph 1

Ein Od Milvado!

"There is nothing other than the One!"

Lesson Four

The substance of creation; the essence of the souls; affinity and difference of form
Paragraphs 7–9 of the Introduction to the Zohar

Prior to beginning this lesson we need to learn some of the basic terms used in the Kabbalah. As we learned in the previous lesson, the will to receive is the desire for the bounty that the One wants to give the created beings. In the language of the Kabbalah the desire is termed 'the vessel', and the bounty that the One wants to give the vessel is termed 'the light'. Here are these terms as brought in an excerpt from *In the Shadow of the Ladder*:

> Light
> In Kabbalah, light is the direct emanation of Divinity. It exists eternally. Its nature is giving benefit. It is referred to as *yesh m'yesh* (is from is). That is to say, it is not something new or created but it always is. "I am God, I do not change" (Mal. 3:6).
>
> Vessel
> The vessel is the will to receive. This is something new, something created, *yesh m'ayin* (something from nothing). It did not exist in an active form in God prior to the creation. It constitutes a lack, so the vessel has the quality of receiving, or desire.
>
> Giving
> The very nature of the light is to give; to bestow; to benefit.
>
> Receiving
> The very nature of the vessel is receiving. If the vessel is empty then it desires to receive. The nature of the vessel is a lack. This is the will to receive.[1]

Let us now continue with the *Introduction to the Zohar*. We start by revising paragraph six:

Introduction to the Zohar   6. Our Sages have taught us that God's only purpose in creating the world was in order to give pleasure to His created beings. It is here that we need to put our

Lesson four

eyes and focus our thoughts because it is the ultimate aim and purpose of the creation of the world. We need to consider that since the purpose of creation was in order to give His created beings pleasure, it was necessary for God to create within the souls an exceedingly large desire to receive all that He planned to give them. After all, the measure of any joy or of any pleasure is proportionate with the measure of our will to receive it, to the extent that as the will to receive grows larger, in like measure, the pleasure received is the greater. Similarly, if the will to receive pleasure is lessened, then, in like measure, the pleasure in its receiving is correspondingly reduced.

The very purpose of creation itself necessitates the creation within the souls of a will to receive that is of the most prodigious measure, compatible with the great amount of joy with which God intends to give delight; for great pleasure and a great will to receive it go together.

7. Now that we know this, we are in a position to understand our second inquiry with complete clarity. We wanted to know, "What is that aspect of reality of which we can be absolutely certain that it is not to be found within God and is not included in the essence of the One, but of which we can say that it is an absolutely new creation, something brought into being which did not exist before?"

Now we know clearly that it was God's purpose in creation, which is to give pleasure to His created beings, that necessitated the creation of the measure of the will to receive from the One all the pleasantness and good that He planned for them. We can now see that it is this will to receive which was most definitely not included in His essence until He created it in the souls, as from whom could the One receive?

So God created something new that does not exist within Himself. It follows directly from the purpose of creation that it was not necessary to create anything else besides this will to receive. This new creation is sufficient for God to fulfill His entire plan of the purpose of creation by which the One intends to give us pleasure. All the content of God's purpose, all the varieties of good which He intends for us, emanate directly from God's essence. He does not create the good anew since it emanates directly from His Being into the large will to receive that is in the souls.

It is thus totally clear that the only created material in the creation itself, from its beginning to its end, is the will to receive.

The entire creation may be expressed in the basic terms of light, and the vessel for the light. What a wonder!

Lesson four

The will to receive, being the substance of creation, is an essential part of the material of every created being.

Consider how this will to receive operates in whichever area you are most familiar with, or with which you have expertise. Look at the ways in which the will to receive manifests itself in the field of psychology; animal behavior; law; governance; politics; the arts; history; medicine; or in simple human behavior as it manifests in the home, within relationships, on the street, or in the daily activities of shopping and going to the bank.

We shall now turn to the book *Talmud Eser haSephirot* (The Study of the Ten Sephirot), in which Rabbi Ashlag defines the essence of the spiritual vessel:

> Commentary on the term *Challal Panui* (empty space)
> In order to explain this term we need, first of all, to know what constitutes the essence of a spiritual vessel. Since the created being receives the bounty of its life-force from the Creator, it has to be the case that it has the will, the desire, to receive this very bounty from Him, may the One be blessed. And you should know that it is the dimension of this will, this desire, that comprises the entire matter of the created being. All that is within the created being aside from this material, is not ascribed to this material, but is attributable to the bounty that the created being receives from the Creator. And not only that, but it is this material that sets the measure of magnitude and stature of every created being, of every spiritual entity, and of every *Sephirah*.
>
> For the emanation of the highest light from the Creator is certainly without measure or dimension, only the created being itself setting a finite dimension to the bounty, since it receives no more and no less than the measure of its desire and will to receive. This is the criterion that operates in spirituality of how much light a vessel may receive, where compulsion is not practised and everything depends on will. Therefore, we designate this 'will to receive' as the created being's vessel for receiving. This vessel is defined as the created being's material aspect, by virtue of which the created being came forth from being included within the Creator, becoming a separate entity. This separate entity is named 'a created being' since it is defined by this material, which is not to be found at all within the Creator. The will to receive certainly does not operate within the Creator, as from whom could the One receive? Understand this well. [2]

Note that when Rabbi Ashlag remarks, "Understand this well," he does not intend that we understand with our minds only. He's actually drawing our attention to some important inner work.

A page from the *Talmud Eser haSephirot*

חלק ראשון
צמצום וקו כולל ב' פרקים

פרק א'

מבאר ענין הצמצום הא' שנצטמצם אור אין סוף ב"ה בכדי להאציל הנאצלים ולברוא הנבראים. ובו ה' ענינים:

א. לפני הצמצום היה אין סוף ממלא כל המציאות. ב. סיבת הבריאה היתה כדי לגלות שמותיו וכינויו. ג. צמצום האור מסביבות נקודה האמצעית. ד. החלל שנשאר אחר הצמצום היה עגול. ה. לפי שאור אין סוף הוא בהשואה, היה הצמצום ג"כ בהשואה שהוא סוד העגול.

לפני הצמצום היה אין סוף ממלא כל המציאות

א) דע כי א טרם שנאצלו הנאצלים ונבראו הנבראים, היה אור ב עליון פשוט ג ממלא כל המציאות. ולא היה שום ד מקום פנוי בבחינת

אור פנימי

מיוסדת על ענינים רוחניים, שאינם תופסים לא מקום ולא זמן, ואין העדר ותמורה נוהג בהם כל עיקר, וכל השינויים הנאמרים בחכמה הזאת, אין זאת אומרת שהבחינה הראשונה נעדרת, ומקבלת צורה אחרת, אלא השינוי האמור, הוא ענין תוספת הצורה לבד, וצורה הראשונה אינה זה ממקומה. כי ההעדר וההשתנות המה מדרכי הגשמיים. וזהו כל הקושי למתחילין, כי תופסים הדברים בביטויים הגשמי בגבולים של זמן ומקום חילוף ותמורה. אשר המחברים השתמשו בהם רק לסימנים בעלמא על שרשיהם העליונים. ולפיכך, אתאמץ לפרש כל מלה ומלה בצביונה הרוחני, המופשט ממקום וזמן וממתמורה, ועל המעיינים מוטל לחקוק היטב בזכרונם את פירוש המלות הזה, כי אי אפשר לחזור עליהן בכל פעם.

א) צורת הזמן הרוחני נתבאר היטב לקמן בהסתכלות פנימית בסופו בד"ה עוד.

ב) היינו האור המתפשט מעצמות הבורא יתברך. ודע, שכל השמות והתוארים הבאים בחכמת הקבלה, אינם ח"ו בעצמות הבורא ית', אלא רק באור המתפשט מעצמותו ית', אמנם בעצמותו ית', אין לנו שום מלה והגה.

* עץ חיים שער א' ענף ב.

כלל. כי זה הכלל, כל מה שלא נשיג לא נדעהו בשם. וזכור זאת ואל תכשל.

ג) ולכאורה תמוה מאד, הלא המדובר כאן הוא בטרם שנבראו העולמות, וא"כ אינו מציאות ישנה כאן, אשר אור העליון צריך למלאותה. והענין הוא, כי כל העולמות וכל הנשמות שישנם העתידים להבראות עם כל מקריהם עד לתכלית תיקונם, הנה הם כולם כבר כלולים בא"ס ב"ה, בכל תפארתם ובכל מלואם. באופן, שיש לנו להבחין ב' עיקרים בכללות המציאות שלפנינו. עיקר א': בבחינת מה שהם קבועים וקיימים בא"ס ב"ה בכל שלימותם ותפארתם. העיקר הב': כמות שהם ערוכים ומשתלשלים ומתחדשים לפנינו מאחר הצמצום הא', בחמשה העולמות המכונים: אדם קדמון, אצילות, בריאה, יצירה, עשיה, כמ"ש להלן. וז"ש הרב, אשר אור העליון הנמשך מעצמותו ית', היה "ממלא את כל המציאות", דהיינו כללות המציאות שבעיקר הא', מבחינת מה שהם ערוכים וקיימים בא"ס ב"ה שמטרם הצמצום. ומשמיענו שאור העליון היה ממלא אותם לגמרי עד שלא נשאר בהם שום מקום פנוי, שיהיה אפשר להוסיף בהם שלימות ותיקון כל שהוא (ועי' היטב בהסת"פ כאן).

ד) פירוש כי בטרם שנבראו העולמות, שהיה אז רק א"ס ב"ה בלבד כנ"ל, לא היה

Lesson four

What inner work can you see in the fact that the Creator is not lacking anything? Does the One need our good deeds? If not, who needs them and why?

Look at the phrase "compulsion is not practised in the spiritual worlds and everything depends on will." Take the time to contemplate this and see how important this principle is, not only in society as a whole, but in our intimate relationships as well. Write on the implications of this statement in your journal, or discuss this statement with your group.

Introduction to the Zohar

8. Now we can come to understand the insight of the Kabbalists of whom we spoke in the third inquiry (lesson 2). We wondered how they could say that the souls are part of God in a way that is equivalent to a stone quarried from a mountain, there being no difference between the stone and the mountain except that one is a part and the other is a whole.

Even if we are to assume that the stone is separated from the mountain by the metal instrument especially designed for this purpose, still, how is it possible to say such a thing regarding God's essence? And by what instrument could the souls become separated from His essence and leave the state of being included within the Creator in order to become the created?

First of all take a moment to meditate on the issue that our truest and deepest essence is actually the same as God's essence. Feel the deep beauty of these words.

Now we shall come to consider what it is that separates us from the Creator. This question concerns the root of all our pain and suffering. In the *Introduction to the Zohar*, Rabbi Ashlag starts by defining the term 'separation' and discusses what causes separation between two spiritual entities.

Introduction to the Zohar

8. (continued) We are now in a position to understand the matter well. Just as a metal instrument cuts and divides a physical object, splitting it into two, so in spirituality, it is difference of form that divides one entity into two. For example, when two people love each other, we may say of them that they cleave to each other as if they were one body. The opposite is also true. When two people hate each other, we say that they are as far from each other as the East is from the West. We are not discussing their locality, whether near or far. Our intention is, whether or not they embody **affinity of form.**

When a person enjoys affinity of form with his or her friend, each one likes what the other one likes and dislikes what his or her friend dislikes. They love each other and are as one with each other. If, however, there is any difference of

Lesson four

form between them, for example, if one loves something even though the friend hates it, then according to the degree of this difference of form, they are removed from each other. Opposition of form occurs when everything that the one loves, the other one hates, and vice versa. Then they are as far away from each other as the East is from the West, at two opposite poles.

Difference of form causes separation, and affinity of form causes togetherness or unity. This is a very important spiritual principle. As we shall see, it is a basic tenet of the wisdom of the Kabbalah.

Take a moment to consider: Is there anyone with whom you embody complete affinity of form? With whom do you embody partial affinity of form? Take a look at someone with whom you manifest differences of form or even opposition of form. List your relationships in your journal. Write down what it is that makes each person similar or different from you.

Do you notice that considering relationships in this way takes out the guilt and the judgment? When we are able to consider differences between ourselves and others as degrees of affinity or difference of form, we can begin to value the one who is different from us without discomfort, criticism, or judgment and to release ourselves from the need to try to change the other person.

Now we go on to consider how this spiritual principle operates with respect to the souls and God.

Introduction to the Zohar

9. Difference of form separates spiritual entities in the same way that a blade separates objects of the physical world, the degree of separation being given by the degree of opposition of form.

From this you may see that the souls have, innately, the will to receive God's pleasure, which, as we have clearly shown, does not exist within God, the Creator—for from whom could the One receive?—And it is this change of form, which the souls acquired, that acts to separate them from His essence, in a way similar to that of the blade that splits the stone from the mountain. It was through this change of form that the souls emerged from the totality of the Creator and became differentiated from Him, thus becoming created beings.

So it is this very will to receive that we have in our nature, planted there in order to fulfill God's purpose of giving us pleasure, which, at the same time separates us from the One! What a paradox!

Lesson four

This paradox is well described by Rabbi Ashlag in his book, *Petichah l'Chochmat haKabbalah* (The Gateway to the Wisdom of the Kabbalah):

> The matter is as follows: Just as physical things are separated from each other through distance in space, so spiritual entities are separated from each other through difference of form between them. You can find this also in this world. An example would be concerning two people who are of like mind. They love each other, and even if they are physically far away from one another, it makes no difference to their relationship. The opposite is also true. If two people are far from each other in their opinions, then they dislike each other, and even if they are physically in proximity to each other it does not bring them any closer together. So difference of form in their way of seeing things distances them from each other, and similarity of form in their way of seeing things brings them close to each other. If, for example, the nature of one person is entirely opposite from the nature of the other, then they are as far away from one another as the East is from the West.
>
> In spirituality this applies in a similar way. All matters of distance, closeness, union and coming together as one, which we discern in the spiritual worlds, are all measures of difference of form. To the degree that spiritual entities are different in form they are separated from each other, and to the degree that they have affinity of form, they join together.
>
> So even that the will to receive is an intrinsic part of every created being, as it is the entire created aspect of the created being, and this is the vessel that is fitted to receive the aim of the thought of creation, nevertheless it is the cause of the created being becoming completely separated from the Creator, as there is a difference of form between it and the Creator, even to the extent of opposition of form. For the Creator is wholly giving and does not have the tiniest spark of receiving, whereas the created being is entirely receiving [in its created nature] and does not have the tiniest spark of giving. There can be no greater difference of form than this. It is thus inevitable that this difference of form separates the created being from the Creator. [3]

How does this separation of the created being from the Creator feel to you? How does this separation express itself and under what circumstances?

When do you feel closer to the Creator? When do you feel further away from the One?

But are we separated from God from His perspective also?

Lesson four

Introduction to the Zohar

9. *(continued)* However, that which the souls attain of God's light comes directly from His Being, from the essence of the One. So from the perspective of God's light, which the souls receive within their vessel—the vessel being the will to receive—no separation exists between the essence of God and between themselves, as the light that they receive is a direct emanation of His Being.

The only difference that exists between the souls and God's essence is that the souls form a portion of the essence of the One. In other words, the measure of light that the souls receive within their vessel, which is their will to receive, is a part which has already separated from God, since it is carried within the will to receive, which has difference of form from the Creator. It is this difference of form that separated the souls from the Creator and made them "a part." Through it, the souls left the aspect of "the whole" and became a part. And so we see that there is no difference between God and the souls, except that one constitutes a whole and the other constitutes a part, just as in the case of a stone quarried from a mountain. Understand this well as there is nothing more to be said in this very high place!

1. *In the Shadow of the Ladder chapter five, pages 206–207*
2. *Talmud Eser haSephirot volume one, chapter one, Or pnimi, paragraph 6*
3. *Petichah l'Chochmat haKabbalah, chapter one, paragraph 13*

Ein Od Milvado!

"There is nothing other than the One!"

Lesson Five

The nature of evil; the different routes that body and soul travel; the purpose of the *mitzvot* in the healing of the will to receive for oneself alone; the means by which the higher levels of the soul are drawn to the person
Paragraphs 10–12 of the Introduction to the Zohar

Introduction to the Zohar

10. Now a doorway has opened for us to understand the fourth inquiry. We asked, "How is it possible that from God's holiness could emerge the whole framework of uncleanness (evil) and the *klipot* ('the shells', the lights which sustain the evil) given that they are absolutely at the opposite pole from God's holiness? How could He possibly support and sustain them?"

As we can see, there are really three aspects to this inquiry: 1) the framework of uncleanness emerges from God's holiness; 2) the framework of uncleanness is in opposition of form from God, who is holy; 3) God sustains the framework of uncleanness and supports it.

Rabbi Ashlag relates to all three aspects, one by one:

Introduction to the Zohar

10. *(continued)* First of all, we need to understand the essential nature of the framework of uncleanness and the *klipot*. These are the great wills to receive that, as we have said, are the substance of the souls' essence inasmuch as they are created; for it is only through their will to receive that the souls are able to receive all the content of the purpose of creation.

This statement is really surprising. Haven't we just learned that the will to receive is the vessel for the light and is consequent to the purpose of creation? Also, that the will to receive is the material of the created being, and that it is the dimension of the vessel which determines the measure of light that the created being is able to receive? We have further learned that from the perfect Creator can only come forth created beings that are perfect; therefore this will to receive must itself be perfect. How then can Rabbi Ashlag define the will to receive as the essence of evil?

Lesson five

In order to begin to answer this question, we first have to define what evil is. We shall study a piece taken from the book *Matan Torah* (The Gift of the Torah) by Rabbi Ashlag.

> In order not to weary the reader, we shall clarify evil and good in a general way. All evil is actually selfish love, which we call 'egoism', since it is in opposition of form to the Creator, may the One be blessed, who has no will to receive for Himself at all, but only desires to give benefit.[1]

We see that evil is selfish love, which is the will to receive for oneself alone without any spark of benefiting others. This is what separates us from the Creator, since such receiving is in opposition of form to God, whose entire will consists only of giving benefit to the created beings.

This is the paradox of the creation. On the one hand, we need the will to receive because it is the vessel that receives within it the light of God. On the other hand, since it is in opposition of form to God, it separates us from God. Furthermore, because of this difference of form that exists between the light and the vessel, the vessel cannot, in practice, receive the light intended for it.

So we are left with the question of how can the souls, who have innately the created nature of the will to receive, ever come into affinity of form with God?

Introduction to the Zohar

10. (*continued*) However, the will to receive does not remain in this form within the souls, for, were it to do so, the souls would, of necessity, be permanently separated from God, because the antipathy of form which is within them would separate them from Him. In order to remedy the matter of this separation that is laid upon the vessels of the souls, God created all the worlds and divided them into two frameworks, according to the inner meaning of the verse, "God made them, one opposed to the other" (Eccles. 7:14). This refers to the four worlds, *Atzilut, Briyah, Yetzirah,* and *Assiyah* of holiness and opposed to them are the four worlds, *Atzilut, Briyah, Yetzirah,* and *Assiyah* of uncleanness. He stamped the will to give benefit within the framework of the four worlds of holiness, removing from them the will to receive for oneself alone, which He placed within the framework of the four worlds of uncleanness, through which they became separated from the Creator and from all the worlds of holiness.

For this reason, that is, because they are separated from holiness, the *klipot* (the lights that sustain the evil) are referred to as 'dead', as in the verse from the Psalms, "They ate the sacrifices of the dead" (Ps. 106:28). The wicked who are attracted to the *klipot* are referred to as 'dead' in the same way. The Sages say that the wicked in their lifetime are called 'dead', as the will to receive for themselves, which has been stamped within the framework of uncleanness, is in opposition of form to God's holiness, thus separating them from the "Life of All Lives."

The framework of uncleanness is at the opposite extreme from the One. God, having no aspect of receiving within Himself, is only giving benefit. The *klipot*, having no aspect of giving benefit, only receive for themselves for their own pleasure. There can be no greater opposition of form than this. We have already seen that spiritual distance starts with a measure of difference of form and ends with opposition of form, which is the ultimate in spiritual distance.

How does the framework of uncleanness manifest in the world around us? Firstly, think of obvious examples, such as the evil dictators the world has known. Then bring it down to our own society. How does the framework of evil manifest in our economic systems, many of which are based on the ethos of everyone for himself or for herself?

Then bring it further down into the more intimate aspects of our lives. How does the framework of uncleanness manifest within families, in relationships that are not honest but which lead to abuse, neglect, violence? Write in your journal on all these aspects. And then finally try and take a few minutes to see how the framework of uncleanness manifests within one's own self, in our thoughts, our feelings, and our acts.

When you have looked at all these levels of the framework of uncleanness and given examples of those aspects which lie outside of us and of those which are within us, write down the opposite of each example in terms of the framework of holiness. "God made them one opposed to the other" is true at every level, even to the smallest detail.

The matter of "one opposed to the other" is illustrated by a parable that appears in the *Zohar*. This parable is called, "The letters of Rav Hamnuna Saba." In it the letters of the Hebrew alphabet represent different vessels for the light, which manifest as different attributes. Since vessels are referred to by the feminine principle in the language of the Kabbalah, I have brought this out in the translation.

Before the creation of the worlds, each letter of the Hebrew alphabet entered before the Holy Blessed One, claiming that God should create the world through her, as she has the very attribute which could bring the world to perfection. However, for each letter it is found she has an equal and opposite negative attribute, leaving the outcome of the world uncertain. The parable examines all the letters, until finally, the Hebrew letter ב *(bet)* appears and maintains that she has the especial attribute, the light of *brachah* ברכה (blessing), which, since it is unopposed by a negative attribute would ensure the world could reach perfection, and thus the Creator should create the world through her. And indeed it is the letter ב which opens the Torah.

Here is the beginning and end of the parable, as it appears in the *Zohar*, accompanied by Rabbi Yehudah Lev Ashlag's commentary on the *Zohar*, the *Perush haSulam* (The Ladder):

Zohar
The Letters of Rabbi Hamnuna Saba
When the Holy Blessed One wanted to create the world, all the letters came before Him, from the last till the first, beginning with the letter ת *(tav)*. She said, "Master of the Worlds, may it be good before You to create the world through me, because I am the seal of Your ring, which is *emet*, אמת (truth) and You are called by the name 'Emet.'" (That is to say that the last letter of the Hebrew word for truth, *emet*, is the letter *tav*.) "It is fitting for the King to begin with a letter of אמת (truth) and to create the world through me." The Holy Blessed One said to her, "You are beautiful and you are honest, but you are not appropriate for the creation of the world because in the future you will be written on the foreheads of those men of faith who keep My Torah from beginning to end, and when they are so written they will die.[2] Furthermore, you seal the word *mavet*, מוות (death), so therefore it is not appropriate to create the world through you." Immediately the letter ת went out.[3]

Perush haSulam
Explanation: This parable of the letters is unfathomably deep. In order to explain it, somewhat, I shall give a short introduction to its scope in this commentary.

The creation of the world implies [the means of] perfecting and existing in such a way that the world will be able to exist and complete the purpose for which it was created. And it is known that "God made them, one opposed to the other" (Eccles. 7:14); meaning that for every power that exists in the framework of holiness, God created an equal and opposite power in the framework of evil, which opposes that which is holy. Just as we have four worlds, *Atzilut*, *Briyah*, *Yetzirah*, and *Assiyah* of holiness, so there are four worlds, *Atzilut*, *Briyah*, *Yetzirah*, and *Assiyah* of uncleanness that oppose them. Therefore, in the world of

Lesson five

Assiyah (which includes this world), one cannot distinguish between one who serves God and one who does not. This implies that there is no clarification at all between holiness and uncleanness. Accordingly, it is very hard for the world to survive, since how can we know how to distinguish between good and evil, between holiness and uncleanness? However, there is one very important clarification, that is, "the false gods are sterile and do not bear fruit." For those who stumble, walking in the ways of the worlds of *Atzilut, Briyah, Yetzirah,* and *Assiyah* of uncleanness, their source dries up and they have no spiritual fruits for blessing. They wither and fade and come to a complete dead end.

The opposite is the case for those who cleave to holiness and merit the blessing of the work of their hands: "And he shall be like the tree planted by rivulets of water, which gives its fruit in its season and whose leaf does not fade, but in all that he does he will succeed" (Ps. 1:3). This is the only clarification in the world of *Assiyah* by which a person may know if he is acting in holiness or, God forbid the opposite. This is the inner meaning of the Scripture, "'And you may test Me by this,' says the Lord of Hosts, 'for surely I shall open for you the storehouses of Heaven and I shall pour out unlimited blessing for you'" (Mal. 3:10). Subsequently the Scripture writes, "Then you will turn and see the difference between the righteous one and the evil one, between the one who serves God and the one who does not serve Him" (Mal. 3:18). It is explicit that there is no way of distinguishing between one who serves God and one who does not serve Him, except through the light of blessing alone and not through anything else, and thus the Scripture writes, "And you may test Me by this."

Here lies the polarity of this entire parable of the letters: They all came before God, without exception, to show that the world may be created through the manifestation of their own particular level in holiness unique to that letter. For the twenty-two letters of the Hebrew alphabet are the individual heads of the spiritual levels found within the four worlds: *Atzilut, Briyah, Yetzirah,* and *Assiyah*. Each letter considered the particular virtue of its own level, showing how by attaining that particular level humankind could bring holiness to prevail over uncleanness, and thus arrive at the desired completion of the *tikkun* (rectification of the creation). However, the Holy Blessed One responded to each letter by showing her that for the positive attribute she represents, there exists an equal and opposite power in the worlds of uncleanness, and therefore through her particular virtue humankind could never achieve any clarification.

Then the letter ב entered, which manifests the virtue of *brachah* ברכה (blessing). There is no opposing force to *brachah* in the framework of uncleanness, because "the false gods are sterile and do not bear fruit." Then the Holy Blessed One said, "Yes, surely, through you I shall create the world," as it is only through

Lesson five

Blessing alone that one is able to clarify and discriminate between one who is serving God and one who is not. Only the virtue of blessing has no opposite force in the *sitra achra* (the 'other side', the framework of uncleanness) and therefore the world can be sure to survive, clarify and cause the framework of holiness to prevail over the framework of uncleanness; until death is swallowed up for ever, and all will come to the end of the *tikkun* (rectification of the world).

The *Zohar* continues the parable by describing for each letter the particular virtue it represents and how each letter entered before the Holy Blessed One, one after the other. But for each letter it was discovered that for the positive force it represented, there exists an equal and opposite negative force from the side of the framework of uncleanness, until the letter ב enters:

In this next section, please note that in the Kabbalah, the "light of wisdom" refers to the light that God wants to give us according to the purpose of creation, and the "light of loving-kindness" is the light the vessel receives when it acts in giving benefit—it is the joy of giving benefit.

Zohar

The letter ב entered and said to the One, "Master of the world, Let it be good before You to create the world through me. For through me we bless You both above and below, as the letter ב represents *brachah* (blessing)."

The Holy Blessed One said to her, "Surely, I shall create the world through you, and you will be the beginning of the creation; the world will be created through you."

Perush haSulam

Explanation: The letter ב has the inner meaning of wisdom (that is to say the loving-kindness of wisdom, such that the light of wisdom is a point enclosed within her temple). For the light of loving-kindness, which is the light of blessing, is the temple for the light of wisdom, in the inner meaning of the Scripture, "I shall pour out unlimited blessing for you" (Mal. 3:10). The light of blessing does not lessen at all as it passes through and cascades down through the spiritual levels. Just as it is at the highest of the levels that is received in the *Ein Sof* (Infinite), so it is in all its magnitude and beauty in the world of *Atzilut*, and so it is right till the end of the world of *Assiyah*. It is unaffected by any of the barriers it passes through.

And this is what the letter ב maintained, "May it be good before You to create the world through me, because through me we bless You both above and below."

That is to say that my light of blessing is equal, both in the higher worlds and in the lower worlds, without any change, because no barrier or density can affect my light in any way. Therefore, my attribute is suitable for the creation of the world as there is no place for the *klipot* (the lights which sustain the framework of uncleanness) to take grasp; for the *klipot* only take hold in a place where there is lack. Since I have no lack, the *klipot* cannot have any hold over me.

The Holy Blessed One said to the letter ב, "Surely, I shall create the world through you, and you will be the beginning of the creation; the world will be created through you."

The One agreed with the letter ב that her attribute of blessing is suitable for the creation of the world. This is the inner meaning of the Scripture, "For I have said, 'a world of loving-kindness shall be built (*yibaneh*)'" (Ps. 89:3).

"The world shall be built"; יבנה (*yibaneh*) implies building (בנין) (*binyan*) and understanding (בינה) (*binah*). (Both words are from the Hebrew root: ב'נ'ה *b.n.h.*) For the One determined the light of blessing to be a sufficient clarification whereby one may distinguish between those who cleave to holiness and those who turn away from God to cleave to a false god. This accords with the inner meaning of the Scripture: "'And you may test Me by this,' says the Lord of Hosts, 'for surely I shall open for you the storehouses of Heaven, and I shall pour out unlimited blessing for you'" (Mal. 3:10). But they who turn away from God and incline to a false god are lacking blessing, for a false god is sterile and does not bear fruit. Thus the prophet concludes, "Then you will turn and see the difference between the righteous one and the evil one, between one who serves God and one who does not serve Him" (Mal 3:18), for surely the world shall be built through loving-kindness. [3]

Blessing is the spiritual fruit we receive when we are on the right path. The world of loving-kindness (*chesed*) is the blessing that comes when we are doing our inner work in a way that is right for our soul. The fruit of the spiritual path are not holy visions or experiences, but the establishment of the world of loving-kindness.

So in our own lives, when we start to put something of our spiritual work into practice, we need to check and see whether we are experiencing and creating more love in our homes and in our relationships, more consideration in our workplace, more patience with our children and our elderly relatives and more kindness among neighbors and friends. If this is so, then we know that our work is blessed and that we are participants with God in creation.

Lesson five

It is only through the blessing, the spiritual fruit, that we can distinguish what is truly good and what is not.

Rabbi Ashlag continues his discussion in the *Introduction to the Zohar* of the two frameworks, of holiness and of uncleanness, and describes them in terms of the different routes that body and soul pass through, from their origin in the *Ein Sof* until they arrive in this world.

Introduction to the Zohar

11. The worlds unfold until we arrive at the reality of this material world where body and soul exist, and likewise a time of spoiling and a time of healing. Our body, which is formed from the will to receive for itself alone, comes forth from its root within the purpose of creation, but it passes via the framework of the worlds of uncleanness, as Scripture says, "A man is born like a wild donkey" (Job 1:12). It remains subject to this framework until a person reaches thirteen years of age. This period is designated "the time of spoiling."

When considering this paragraph we need to understand exactly what is meant by the term 'the body'? What is meant by the term 'material'? Let us look at the *Petichah l'Chochmat haKabbalah* (The Gateway to the Wisdom of the Kabbalah) for Rabbi Ashlag's definition of these words:

> As we have said, the will to receive is inevitably included immediately in the thought of creation—with all the many orders that are in it—together with the great bounty that God planned to bestow, in order to give pleasure to the created beings.
>
> You should know that this is the inner meaning of the words 'light' and 'vessel' as we discern them in the upper worlds. For they come inevitably bound together and cascade down together from stage to stage.
>
> According to the measure that the stages descend from the direct revelation of God's light, becoming estranged from the Blessed One, so corresponds the measure of materialization of the will to receive that is included within the bounty. It is also possible to say the opposite, that according to the measure of materialization of the will to receive that is included within the bounty, so does it descend from stage to stage, until it reaches the lowest place of all in which the will to receive has materialized to its most appropriate measure. This stage is designated by the name of the world of *Assiyah*, and the will to receive is designated as the body of a person. The bounty that the body receives within it is designated as the dimension of life force that is in the body.
>
> Similarly, this process holds for all the other created beings of this world. The distinction between the upper worlds and this world is that so long as the will

to receive that is included within God's bounty has not yet materialized into its final form, it is designated as still being in the spiritual worlds, which are higher than this world. Once the will to receive has materialized into its final form it is designated as being already within this world. [4]

Rabbi Baruch Shalom haLevi Ashlag comments on the above paragraph in his explanation, *Or Shalom* on the *Petichah l'Chochmat haKabbalah* as follows: (The words of Rabbi Yehudah Lev Ashlag from the *Petichah* are in boldface.)

You should know that this is the inner meaning of the words 'light' and 'vessel' as we discern them in the upper worlds. The will to receive at every level is called 'the vessel' and is designated as a new creation (*yesh m'ayin*), and the bounty that comes into the will to receive is called 'the light', which is not created (*yesh m'yesh*). **Inevitably they come bound together,** that is, it is impossible to receive the light if there is no desire to do so. **According to the measure that the stages descend from the direct revelation of God's light and become estranged from the Blessed One, so corresponds the measure of materialization of the will to receive that is included within the bounty.** Here Rabbi Ashlag is saying something new: There is a difference between the One who gives the bounty, and the will to receive the bounty.

When is the will to receive recognizable as a reality in its own right? That depends on the measure of estrangement between itself and the Creator, may the One be blessed. **It is also possible to say the opposite, that according to the measure of materialization of the will to receive that is included within the bounty, so does it descend from stage to stage until it reaches the lowest place of all, in which the will to receive has materialized to its most appropriate measure,** that is to say, it only wants to receive and not to give at all.

At first Rabbi Ashlag said that according to the measure of estrangement so the will to receive materializes; now is he saying the opposite? However, one must say that these two aspects come together; the degree of estrangement from the Creator, and the degree of materialization are equivalent. If we say that the will to receive is in proximity to the Creator, this implies that it has sparks of giving benefit and therefore has affinity of form; if it is estranged, then it has change of form with respect to the Creator. From this it follows that when the created being does not have any sparks of giving benefit it is designated as being totally estranged from the Creator since it is intent only on receiving, whereas the Creator's intention is wholly that of giving benefit. **This stage is designated by the name of the world of *Assiyah*, and the will to receive is designated as**

Lesson five

the body of a person. That is to say, there is a generality (the world), and there are individuals (the body of the human).

The bounty that the body receives within it is designated as the dimension of life-force that is in the body and is called the animal soul (*nefesh behami*). **Similarly, this process holds for all the other created beings of this world.** In this context, when Rabbi Ashlag says, "the world of *Assiyah*," he is actually referring to this world; he refers to this world as the world of *Assiyah* because this world is close to the world of *Assiyah*, and this is the world of doing things in practice. ("*Assiyah*" in Hebrew means doing.) However, the world of *Assiyah* is actually a spiritual world.

In this world, when we look at ourselves or at others, we see that everyone has a will to receive for himself alone. And when we speak of the will to give benefit to others, we do not really understand what this is. Of course we feel it must be a good thing, but what is it? What will I receive in return …?

The general consciousness of this world is that what I want is certainly for my own benefit and there is no need to think twice about it. Beyond this we have difficulty understanding. We can only understand giving benefit if, as a result, we are going to receive in exchange something better than what we already have.

The distinction between the upper worlds and this world is that so long as the will to receive that is included within God's bounty has not yet materialized into its final form, then it is still designated as being in the spiritual worlds, which are higher than this world. Once the will to receive has materialized into its final form it is designated as being already within this world. That is to say, if the will to receive is designated as having materialized, it implies that we can see it.

The will to give benefit is designated as being spiritual, which implies that we still cannot see it. [5]

From this passage we can see that the term 'the body', as used here, actually refers to the will to receive for oneself alone. This is the form of the will to receive that is in opposition of form to God. This will to receive for oneself alone can manifest as the physical will to receive for oneself alone, the emotional will to receive for oneself alone, the mental will to receive for oneself alone, or even the will to receive for oneself alone in the spiritual realm.

While it is true that many of our wills to receive for ourselves alone are generated by our physical body and its desires, supplying our basic physical needs for food, shelter, and so forth, is not considered as a will to receive for oneself alone and does not cause us to be in opposition of form to our Creator. It is when we go beyond our basic needs into greed or thoughtlessness at other people's

Lesson five

expense that the will to receive becomes the will to receive for oneself alone, and we end up in separation from our Creator.

With regard to the emotional wills to receive, Rabbi Baruch Shalom haLevi Ashlag teaches us that the will to receive happiness is a basic need that all people have. Without happiness, or the hope for happiness, a person has no life-force and does not wish to live. Sadly, we see this in small, uncared-for children who, when they do not receive their basic needs for happiness, fail to grow and may even die. When we pin our happiness on outside circumstances, these may change, either for the better, or for the worse, and we may lose our joy. As we grow in spirituality it becomes possible to satisfy our basic need for happiness from within ourselves. We may do this because we have within us a holy soul that has, at its core, a basic happiness. The more we identify with our soul by acting in accordance with the soul's desires, the more we experience a true lasting happiness that is not dependent on external circumstances. Trying to supply our need for happiness through actions that separate ourselves from our Selves, and thus from the One, may distract us for a while, but ultimately cannot produce any lasting happiness.

The mental will to receive is one of the greatest wills to receive that humankind has. It is the motivating force behind the great discoveries in science and technology. But when it is used for itself alone, it produces technologies which endanger our very existence and indeed the whole planet.

The will to receive in the spiritual realm only develops after the age of Bar or Bat Mitzvah but it is not a basic need in everyone. However, if it is used in opposition of form to God, then it likewise constitutes part of the body. Rabbi Ashlag will be dealing with the spiritual will to receive and its development further on in this *Introduction*.

As regards the term 'materialization', we can now understand that this is *not* synonymous with the physicality of this world. It is a state of consciousness. The more concerned we are with our wills to receive for ourselves alone, the more materialized we have become and the more connected we are with the default consciousness of this world, which is that of the will to receive for oneself alone.

Let us now study the definition of the word 'materialization' according to Rabbi Ashlag's description in the *Petichah l'Chochmat haKabbalah*. (In order to understand the passage that follows, we need to know that the vessel, that is to say,

Lesson five

the will to receive, develops through four stages, the completed vessel being the fourth stage.)

> Now you may understand the true definition by which one may distinguish between spirituality and materialism. Everything that has a complete will to receive in all its aspects, which is the fourth level of the will to receive, is called 'material' and is to be found in every aspect of reality arrayed before us in this world. Anything that is higher than this great measure of the will to receive is called 'spiritual' and belongs to the worlds of *Atzilut, Briyah, Yetzirah*, and *Assiyah* and all their reality, which are higher than this world. From this you may understand that the whole matter of ascent and descent that are referred to in the higher worlds do not ever refer to an imaginary place, God forbid, but they refer only to these four modalities of the will to receive. For inasmuch as something is distant from the fourth stage it is considered to be higher, and inasmuch as it comes near to the fourth stage it is considered to be lower. [6]

Rabbi Baruch Shalom haLevi Ashlag comments on this paragraph in his work *Or Shalom* on the *Petichah l'Chochmat haKabbalah*:

> **Now you may understand the true definition by which one may distinguish between spirituality and materialism. Everything that has a complete will to receive in all its aspects, which is the fourth level of the will to receive, is called 'material' and is to be found in every aspect of reality arrayed before us in this world.** A complete will to receive is one that has no spark of giving benefit and has no will to give unconditionally. Such is the reality of the consciousness of this world.
>
> Question: Are the spiritual worlds of *Briyah, Yetzirah*, and *Assiyah* of the framework of uncleanness, which do not have a spark of unconditional giving in them, designated as being material or spiritual?
>
> Answer: They are designated as material. When Rabbi Ashlag says "this world," he does not mean this physical planet, but he means a certain modality of consciousness. For example, take a person wearing a *talit* (prayer shawl): If his intention in doing the *mitzvah* (a prescribed act in accordance with Jewish Law) is to receive the reward of the *mitzvah* for himself, his action is designated as being material. If his sole intention concerning the *mitzvah* is in order to give pleasure to the Creator, his action is designated as being spiritual.
>
> Question: What is the designation of the inanimate, plant, and animal components of this world?

Lesson five

Answer: They do not have any designated value in themselves, they ascend or descend according to the person. That is, if the person goes up in consciousness, they go up with him; likewise, if he descends in consciousness they descend with him. For example, the Holy of Holies was the one place in which it was totally forbidden for anyone to tread except on *Yom Kippur* (the Day of Atonement) when it was permitted for the High Priest alone to enter there. Consider how worthy his clothes were—they merited that which many good and conscious men never attained!

And this [fourth modality of the will to receive for oneself alone] is to be found in every aspect of reality arrayed before us in this world. Anything that is higher than this great measure of the will to receive is called 'spiritual' … . 'Higher' implies something that has an aspect of the will to give unconditionally; inasmuch as [the will to receive for oneself alone] comes near to the fourth stage it is considered to be lower. This will to receive is designated as being lower for two reasons: 1) It is of lesser importance than the Creator, who is the Giver; 2) it is impossible to use it to receive anything (because of the opposition of form between it and the light). So we see that designating something as being higher implies that it has a little of the will to give unconditionally and can therefore be used to receive somewhat.

Accordingly, we may understand the usage of the terms 'ascending' and 'descending'. 'Ascending' refers to the will to give unconditionally, 'descending' refers to the will to receive.

Generally speaking, there are four stages of giving benefit and of receiving: A person has two powers, 1) that of receiving pleasure, and 2) that of giving unconditionally; upon these lie two possible intentions, 1) that of gratifying his lack (his desire) by giving pleasure to himself, or 2) that of giving pleasure to his fellow or to the Creator.

Here are the four stages set out in detail:

1) A person receives; his intention in this receiving is to give pleasure only to himself. This is called 'receiving for the sake of receiving'.

2) A person receives; his intention in the act of receiving is to give pleasure to his fellow. This is termed 'receiving for the sake of giving benefit'.

Rabbi Yehudah Lev Ashlag gives an example of this type of receiving taken from the Talmud.[7] The subject is a marriage in which a man of some importance is marrying a woman of lesser social standing.

Concerning marriages in general, the Talmud derives from the Scripture (Deut. 24:3) that the man should give an object, usually a ring, worth at least a coin, to the woman. The woman is not considered to be married unless the bridegroom gives her such an object, and with this she is married. Then the husband says,

69

Lesson five

"You are sanctified to me … ." In the case where the woman gives the monetary object, even if the man says, "You are sanctified to me …," the marriage is invalid since she is the one who is giving.

In the case we are considering here, which concerns a man of importance, the Talmud says the law changes: Even though the woman gives the object to the man the marriage is valid. Why? Through his accepting the object from her, and thus signifying he will marry her, she receives great pleasure. Through the pleasure that he gives her she is sanctified. This is the case, because even though the man is actually receiving the object from the woman, since his intention in that receiving is to give her pleasure, he is designated as the giver.

So we have proved that there is such a thing as receiving with the intention of giving benefit. Even though we are taking into consideration only the intention, in this case the person receiving is designated as a giver.

3) A person gives benefit; his or her intention through giving is to give pleasure to the other. This is called 'giving benefit for the sake of giving benefit'.

4) A person gives benefit; his or her intention in the act of giving is actually to derive personal pleasure or recompense. This is designated as 'giving for the sake of receiving'. This is possible to see in the above example from the Talmud. The woman is giving the object, but since in actuality her intention in giving the object is to receive pleasure from the important man, she is designated as being the receiver.

Accordingly, we may now understand the terms used to describe the Torah. There is the 'revealed' Torah and the 'hidden' Torah. 'Revealed' refers to practical acts because they are revealed to all. The revealed Torah teaches us how to do deeds. 'Hidden' refers to intentions, since no one can know the intention of another. For example, a person may be a great benefactor, but the intention behind his acts is actually that of receiving; or a person receives, but the intention behind his receiving is actually that of giving benefit. So the hidden Torah deals with intentions. [8]

Can you look at your day and find some examples when you were situated fairly and squarely in the consciousness of this world (that is to say only thinking of the will to receive for oneself alone)? Write these examples in your journal. The more one starts to look, the more one finds. Don't be dismayed. It is part of the process of creation, and part of each and everyone's spiritual journey, as we are going on to discover. It is important to look at our real motives, for without doing so we cannot move from this consciousness.

Lesson five

What does it mean to you to think that materialization and physicality are not synonymous? Can you appreciate that the spiritual worlds may be accessed by states of mind and by our intentions? Consider that physicality may be spiritual. Write what that implies for you.

Rabbi Yehudah Lev Ashlag continues the *Introduction to the Zohar* by discussing how we can rectify the will to receive for oneself alone.

Introduction to the Zohar

11. *(continued)* Then, from the age of thirteen onwards, through performing *mitzvot* (prescribed acts in accordance with Jewish law), which he does in order to give benefit to others and pleasure to the Creator, the person begins to purify the will to receive for oneself that is inherent within him. The person gradually transforms the will to receive for oneself alone into a will to give benefit.

This statement requires some explanation. What is included in the term "Torah and *mitzvot*"? What is special about Torah and *mitzvot* that they have the power to correct or purify the will to receive for oneself alone, which is our very nature? Does Rabbi Ashlag imply that only a religious person can correct himself or herself and come into union with the Creator? What about the secular person? What is special about the age of thirteen?

We need to consider these questions one by one:

Our first question is, What does the term 'Torah and *mitzvot*' include?

Rabbi Ashlag uses the term 'Torah and *mitzvot*' in a number of ways. These are: *a)* acts of loving-kindness that we do for each other, according to our changing circumstances, which cannot be prescribed prior to the circumstance; *b)* the keeping of *mitzvot* according to the *halachah* (prescribed law), including both the *mitzvot* enacted between a person and the Creator and those enacted between a person and his or her fellow; *c)* learning the Torah as a guide to one's inner consciousness.

We shall be further considering the content of Torah and *mitzvot* later in this study.

Our second question is, What is so special about Torah and *mitzvot* that they have the power to purify the will to receive for oneself alone, which is stamped within our nature? Rabbi Baruch Shalom haLevi Ashlag discusses this in his commentary *Or Shalom* on the *Petichah l'Chochmat HaKabbalah*:

Once my esteemed father asked, "What does a person gain from the light of Torah?" He replied, "A person does not want to harm himself. This is a general principle. Therefore, until a person feels that his will to receive for himself alone is evil how can he throw it away? Only through Torah is it possible to see that the will to receive for oneself alone is actually damaging. Without the Torah we cannot see this. This is what Rabbi Hananiah Ben Akashiah meant when he said, 'The Holy Blessed One wanted to give merit to Israel,' that is through the Torah." [9]

One needs to know that the Torah is not just a type of technical spiritual information, but is actually an emanation of the light of God, the goodness of the One. The essence of the Torah and the essence of God are one. Therefore, the Torah has an especial power that the light within it may lead a person back to the right way. Just as the Sages taught, "I created the evil inclination, I created the healing spice of Torah." [10] However, in order that the light of Torah should enlighten a person and not blind him, the practice of Torah must be carried out through the intention of giving benefit and not through the intention of the will to receive for oneself alone.

On the inside cover of his books, Rabbi Baruch Shalom haLevi Ashlag wrote the following:

> The Rabbi of Spinka, in the introduction to his book *Imrei Yoseph* (The Sayings of Joseph), quotes the holy Rabbi Chayim of Sanz on the verse: "The glory of God, hide the matter; the glory of Kings, research the matter" (Prov. 25:2).
> "If a person wants to learn the wisdom of the Kabbalah in order to know how many worlds and how many *Sephirot* there are, that is, he wants to know the glory of God because he wants to know how great is the glory of the Lord, may the One be blessed, then hide the matter. But if he wants to learn this wisdom in order to know how to make God his King; how to serve the One with intention, sanctifying all his limbs and making them into a vehicle for holiness—that is the glory of Kings—how one may crown Him the King and serve Him, then research the matter."

Rabbi Yehudah Lev Ashlag will enlarge on this point later on in the *Introduction to the Zohar*.

The third question we asked above is: Is Rabbi Ashlag addressing only the religious Jew or is he also addressing Jews who lead a secular lifestyle?

Lesson five

When the will to become one with the Creator awakens, one feels like a baby that has just been born. The person says to himself or to herself, "I know that I want to cling to Him and I don't want to live in this dreadful separation any longer, but I don't know what I need to do and where I need to begin." This question awakens in the secular and in the religious Jew alike.

Although the religious Jew observes the practice of Torah and *mitzvot* as prescribed by *halachah*, he or she also needs to begin to practise Torah and *mitzvot*, not from habit or from the education received, but as something completely new. Learning Torah surrounds the soul with the light of God and awakens it to return to its Source. The Torah itself is all one light but it appears in different garbs for the needs of the different souls.

What are the *mitzvot* and how do we do them? This has been taught to us by our Sages of blessed memory, who taught us how to find our way back from this dreadful separation. The outstanding difference between the religious Jew and the secular Jew is that the secular Jew concentrates primarily on the commandments that are practised between one person and another, whereas the religious Jew also fulfills those commandments that are practised between oneself and God. From the perspective of bringing a person into affinity of form with the Creator the difference between them is not so great, as Rabbi Ashlag writes in his essay *Matan Torah*:

> There are in fact two parts to the Torah: a) *mitzvot* that are practised between oneself and God, may the One be blessed, and b) *mitzvot* that are practised between oneself and one's fellow. Both of them address one issue, that is, how to bring the created being to the ultimate purpose of coming into unity with the blessed One.
>
> Even the practical side of these two types of *mitzvot* are one; because when a person does his work for its own sake, without involving selfish love, without gaining anything for himself, then a person does not in fact feel any difference in his acts, whether he is working for love of his fellow, or whether he is working for love of God. [11]

Thus we see that the practice of Torah and *mitzvot* is directed towards every man and every woman of every background or group.

Lesson five

Here follows a section taken from one of the articles on the inner work that Rabbi Baruch Shalom haLevi Ashlag published in the book *Bircat Shalom, Sefer haMa'amarim* (Book of Articles), on the subject of Torah and *mitzvot*.

In this article Rabbi Baruch Shalom haLevi Ashlag uses the concept of 613 *mitzvot*. This is the total number of the *mitzvot*, but we need to know that 613 *mitzvot* are not meant to be carried out by any one person. There are *mitzvot* that are carried out by specific people only, like a king or a *cohen* (priest), or *mitzvot* that may be carried out only in certain specific situations, as for example during the time of the Temple. We shall discuss the concept of 613 *mitzvot* later on in this study. Another concept that Rabbi Baruch Shalom haLevi Ashlag refers to in this article is that the reason the will to receive requires *tikkun* is due to the shame that arises in the vessel as a consequence of the difference of form that exists between the Creator, the Giver, and the created being who is the receiver.

> And we shall expound on the issue of the evil inclination: It is known that the purpose of creation is to give good to the created beings; therefore, God created in them a will and desire to receive pleasure and joy. In order that the created beings would have wholeness at the time when they receive the joy, they should not feel any aspect of shame when so doing. Thus, the *tikkun* that is called 'with the intention of giving benefit' was instituted, which means that the created beings should not want anything for themselves, but they only want to benefit the Creator. In this way they will not feel any shame, since they are not receiving anything for their own benefit, but are only receiving for the benefit of the Creator and not for their own utility.
>
> But we need to know what we may give to the Creator so that the One may have pleasure. Therefore, the Holy One let us know this through Moses our Teacher. He gave us 613 *mitzvot* so we may fulfill these *mitzvot* with the intention of giving pleasure to the One. Only then can the One give us all His Good, and not prior to this, because the vessels of the created beings, which are designated as being the wills to receive for oneself alone, are termed evil—they separate the created beings from the One, May He be blessed—and they are not suited to receive the good and the joy. The will to receive for oneself alone is designated as 'evil' because it is this that causes all the destruction, theft, murders, and suchlike.
>
> But we need to know that the will to receive for oneself alone is also detrimental to ourselves personally. Apart from the fact that it causes harm in the physical world, it ruins our spiritual state so that we can no longer arrive at the purpose of creation, wherein the Creator wants to give goodness to the created

Lesson five

beings and we need to receive the goodness and the joy. This is because the will to receive for oneself alone is in opposition of form to the will to give benefit. That is to say, the Creator is the Giver—whereas we want to receive. Without affinity of form we cannot be in union with the One and cannot receive His Goodness.

However, we can rejoice over the fact that the One let us know, through Moses our Teacher, that by fulfilling Torah and *mitzvot* we can acquire the *tikkun* that is called 'affinity of form'. If the One had not let us know what He wants us to give, we would not know what to give Him. However, since the One told us that we may fulfill the 613 *mitzvot*, we know what we may give Him.

This is like a vegetarian who enjoys eating just fruit and vegetables, and who invites an important person to his home and wants to prepare a meal for him. But being vegetarian himself, he is not used to preparing a regular meal that includes all types of food that vegetarians do not eat. Consequently, he has to go to great pains to find out what this important guest is used to eating. If the guest were to provide him with a menu of the type of food he likes to eat, how happy he would be, as now he would know what to prepare for the guest's meal.

Therefore, we need to be happy that the One told us through Moses, our Teacher, what gives Him pleasure, so that we do not have to go to the trouble of finding out how we can give the One pleasure. This is the essence of the 613 *mitzvot* that He gave us to fulfill. If we have the intention of giving pleasure to Him when practising Torah and *mitzvot*, then we may come into affinity of form with the One. This is called 'clinging to His attributes', through which we merit *dvekut* (union) with the Creator.

However, we need to question the whole issue that He wants *us* to give to *Him*. Could the One be lacking something that we could give Him which would give Him pleasure?! It has already been explained in several places that this is a *tikkun* for *our* benefit so that the good and the joy that the One wants to give us should not be mixed with the feeling of shame.

Why did the One choose these 613 *mitzvot*? The Sages teach that it is just these particular acts that help us reach the stage of giving benefit, leaving the domination of selfish love. The stage of giving unconditionally is a new personal trait that is not in our nature. [12]

Here we have to take care in our understanding: Rabbi Baruch Shalom haLevi Ashlag writes that we fulfill the Torah and *mitzvot* in order to give pleasure to the Creator. We could make the mistake of thinking that the One lacks something that we could give Him and that He "needs" the human and our kindnesses! But the words "giving pleasure to the Creator" imply that when we fulfill

Lesson five

the Torah and *mitzvot* for their own sake we achieve affinity of form with the Creator. Consequently, we become an infinite channel through which we may receive all that the Creator wants to give us, as we give to all. Thus we are giving pleasure to the Creator by providing the conditions through which the purpose of Creation can be fulfilled. This is the meaning of "giving pleasure to the Creator."

Our fourth question is: What is special about the age thirteen? The importance of this age will be studied later in the *Introduction to the Zohar*.

Now we shall continue our study of the *Introduction to the Zohar*, starting again from the beginning of paragraph 11:

Introduction to the Zohar

11. The worlds unfold until we arrive at the reality of this material world where body and soul exist, and likewise a time of spoiling and a time of healing. Our body, which is formed from the will to receive for oneself alone, comes forth from its root within the purpose of creation, but it passes via the framework of the worlds of uncleanness, as Scripture says, "A man is born like a wild donkey" (Job 1:12). It remains subject to this framework until a person reaches thirteen years of age. This period is designated 'the time of spoiling'. Then, from the age of thirteen onwards, through performing *mitzvot*, in order to give benefit to others and pleasure to the Creator, the person begins to purify the will to receive for himself which is inherent within him. The person gradually transforms the will to receive for oneself alone into a will to give benefit. By this means, a person progressively attracts to himself a holy soul from its root within the purpose of creation. This soul passes through the framework of the worlds of holiness and enclothes itself within the body, and this is the time of healing.

From this we can see that both the body and the soul have their origin in the root of creation, but they follow different paths. The body coming to us through the framework of uncleanness, which manifests the will to receive for oneself alone, and the soul coming to us through the framework of holiness, which manifests the will to give.

Introduction to the Zohar

11. (*continued*) So the person carries on, continuing to acquire and attain higher levels of holiness drawn from the purpose of creation within the *Ein Sof* (Infinite). These higher levels of holiness help the person to transform the will to receive for oneself alone until it has entirely transformed into the will to receive in order to give pleasure to the Creator, without including his own self-benefit. It is by this means that the individual acquires affinity of form with the Creator.

Lesson five

For receiving only for the purpose of giving benefit to others or to God is considered as having exactly the same form as pure giving.

As we learn in the Talmud in the laws of marriage[7] concerning an important person: [A woman of lower social standing] gives [the ring for marriage to an important man, in contrast to ordinary marriages in which the man provides the ring for the marriage]. And he says, ["With this ring you are sanctified to me,"] then she is sanctified [and the marriage is valid]. The receiving [by the man] in order to give pleasure to her is considered as pure giving to her.

Thus when a person receives with the intention of giving benefit, he acquires complete unity with God because spiritual unity is none other than affinity of form. As the Sages have taught: How can a person become united with the One? Only by becoming one with His qualities. Just as the One is merciful and compassionate, so should you be merciful and compassionate.[13] It is by this means that a person becomes fit to receive all the good, the pleasantness and the tenderness that is implicit in the purpose of creation.

We need to go a little further into the term 'receiving for the sake of giving benefit' or 'receiving with the intention of giving benefit'. It is a common mistake among students to take these words to mean, "firstly I need to receive, *then* I may give." But in actual fact the action of giving has to *precede* that of receiving, for the simple reason that we all have within our nature the will to receive for ourselves alone. If we do not preclude receiving by prior giving, we have no choice other than to receive for ourselves alone.

Rabbi Yehudah Lev Ashlag illustrates this essential point in a parable he brings in the *Petichah l'Chochmat haKabbalah*:

> I shall explain this to you with an example from this world: It is in the nature of a person to value and hold dear the quality of giving benefit, and to be disgusted by and despise the quality of taking from one's equal. Therefore, if somebody comes to another person's house and the host asks him to eat, even if the guest is very hungry he will refuse to eat, as it seems to him contemptible or inferior to be taking a gift from an equal. However, when his friend repeatedly beseeches him to join him in a meal to a sufficient measure, that is, he beseeches him until it is clear to him that he will be doing the host a great favor if he eats his food, then he is agreeable and eats with him. He no longer feels that he is receiving a gift and that his friend is giving to him. Rather, he feels the opposite. He now feels that he is the giver, and he is the one who is doing his friend a favour by accepting the meal.

Lesson five

So here we see that even though hunger and appetite are the particular vessels for receiving food, and this man had sufficient hunger and appetite to receive his friend's meal, nevertheless, he was unable to taste even the smallest thing in his friend's house on account of his feelings of shame. However, when his friend began to entreat him, and he began to refuse, there began to form within him new vessels for receiving the meal. The power of the host's entreaties and the power of the guest's refusals grew stronger, until in the end they grew sufficient to transform his quality of receiving to a quality of giving, until the guest was able to believe that he was doing a favor and bringing great satisfaction to his host by virtue of his eating. Thus new vessels for receiving his friend's meal were formed. It transpires that the force of his refusal became the main vessel for receiving the meal, in place of the hunger and the appetite, even though they are truly the customary vessels. [14]

Explanation: In this parable, the appetite is the vessel, the food is the light; the host represents the Creator as the giver of good. If the guest were to receive the food with his appetite alone then we find that he would be in opposition of form with respect to his host, as he would be receiving, and the host, giving. However, as the guest refuses the food, he is giving up the opportunity to eat just in order to fulfill his hunger. This is a movement away from himself and his own needs. This refusal to take from his host stops him from being in opposition of form from him and sets up a new dynamic. Now the host starts to plead with the guest that he should receive from him. Only when the guest understands that through his receiving the meal he is actually *giving pleasure* to the host, does he agree to eat. It is the guest's first action of refusing the food that allows the new possibility to arise whereby, instead of eating for the sake of eating, he is able to receive the meal for the sake of giving pleasure to his host, and remain in affinity of form with his host. Thus we see that giving as a prior act, or, as in this example, refraining from receiving, provides the framework for receiving with the intention of giving.

Define for yourself the terms 'affinity of form', 'difference of form', and finally 'opposition of form'. Which type of will to receive leads to affinity of form, which leads to difference of form, and which leads to opposition of form? Can you find examples within your own life of these three types of the will to receive?

Now let us reinforce our learning by revising the definitions of these terms as they appear in *In the Shadow of the Ladder*. It is essential to have these definitions completely clear, as these terms appear throughout this and all other works of Rabbi Ashlag's.

Affinity of Form; Difference of Form

When two spiritual entities act in an identical way, or have identical desires, they are said to have affinity of form and thus to be at one with each other. Two spiritual entities which act in different, or opposite ways have difference of form. Thus affinity of form leads to *dvekut* and unity, while difference of form leads to separation and spiritual distance.

The will to receive for oneself alone

Now we can understand that if the very nature of the light is giving benefit and the very nature of the vessel is receiving, this is the basis of the difference of form and separation that exists between ourselves (the vessels) and God (the light). And indeed, if we act as pure receivers, using the will to receive for ourselves alone, only receiving according to the dictates of our own desires or egos, we could not be further away spiritually from God. This is called the 'will to receive for oneself alone', and is often referred to in the Kabbalah as 'the body'.

The will to give with the intention of receiving

This is the first stage in which a person begins to emerge from pure receiving and starts to occupy himself with giving. At this stage the person is still serving himself, in the sense that his intention is to improve his situation, such that through his giving he will receive honor, or gain of some other kind, either in this world or in the next. Nevertheless, this is still considered to be an important stage because it is an intermediate stage between receiving for oneself alone and between the stage of giving unconditionally. Since the person's intention in his giving is actually for the sake of receiving something, his giving does not belong to the framework of holiness. This stage is also called in the Kabbalah by the name of 'Torah which is practised, not for its own sake'.

The will to give for the sake of giving benefit

This is the first stage in the framework of holiness. Note that giving benefit to one's fellow, as in "Love your neighbor as yourself," is considered the same as giving benefit to the Creator from the perspective of affinity of form with the Creator. In this stage a person's focus has moved from being interested in what he receives, to focusing on what may benefit the other. The person's desire is to do good; this is the desire of the soul as opposed to that of the body. Giving with the intention of giving benefit is the first stage of the *Tzaddik*, in that this type of giving is in union and affinity of form with the Creator. This stage is termed in the language of the Kabbalah, 'the *tikkun* of the creation'.

Lesson five

The will to receive in order to give pleasure to the Creator

Despite the fact that the will to give for the sake of giving benefit is a stage of union with the Creator, there is still one further development of the vessel, and that is the will to receive for the sake of giving benefit. In this form the vessel now fulfills the ultimate purpose of creation, in that it enables God to give pleasure to His created beings, without leading to separation between the vessel and the light.

The purpose of creation (also called "the thought of creation")

The purpose of creation is that God wants to give pleasure to His created beings.

Tikkun (The healing of creation)

The *tikkun* of the creation is to change the direction of the vessel from receiving for itself alone, which separates it from the Creator, to giving benefit, such that the vessel achieves affinity of form with the Creator. This work of *tikkun* is done by the souls while they are present in their many incarnations in this world.[15]

We shall continue with the *Introduction to the Zohar*:

Introduction to the Zohar

12. So now we have clarified the healing of the will to receive that is inherent in the souls as a consequence of the purpose of creation. For the sake of the souls, God created the two frameworks described above, one opposed to the other, which the souls pass through, dividing into two aspects, body and soul, that enclothe one another.

Through the practice of Torah and *mitzvot*, the will to receive is eventually transformed into the will to give. Then the souls are able to receive all the good that is implicit in the thought of creation. With this, they merit to a wondrous unity with God, since they have earned affinity of form with their Creator through their work in Torah and *mitzvot*. This state is designated as the end of the healing process (*tikkun*).

Then, since there will no longer be any need for the other side, the unclean side, it will disappear from the earth, and death will be swallowed up forever. The work of Torah and *mitzvot* which is given to the totality of the world during the time period of its existence, and likewise, to each individual during the years of his or her life, has as its only purpose to bring us all to this final healing in which we come into affinity of form with the Divine.

Now we have also explained how the framework of the *klipot* and uncleanness is created and emerges from God's holiness. We have seen that this was necessary so as to allow the creation of the body which a person can subsequently heal through the work of Torah and *mitzvot*. If we did not have such bodies, which contain within them the defective will to receive provided by the framework of uncleanness, we would never be able to heal it, as one cannot heal anything that one does not have within oneself.

The idea that we have darkness within us as well as light is actually something that takes time to comprehend. We tend to push the darkness away, or project it onto someone else. In actual fact, Rabbi Ashlag taught that God covers up our own darkness from us until such a time as we are ready to deal with it. When we begin to see it, this is taken as a gift from God, as it is only when we can see it that we can start to work to transform it. The darkness that is within us that we discover as we go along the spiritual path is not something new; rather, it is something we always had within us, except we did not know it.

Still, when we start noticing our own real motives, our behaviors, and our thoughts, it can be shocking. Always remember that it was God who created the vessel called the will to receive for oneself alone, so there is no need to feel guilty. On the contrary, this will to receive for oneself alone has an important role to play, as we shall learn further. When we start to become aware of it, we should not get depressed; on the contrary, it is a good sign. Now we can roll up our sleeves and start work!

Try out different strategies to help yourself in transforming the direction of the will to receive. The most important ones are studying the wisdom of the Torah, praying for help, and joining with others who are also working in the same way.

1. *Mahut haDat uMataratah* (The Essence of Religion and its Purpose)
2. *Shabbat 55a*
3. *Zohar*, volume one, Introduction to the Zohar, *Perush haSulam*, paragraphs 23–37
4. *Petichah l'Chochmat haKabbalah*, paragraph 2
5. *Or Shalom on the Petichah l'Chochmat haKabbalah*, paragraph 2
6. *Petichah l'Chochmat haKabbalah*, paragraph 11
7. *Kiddushin 7* (marriage laws), see also *Talmud Eser haSephirot*, volume one, chapter one
8. *Or Shalom on the Petichah l'Chochmat haKabbalah*, paragraph 11
9. *Or Shalom on the Petichah l'Chochmat haKabbalah*, paragraph 2
10. *Kiddushin 30b*
11. *Matan Torah*, paragraph 13
12. *Sefer haMa'amerim, Bircat Shalom*, volume one, article twenty-one, Chukat, year 5747
13. *Shabbat 133b*
14. *Petichah l'Chochmat haKabbalah*, paragraph 15
15. *In the Shadow of the Ladder*, chapter five

Ein Od Milvado!

"There is nothing other than the One!"

Lesson Six

The states in which the souls exist simultaneously; free will; the nature and purpose of suffering

Paragraphs 13–16 of the Introduction to the Zohar

Rabbi Ashlag continues his discussion in the *Introduction to the Zohar* by looking at the different states in which the souls exist: 1) in the *Ein Sof*, 2) during the evolving of the worlds, and 3) at the end of the *tikkun*.

Introduction to the Zohar

13. However, we have yet to understand how it could be that the will to receive for oneself alone, since it is so defective and distorted, could possibly have issued forth from the thought of creation in the *Ein Sof* (Infinite), whose unity is so wondrous that no thought or word can express it.

The truth of the matter is, that at the very moment that God had the thought to create the souls, His thoughts completed creation instantly, God having no need of physical action as we do. Immediately, all the souls, together with all the worlds that were yet to be created, emerged, filled with all the goodness, delight, and tenderness that God planned for them, in the same complete and total perfection that the souls are destined to receive at the end of the healing time (the end of the *tikkun*).

This will come about when the will to receive that is within the souls has received all its healing to completion and transformed into pure giving, in total affinity of form with the Creator.

In the eternity of God, the past, present, and future function as one. The future functions as the present, as God does not require time.

Zohar
At the time when the Holy Blessed One wanted to create the world, His Will arose before Him and portrayed all the future souls that were to be given subsequently to humankind. All of them were portrayed before Him in the actual form that they would finally attain in the children of Man, and He saw each and every one.[1]

Zohar
Rabbi Shimon said, "When the thought arose to create the worlds, at that very moment all the higher worlds and the lower worlds and all that is in them were created.[2]

Lesson six

Introduction to the Zohar

13. *(continued)* It is for this reason that the defective will to receive that manifests in the form which is separated from God **never existed at all in the *Ein Sof*. On the contrary, it is the very same affinity of form with God, destined to be revealed in the future, at the very end of the healing process, that appeared instantly in God's eternity.** It was concerning this that the Sages said, "Before the world was created, He and His Name were One."[3] The separated form of the will to receive did not manifest in any way in the souls' reality as they emanated according to the thought of creation, but they were one with Him in affinity of form, according to the inner meaning of, "He and His Name are One." ('He'—the light, 'His Name'—the will to receive, 'One'—in affinity of form.) Look in the *Talmud Eser haSephirot* (The Study of the Ten *Sephirot*) part one:

> Before the four worlds there was the *Ein Sof*, He and His Name are One, in wondrous and hidden unity, may the One be blessed.[4]

Rabbi Yehudah Lev Ashlag enlarges on the difference that exists between the *Ein Sof*, in which the light and the vessel are in simple unity, and the worlds, in which the will to receive manifests in the following excerpt from his commentary *Or Pnimi* (Inner Light) on the *Etz Chayim* (Tree of Life) of the Ari that appears in the *Talmud Eser haSephirot*:

Etz Chayim
Know that before the worlds were created there was the one simple light filling all reality.[5]

Or Pnimi
Filling all reality: Seemingly this is a very strange statement. Are we not talking of *before* the worlds were created? If so, what reality is the Ari referring to, that the highest light needs to fill?

All the worlds and all the souls, that there are and that will be created in the future, with all that happens to them until the complete *tikkun*, are already included, in all their glory and in complete fulfillment, in the *Ein Sof*, in such a way that we may discern two general principles in the reality which is before us: The first principle is the modality wherein the worlds and the souls are permanent, existing in the *Ein Sof*, whole and in all their glory. The second principle is the modality in which the worlds and the souls are arrayed, evolve, and are renewed in the five worlds after the first *Tzimzum* (an early event preceding the cascade of the worlds). These five worlds are called *Adam Kadmon*, *Atzilut*, *Briyah*, *Yetzirah*, and *Assiyah*, as we shall explain further on.[6]

Lesson six

These two principles, which are two realities, exist side by side in parallel. We shall continue to investigate this matter in the *Introduction to the Zohar:*

Introduction to the Zohar

14. Therefore we find that the souls have three overall states of being. The first state is their existence within the *Ein Sof*, according to the thought of creation, where they already possess their future form, which belongs to the completion of their healing. The second state is their reality during their worldly state, in which they are divided by the two frameworks of uncleanness and holiness into body and soul. Here, they are given the work of Torah and *mitzvot* in order to transform the will to receive that is within them and to convert it into the will to give pleasure to their Creator, not using it for themselves at all. During the period of this state, the healing work (*tikkun*) is done on the souls alone, not on the bodies. That is to say, the souls need to remove every element of receiving for themselves, which is the characteristic of the body, remaining only with a will to give benefit. This is the form of the will as expressed by the soul. It is taught that even the souls of the righteous cannot enjoy the delights of the Garden of Eden after their death until their bodies have completely finished disintegrating into dust.

That is to say that in our state two, our chief work is to reach the stage of giving benefit only for the sake of giving benefit (giving unconditionally), not using our wills to receive for oneself at all. This stage is called, in the language of the Kabbalah, 'the *tikkun* of the creation' in which the souls are rectified (healed), using their wills to receive only to supply their most basic needs. The focus in this stage is entirely on giving benefit to the other.

Introduction to the Zohar

14. (*continued*) The third state is the completion of the healing of the souls after the revival of the dead, when a complete healing will come to the bodies as well. Then the receiving itself, which is the form of the body, comes under the influence of pure giving, and the souls thus become fit to receive all the good, delight and pleasantness implied in the thought of creation. Additionally, they merit oneness with God through their affinity of form with their Creator. All this they receive, not with their will to receive for themselves alone, but only through their will to give pleasure to their Creator, as God takes delight when we receive from Him.

From now on, for the sake of brevity, I shall refer to these states of the souls as 'state one', 'state two' and 'state three'. You must remember everything that has been explained here every time we use these terms.

In summary: State one is the existence of the souls in the *Ein Sof* according to the purpose of creation, in which they are already in their future perfected form as it will manifest in state three, at the end of the *tikkun*. State two is the reality of the souls as they exist in this world. State three is the completed *tikkun* of all the souls.

Introduction to the Zohar

15. When we look at these three states, we see that the existence of every one of them implies the existence of each of the others with total certainty. If you could imagine any aspect of one of these states not existing, then none of these states could exist.

For example, state three represents the complete transformation of the form of receiving into the form of giving benefit. If this state were not to become manifest, then state one, which is in the *Ein Sof*, could not have come into being. This is because all the perfection, which, in the future, will be expressed by state three, **already functions as the present within the eternity of God.** Thus, all the perfection implied in state one is like a copy taken from the future into the present of the *Ein Sof*, such that if it were possible that the future were to be abolished, then there could not be a reality within the present of the *Ein Sof*. Thus state three implies the existence of all that is in state one.

This is equally true if something were to be abolished from state two. State two is the reality of the work which is destined to be completed in the third state. This is the work of the spoiling and of the healing and of the bringing forth into incarnation the various levels of the soul. How could the third state come into being if the second state were left incomplete?

Thus the second state implies the third state. Likewise, the existence of the first state that is in the *Ein Sof*, wherein all the perfection of the third state already operates, requires that state two and state three should become manifest with exactly the same degree of perfection that exists in the *Ein Sof*, no more and no less.

So it is the first state itself that obligates the emergence of the two frameworks, of holiness and of uncleanness, one opposed to the other, within the second state. It is thus the first state itself that allows the existence of the body, with its defective will to receive, to develop via the framework of uncleanness, in order that we may repair it. If this framework of the worlds of uncleanness did not exist, then we would not have this will to receive, and we would not be able to heal it and arrive at stage three, since one cannot heal something unless it is within one. You might want to ask—but it would not be a good question—"How is it that the framework of uncleanness is created from the first state?" On the contrary, it is the first state itself that requires that the framework of uncleanness should exist and be sustained during the second state.

Lesson six

We are obliged to reach our perfection, as our perfection already exists. We exist simultaneously both whole and perfected in state one in the *Ein Sof* and in the reality of state two, of which this world is a part.

In order to understand how these two principles exist side by side in reality it is worth looking at the words with which Rabbi Ashlag opens his commentary *Or Pnimi* on the *Talmud Eser haSephirot*:

> We need to remember that the whole of the wisdom of the Kabbalah is based on spiritual matters that do not occupy place or time. Furthermore, absence or exchange plays no part in them; such that all the changes that are described in this wisdom do not imply that the first state disappears as it acquires another form, but that the stated change is only an additional form, and the first state is left intact.

At the same time that we experience the travails of our lives in this world in state two, we already exist in our eternal wholeness in the *Ein Sof*. We are talking about parallel existence in parallel worlds, or, as the Kabbalah puts it, additional states that the souls and worlds exist in simultaneously.

There is a strong message of hope and joy in these passages, for we already exist in our final perfection in the *Ein Sof*, which will manifest in our reality in the future, in state three; from this we can derive hope, joy, and faith.

When we look at the state of the world, it is easy to fall into either denial or despair, and believe, God forbid, that there is no future. It takes hope and faith to face the true state of the world while maintaining our inner joy. Yet we can do so by drawing on this tremendous message, that we and the world with us are already existing in our ultimate perfection in the *Ein Sof*. Take time to meditate on this.

Likewise, it is possible to see that all the spoiling and separation that we experience in state two has to be within us, otherwise we cannot arrive at state three in actual practice. A person can only correct that which is within him or her, therefore this obligates the existence of evil within us. Thus even in our present state, in this world, with all the good and the evil that is in us, we do have to say, "so it has to be."

Rabbi Ashlag now raises the question in the *Introduction to the Zohar*, that since all creation already exists in complete perfection, is there a place for free choice, and, if so, where does it lie?

Lesson six

Introduction to the Zohar

16. We might feel that according to the above, free will is negated, since we are obliged to come to our perfection in the third state as this third state already exists within the first state. However, the matter is as follows: God prepared two pathways within the context of state two with which to bring us to state three. The first path lies through the practice of Torah and *mitzvot* in the way that we have explained above (paragraphs 11 and 12), and the second path is via the path of suffering. Suffering in itself cleanses the body (the will to receive for oneself alone) and forces us finally to transform the will to receive which is within us and to accept the form of the will to give, bringing us to cleave to God. This is according to the saying of the Sages, "If you reform, that is good, and if not I shall set a king like Haman [7] over you who will force you to reform."

Now read the following passage from the Talmud in which the Sages, in their typically metaphorical way, are discussing the two possible ways we can come to the end of the *tikkun* (redemption). One is through repentance (free choice), the other is through mourning (suffering):

Rav said, "All hope is lost, and the matter only depends on repentance and good deeds. When Israel will turn in repentance (come into affinity of form through free choice) they will be redeemed."

Shmuel said, "It is enough for the mourner that he mourns; that is to say, even without repentance they will be redeemed."

Rabbi Eliezer said, "If Israel would repent they will be redeemed, but if not, they will not be redeemed."

Rabbi Joshua said to him, "How can it be possible that if they do not repent of their own accord they will not be redeemed?! But the Holy Blessed One will put a king over them, whose decrees are worse than Haman's, and will thus compel them to repent and come to the good way." [8]

Rabbi Ashlag goes further into this paragraph from the Talmud in his commentary, the *Perush haSulam* on the *Zohar* as follows:

And it is known what the Sages of blessed memory said on the Scripture, "'I am the Lord; in its due time, I shall hasten it' (Isa. 60:22). If they merit, I shall hasten it [the redemption], and if they do not merit, [the redemption will come] in its due time." [9] We need to understand how Israel can be redeemed, even if they do not merit it and are still persisting in their rebelliousness.

The exile comes about because, through their sins, Israel cause the left-hand side (the will to receive for oneself alone) to prevail over the right-hand side (the will to give benefit), leaving the left-hand side to rule alone. Then the right-hand side removes her loving-kindness from Israel. Therefore, when Israel turn in repentance, cleaving to the Holy Blessed One, which is the middle line, then the middle line returns and unites the right and the left and establishes the lights of *both* sides, and wisdom is enclothed in loving-kindness (the light is received with the intention of giving unconditionally). Then Israel are redeemed with the light and receive all the good reward. This is the inner meaning of, "If they merit, I shall hasten it." Therefore there is no set time for the redemption, but when they make repentance they will be redeemed.

However, if they do not repent, then there is a set time when the redemption will come even if they still have not repented. This will be at the time when it is possible to gather together all the harsh decrees that Israel suffered during the time of the exile to a complete measure, sufficient for Israel to be afraid to let the left-hand side prevail over the right-hand side—they would be afraid to let their will to receive for oneself alone prevail over the will to give, as they did at the time of the destruction of the Temple. Then they will be fit to receive the redemption, even without repentance, because even without repentance they can now be sure that they will never return to their foolishness again because of the harsh decrees they have suffered.

And this is the inner meaning of, "If they do not merit, then in its own time," that the redemption will occur in any case, when the harsh decrees of the exile have come to a sufficient measure. Thus it is not required that Israel will awaken with repentance.[10]

Introduction to the Zohar

16. (*continued*) The rabbis further commented on the Scripture, "In its due time, I shall hasten it" (Isa. 60:22), saying, "If they are worthy, I shall hasten it, and if not, it will come in its due time." In other words, if we merit to travel on the first path, which is the path of the practice of Torah and *mitzvot*, then we hasten our healing. We do not then need hard and bitter suffering and the longer time required for suffering to transform us against our will. If we take the way of suffering, healing will come, but in its own time. That is, only at the time when the suffering has completed our healing, and we arrive at this healing against our will.

The choice is ours. Whichever way we choose, the final healing, which is state three, must most certainly come about because its existence is implied by state one, and the only choice that we have is whether to take the path of suffering or the path of Torah and *mitzvot*.

So now we have clarified how these three states of the souls are connected to each other and obligate each other's existence.

Lesson six

However, we need to question whether the choice between taking the path of Torah and *mitzvot*, or that of taking the path of suffering, can truly be considered a free choice. After all, only someone who is insane would consciously choose a path of suffering of his own free will!

One can answer this with a parable: A person has a garden, but he does not look after it or plant nice plants in it. Consequently weeds spring up. Did he choose to have a garden of weeds? Although he did not choose this directly, he did so indirectly. By not actively choosing the positive, the weeds sprang up of themselves.

The analogy is clear. A person does not consciously choose the path of suffering. But by ignoring the positive steps he needs to take in his life he is in fact choosing the path of suffering.

The path of suffering is an unconscious choice made by the soul, whereas the path of Torah and *mitzvot* is a conscious choice. Naturally, we are speaking of Torah and *mitzvot* as positive actions that are carried out with the intention of giving unconditionally, through which a person acquires affinity of form with the Creator.

The purpose of suffering, as we see here, is to cleanse the will to receive from receiving for oneself alone. This is a difficult idea to accept. Each and everyone of us goes through suffering in our lives, both on our individual path and as members of the community within which we live. No one in their right mind chooses the path of suffering as a conscious choice, yet it is clear that in the subconscious this is a choice we choose. The soul is searching for the light it receives through the suffering. The suffering releases it from the bondage of the will to receive for oneself alone that we are trapped in. When we wake up to the unconscious choices we have made, we are given the possibility to choose anew, to move over to a more conscious choice and to deal with the will to receive for oneself alone through Torah and *mitzvot*.

Rabbi Baruch Shalom haLevi Ashlag explains these two ways in an explanation which appears in the biographical work *haSulam* by Rabbi Abraham Mordecai Gottlieb:

> If you want to catch fish, you have two possibilities: You can either take the fish out of the water, or you can drain the water from the fish.
>
> Moral: If a person wants to stop using his or her selfish love, then he can take himself away from material enjoyment, and cleave to Torah. However, if the

person does not do this himself, then he inevitably receives the path of suffering; the Holy Blessed One will take the joys and satisfaction out of the material world for him, and he is left with complete emptiness. Then he is forced to go and search out a new source of sustenance."

In his book *Matan Torah* Rabbi Yehudah Lev Ashlag writes as follows:

Conscious and Unconscious Development
Know that there are two forces given to us from Above that push us to climb up and ascend the rungs of the spiritual ladder until we reach the heavenly top that is our destination—namely, our similarity of form with our Creator, may the One be blessed.

The first of these forces pushes us without our intent, which is to say, without our personal choice. This force pushes us from behind. We have defined it as 'the way of suffering', or 'the way of nature'. From it stems the philosophy of moral conduct that is called 'ethics', which is based on experiential knowledge acquired by critical analysis of situations that arise in practice. This ethical law is in essence a summary of the damage that has become obvious to us and which is caused by the core of egoism within us. These experiences came to us seemingly by chance, without our intending them or choosing them. However, they are sure in their purpose, because the character that evil takes becomes clearer to our senses. According to the measure that we recognize the damage the evil causes, we remove ourselves from it and thus arrive at a higher rung on the ladder.

The second force pulls us consciously, that is through the power of our own choice. This force pulls us forward from ahead. We have designated this force as being the path of Torah and *mitzvot* for the sake of giving benefit. For through the practice of the *mitzvot* and the work of giving satisfaction to the Creator we find that there develops within us, with marvellous rapidity, the same sense of recognition of the evil. We thereby profit in two ways: Firstly, we do not have to wait for the vicissitudes of life to push us from behind, for the incentive they give rise to is measured only by the amount of pain and destruction they cause us, which comes upon us through the presence of the evil within us. Through the path of service to God, may the One be blessed, the same recognition of the evil within us develops without any prior suffering or destruction. On the contrary, through the pleasantness and refinement that we feel at the time of our pure service to God, which we do only in order to give satisfaction to Him, there develops within us a relative ability to recognize the baseness of the sparks of light that we gain through selfish love, that hinder us on our journey towards receiving this refined taste of serving the One unconditionally. This gradual sense of the recognition of the evil increases and develops within us through the periods of delight and great tranquility we receive periodically, consequent on our service to God, may the One be blessed, and from our experiencing the pleasantness and refinement that comes to us consequent on our affinity of form with our Creator. Secondly, we save time, as this process functions with our intent, and we have it within our ability to increase our practice of Torah and *mitzvot*, and so hurry up the time our healing takes as much as we wish. [12]

It can be a deeply moving exercise to look back on some difficulty or suffering that you have personally experienced in your life and to see what you have gained from it; how you grew spiritually, and what layers it peeled off. Describe such an experience and the effect it had on you in your journal.

The idea that suffering is purposeful and not meaningless is an important one. Whatever happens to us is at the hand of the *hashgacha pratit* (the Divine Providence); it is neither random nor meaningless. This perception of the Divine Providence may not be our present one. Nevertheless, our perception changes as we change and grow in our faith and understanding.

Now take a moment to write in your journal of a time when you experienced delight and tranquility after performing an altruistic act. It's important to pay attention to the good feelings consequent on such an action and to allow yourself to enjoy the pleasure you have earned.

The issue of how we perceive God in relation to the sufferings we undergo is discussed at great length in the *Hakdamah l'Talmud Eser haSephirot* (Introduction to the Study of the Ten *Sephirot*). It is not possible to bring the entire discussion here, so I have just brought one salient paragraph:

> You need to know that the distance that we feel ourselves as being so far away from God that makes us so liable to sin has only one single cause. It is the source of all the pains and sufferings we experience and is the source of all our arrogant acts and mistakes over which we stumble. It is obvious that if we were able to remove this one single cause, then we would instantly be free of all our suffering, and we would immediately merit to cleave to God with all our heart, soul, and might. I say to you that this root cause is none other than the minimal understanding that we possess of the way that God involves Himself in the life of His created beings, which is termed 'His Divine Providence'. We do not understand the One as is fitting. [13]

Lesson six

We do not understand the Divine Providence, the way the One relates to us, the created beings, because we do not understand His unity, and the different ways His unity expresses itself in practice.

Here is an excerpt from the *Histaclut Pnimit* (Inner Look), which forms part of the *Talmud Eser HaSephirot*. In this excerpt, Rabbi Yehudah Lev Ashlag discusses the subject of the unity of the One. Part of it is difficult to understand, but Rabbi Baruch Shalom haLevi Ashlag explains it simply in his wonderful explanation *Or Shalom*, which follows subsequently:

> *Histaclut Pnimit*
> There is nothing in the whole of reality that is not included within the *Ein Sof*. Concepts which we perceive as opposites are included comprehensively within Him in the inner meaning of *Echad, Yachid, uMeyuchad* (One, Single and Unity).
>
> Know that there is no essence of any being in the world, either of those that are perceived with our senses, or of those conceived by our minds, that is not included within the Creator, may the One be blessed. For all of them come to us from Him, may the One be blessed, and the One cannot give out that which is not within Him to give.
>
> This matter has already been well explained in the holy books. But we need to understand that concepts, which for us are separate or even opposite, are included as one within Him. For example, the concept of wisdom is, for us, different from the concept of sweetness. Wisdom and sweetness are two separate ideas. Likewise, the concept of the worker is certainly different from the concept of the action. For us, the worker and his action are two separate entities. This is even more so for concepts that we perceive as being opposites, such as bitterness, sweetness, and suchlike. For us, these are certainly differentiated one from the other. However, within Him, may the One be blessed, wisdom, joy, sweetness, pungency, the worker, the action, and so forth, which, for us, make up different or opposite forms, are all included in His simple light as one, without any recognition of the differences between them at all. They are all included within the concept of *Echad, Yachid, uMeyuchad*.
>
> *Echad* (**One**) teaches that He is in equivalence. *Yachid* (**Single**) teaches that everything comes from Him. All pluralities, are, within Him, single in form, as is His essence. *Meyuchad* (**Unity**) teaches that even though He acts in a multiplicity of actions, only one force drives all these, and all of them return and reunite in the one single form, such that this one single form swallows up all the forms that appear in His actions.
>
> This is a very subtle matter, and not every mind can comprehend it.

Lesson six

Nachmanides, likewise, explained the issue of His Oneness, may He be blessed, in the inner meaning of *Echad, Yachid, uMeyuchad* (One, Single, and Unity). This is what he writes in his commentary on the *Sefer haYetzirah* (The Book of Formation):

"We need to explain the terms *Echad, Yachid*, and *Meyuchad*: When God unites to act with one power He is called '*Meyuchad*'. When He acts in ways that seem different to us He is called '*Yachid*', and when He is in one equivalence He is called '*Echad*'." Here ends his very pure language.

Explanation: **God unites to act with one power (*Meyuchad*):** Here Nachmanides wants to say that the purpose of His actions is to do good, as is fitting for His unity, and there is no essential difference in His actions.

When He acts in ways that seem different to us, then He is called *Yachid*: His actions differ from each other, and He appears as a worker for good or, God forbid, as one who works evil. He is called *Yachid*, because all His different acts have one single result, which is to do good. So we find that He is single in each and every action and He does not change due to His different actions.

When He is in one equivalence He is called *Echad*: That is to say *Echad* teaches us about His essence, may the One be blessed, that by Him all the different opposite forms are in one equivalence, as it is written above.

Maimonides wrote: Regarding God's essence, the Knower, what is known, and the knowledge are one, for His thoughts are higher than our thoughts and His ways are higher than our ways. [14]

Rabbi Baruch Shalom haLevi Ashlag comments as follows:

Echad: As the One is in His essence—no thought can grasp Him at all. All that we can speak of the One stems only from the aspect of "from Your works we know You," that is, from the light that emanates from Him. What is revealed is that He is One, which is to say that He has one desire—to give goodness to His created beings.

Yachid: From the aspect of "One" is revealed "many." That is, acts which are good and acts which are bad. The created beings receive pleasure and suffer pain. Thus the question is raised: "If His will is to do good to the created beings why is there suffering? Answer: "God is *Yachid*." Over every action rides the form of the single mind. In other words, we need to believe that all our suffering has a purpose, which is to bring a person closer to his real objective, which is to achieve wholeness wherein he will be able to receive the true good and delight.

Once I told a parable about this: There was once a man who was walking along the street when suddenly he was attacked by someone with a knife. The attacker was caught and taken to the police station where he sat in jail until it was time for him to be brought to court. During his trial he said in his defence, "But I only cut the passer-by a little! I myself have seen how a surgeon in the hospital cut the belly of a patient with a great big cut and the patient even paid the surgeon money for it, whereas you put me in jail just for the little cut that I made?!"

The judge explained to him, "When the surgeon cuts the abdomen of a patient, his intention is that the patient will benefit. That is to say, the suffering caused by the cut comes about only in order to bring about an improvement and an amelioration in the state of the patient. So we see that the doctor is acting kindly, even though suffering is involved. That is why we need to pay him for it. However, when you cut the passer-by, you intended to inflict harm, you intended to satisfy your own selfish purposes, therefore you must pay the penalty of your action."

Analogy: We need to know that the form of *Yachid* overrides even the evils that are to be found in the world. This is the suffering with which the created beings suffer. The suffering has the purpose of bringing us to the fulfillment of the single desire, which is the desire of the One to give goodness to the created beings.

Meyuchad: This is the state achieved when a person merits **to see** that all the sufferings he suffered in the past had only one purpose, and that was to bring him to wholeness. (That is he now *sees* that this is so and no longer has to *believe* that this is so, as in the case of *Yachid*.) [15]

Here are some further questions for you to consider. Write your answers in your journal, giving concrete examples from your own life, if possible:

Looking at the reality of suffering, can you see how it is the will to receive for oneself alone that is the cause of all suffering? Can you see how the use of the will to receive for oneself alone separates us from our Source, from our Selves, and causes the worst of all spiritual suffering? Can you see how the effects of suffering help us to soften, transform, and change the will to receive for oneself alone to a vessel that's fit to receive the light of God?

In order to look further into these questions, here follows a piece taken from the *Zohar*:

(We need to know that the language the *Zohar* is written in is a type of code called the "language of the branches." The words of the *Zohar* are not meant to be understood in their literal sense. We shall be studying the language of the branches more deeply in lesson nine.)

Zohar

From this light of *Ruach*, purity, go forth seventy lights, all of them sparkling at once, and all of them giving light, in the modality of the round *Sephirot*—because they do not emanate to give light from above to below like other lights. Cleaving one to another, giving light to each other, uniting with each other. All the merits of the world exist within these lights. From all of them go forth two lights which are balanced as one, which stand already before them.

Perush haSulam

Cleaving one to another, giving light to each other, uniting with each other. "The lights cleaving to each other" implies that they have equivalence of form, because cleaving to each other (*dvekut*) in spirituality is nothing other than affinity of form. **Giving light to each other** implies that the lights mix with each other to give light together as one. **Uniting with each other** implies that they need each other, such that one cannot give light without the other, or if one were missing they would not be able to give out their light. **All the merits of the world exist within these lights.** That is to say, through their light all the sins of the world transform into positive acts.

Explanation: For the Sages have said, "There was no joy before Him like unto the day that the heaven and the earth were created."[16] This means that all the created beings of the world exist in their complete perfection, to such an extent that there was no joy before Him like unto the day the heavens and the earth were created. However, it is impossible for a human being to participate in God's great joy until he has come to the complete *teshuvah* (transformation) from love. (He has achieved the stage of the will to receive with the intention of giving benefit.) Before this he can neither rejoice in himself nor in the created beings of the world. On the contrary, the person feels the world with which he is confronted to be full of suffering and pain, until he says, (as in Job 9:24), "the land is given over to the wicked." Both bodily pain and emotional pain, which are caused by the sins that people do, come to them because they are going along a path that is contrary to the purpose of creation. For the world was created according to the inner intention of giving unconditionally, that is for us to practise Torah and good deeds in order to give pleasure to the Creator, and not for pleasuring ourselves, as it is written, "All that God creates is for His sake" (Prov. 15:4), that is to say, in order that the created beings should give Him pleasure.

But in the beginning, "A human being is born as a wild ass" (Job 11:12), which means that the only thing that interests a person is to pleasure himself and he has no desire to give benefit to another at all. Thus the person maintains, "Everything that God made, He made for me and my self-enjoyment," and therefore he wants to swallow the world, and all that is in it, for his own good and his own purpose.

Therefore, the Creator implanted harsh and bitter suffering to be inherent in the matter of receiving for oneself alone, which is the nature a human being has from birth, including both physical and emotional suffering. If he were to occupy himself with Torah and *mitzvot*, even for his own pleasure, through the light that is in them he would, at least, perceive the paucity and the dreadful destructive nature of the will to receive for oneself alone. Then the person may give his heart over to the issue of separating himself from the nature of this type of receiving, and dedicate himself completely to working, solely with the intention of giving pleasure to the Creator, according to the measure of the Scripture, "All that God has worked is for His sake." And then God will open the person's eyes and he will see before him a full world, perfectly whole, which has no lack. Then he will be able to partake in the joy that God had when the One created the world. And this is what the Sages have said: "One who merits, has tilted the balance of himself and the whole world to the side of merit."[17] For wherever he looks he only sees goodness and perfection, and he does not see any deficiencies in God's work, but he sees that everything is meritorious.

There are two ways by which one may consider the suffering, both physical and spiritual, that the person suffers before he or she repented, (before reaching affinity of form with the Creator):

Firstly, all that the Merciful One does is to benefit. For now the person sees with his own eyes that if it were not for the dreadful pain that he suffered, because he was sunk in receiving for himself alone, he would never have merited that repentance, and so he blesses the evil in exactly the same way as he blesses the good. So we see that everything that God does, He does in order to do good. That is to say, in order to give rise to the good.

Secondly, there is the aspect of: "This is also good." That is, not only do the evil acts give rise to good, but the evil acts themselves are transformed and become good in themselves. That is, the Creator, may the One be blessed, through the means of very great light, illuminates all these evil acts until they are transformed into good acts. This applies to both physical suffering and to emotional suffering, which are sins. In this way all the sins transform and receive the form of merit. The lights that transform the sins into merits are the seventy lights in this temple, (as referred to above in the *Zohar*).[18]

1. Zohar, Perush haSulam, Parshat Mishpatim, paragraph 51
2. Zohar Chadash, Perush haSulam, Bereshit, paragraph 243
3. Pirkei d'Rabbi Eliezer, chapter one

Lesson six

4. *Talmud Eser haSephirot*, part one, chapter two

5. *Talmud Eser haSephirot*, part one, chapter two

6. *Talmud Eser haSephirot*, Or Pnimi, paragraph 3

7. Haman was an evil counsellor at the time the Jews were in exile in the Persian Empire before the rebuilding of the second temple. He sought to destroy all the Jews. The story is told in the Book of Esther.

8. *Sanhedrin 97b*

9. *Sanhedrin 98a*

10. *Zohar, Perush haSulam, Parashat Shelach Lecha*, paragraph 303

11. *HaSulam*, page 46

12. *Matan Torah*, page 54 in the Or Ganuz edition

13. *Hakdamah l'Talmud Eser haSephirot* paragraph 42 (The whole discussion may be found in paragraphs 42–64 published in *In the Shadow of the Ladder*.)

14. *Talmud Eser haSephirot, Histaclut Pnimit*, part one, beginning

15. *Talmud Eser haSephirot, Histaclut Pnimit, Or Shalom*, part one

16. *Sifrei VaYikra, Parasha Shmini, parasha 1*

17. *Talmud, Kiddushin 40b*

18. *Zohar, Perush haSulam, Bereshit B*, paragraph 103

Ein Od Milvado!

"There is nothing other than the One!"

Lesson Seven

The true nature of the body and its purpose; the end of suffering; where am I acting from?
Paragraphs 17–19 of the Introduction to the Zohar

Introduction to the Zohar

17. On the basis of what we have now explained, we are able to answer the third question that we asked above (paragraph 1). We noted that when we look at ourselves, we feel that we are defective and fallen, to the extent that there can be none as despicable as ourselves. But when we look at our Creator who made us, we find that we must really be creations of such a high degree that there are none more praiseworthy than ourselves, as is fitting for the Creator who created us. It is in the nature of a perfect Creator that His works should be perfect.

From what we have learned, it can now be understood that our present body with all its occurrences and insignificant acquisitions is not our true body at all! Our true body, that is to say our eternal body, which is perfect with all manner of perfections, is already available, existing and established within the *Ein Sof* in its aspect of state one. There, it is already receiving its perfected form, taken from the future yet to be manifest in state three. Its receiving is in the form of giving benefit, and thus it is in affinity of form with the *Ein Sof*, blessed be the One.

So if our first state itself necessitates that in the second state we should be given the shell of our body in its contemptible and spoiled form of the will to receive for ourselves alone, which causes separation from the *Ein Sof*, we should not complain. It is to enable us to repair it and to make it possible for us to receive our eternal body in the third state in all actuality. We do not need to complain about this at all, as our work can only be carried out while in this temporal and worthless body, **as one cannot heal anything that is not within one.**

So, even in this, our state two, we do in fact exist in the measure of total perfection that is fitting and appropriate to the perfect Creator who made us. This body does not damage us in any way as it is destined to die and to be negated. We only have it for the limited time which is necessary to nullify it and to receive our eternal form.

Even in our imperfection we are perfect! It is our body, that is to say our will to receive for oneself alone, in all its manifestations, physical, mental, emotional,

Lesson seven

and spiritual, that gives us the work of rectification and thus gives us the opportunity to fulfill the purpose of creation in actuality—state three. Thus we need this defective will to receive, because a person cannot heal that which he or she does not have within himself or herself.

This is an important principle: We are so good at seeing what is wrong with our fellow, giving all manner of advice and suggestions to the other as to how he or she may rectify himself or herself, whereas regarding our own selves we may be quite blind. The truth that we cannot heal something unless it is within us is so hard to accept. It is hard to accept that I myself have anything within me that needs fixing!

It is hard to look truthfully at our own wills to receive for ourselves alone because this immediately brings up feelings of fear, shame, self-criticism, and unworthiness. These feelings constitute a huge barrier to our own spiritual progress. At these difficult moments it is helpful to fix our minds on what Rabbi Ashlag states here: "Even in this, our state two, we do in fact exist in the measure of total perfection that is fitting and appropriate to the perfect Creator who made us." So when we discover something about ourselves that requires healing, or *tikkun*, yes, we can be happy about it. It was placed within us for the specific purpose of having us do the work of rectifying it. And in so doing we are fulfilling our role of bringing about the complete *tikkun* for the whole of humankind.

Here follows an excerpt of the account of my first encounter with this inner work, as printed in *In the Shadow of the Ladder*:

> I started to study with my friend. Right from the start it was clear to me that this was no intellectual study. Used to learning, I nevertheless suddenly found myself unable to understand seemingly simple ideas. I found myself asking my friend again and again, "But what is the will to receive?" My difficulty did not lie in my inability to understand with my brain, but rather, in my inability to see that I also acted from a will to receive for myself alone.
>
> So my first exercise was simply to become an observer of myself. I began to try to see where I was acting from. What were the motives that lay behind my words and actions? This was hard for me. I had been so used to criticizing and judging myself and living up to high standards that simply asking myself the question, "Where am I acting from?" was not an easy task! What encouraged me was my knowledge, brought from the teaching of Rabbi Ashlag, that the ego is a necessary and precious part of God's creation. It is the raw material for

the transformed vessel that will one day receive God's light. I no longer needed to judge myself or feel guilty. If I acted from my ego it was, after all, God who had placed the vessel within me! This helped relieve the difficult feelings of guilt and self-criticism with which I had always lived. The simple question, "Where am I acting from?" became more a matter of curiosity, interest, and self-awareness. It was important at the beginning to ask this question without any hidden impulsion or compulsion to act differently; simply to grow in non-judgmental awareness.[1]

If you would like to, take on the exercise "Where am I acting from?" in your daily life. Jot down your discoveries in your journal.

Here follows an article taken from Rabbi Ashlag's commentary on the *Zohar*, the *Perush haSulam*, which discusses the creation of the human, who contains within himself both the light and the dark.

> Everything that you find in the work of creation is a matter of differentiation and clarification. For example, "and God differentiated between the light and the darkness" (Gen. 1:5); likewise He differentiated between the [upper] water and the [lower] water, also between the water and the dry land. Likewise, regarding the earth bringing forth herbs, the issue of "each according to his own kind" is a differentiation. One can say the same regarding the governance of the day and the governance of the night; equally, regarding the emergence of the animals from the water and from the land, such that all these distinctions teach the clarification of the holy from the shells, or the good from the evil. All that is thus clarified becomes an aspect of existing reality, as is fitting to the Creator in holiness.
>
> This is the inner meaning of the saying of the Sages that the entire work of creation is included in the declaration of the first day, "Let there be light." For within that declaration is included the whole differentiation between the light and the darkness, wherein the holiness is called 'light', and the *klipot* (shells) are called 'dark'. All the other descriptions of the differentiation between the framework of holiness and the *klipot* are details and branches of the overall differentiation between the light and the dark.
>
> However, despite this differentiation between the light and the dark, with which all the created beings of the creation were clarified, the *tikkun* is still left incomplete. The entire aspect of evil or dark appears as something for which there is no use, and this is not at all fitting for His perfection, may the One be blessed. The *tikkun* of creation will only be complete in accordance with the

Lesson seven

inner meaning of the phrase, "Even darkness will not cause dark to come from You, and the night will give light as day, the darkness will shine as much as the light" (Ps. 139:12).

In order to correct this darkness the human being was created, who includes everything from the uttermost evil to the ultimate good. Through his hand the *tikkun* will be finished to the required perfection, that is, the evil will transform into good, the bitterness into sweet, the darkness will shine like the light, death will be swallowed up for ever, and the Lord will be King over all the earth … .

And this is the inner meaning of "Let us make Man in our image (*b'tzalmeinu*), like us (*k'dmuteinu*)" (Genesis 1:26). The light is called the *tzelem* and the darkness is called *dmut*, such that Man will be created from both of these forces, *tzelem* and *dmut*, and through this means all the *tikkun* will be completed by the human. The *Malchut* (the rectified vessel of receiving) will then emanate in her holiness over all the will to receive, and the Lord will be One and His Name will be One, for the darkness in the *Malchut* will then have been transformed into complete light. [2]

Amen.

From here we see that the *tikkun* of the evil of each individual is valuable, not only for his personal *tikkun*, but as each individual rectifies his own aspect of darkness he participates in the communal *tikkun* of the darkness of the creation as a whole. This provides us with a very significant motivation for all of us to continue and persevere in our attempts to deal with our own personal difficulties. The body, which is the ego, opposes our efforts to work on our *tikkun* and therefore invents all manner of excuses why not to do it. One of the best ways to ignore its complaints and still carry on with the work is to remember that each of us is part of the *tikkun* of the whole of humanity. The efforts I make are unique to me, and therefore I contribute a part in the collective effort that no one else can do in my stead.

We shall now continue with our learning of the *Introduction to the Zohar*:

Introduction to the Zohar

18. Together with this, we have now settled the fifth question that we asked (paragraph 1). We wanted to know, "How is it possible that from an Eternal Being could issue forth created beings that are transient, destructive, and harmful?" From the explanations we have already given, we can understand that the truth is that we have already come forth from God as eternal created beings in all perfection in a way that is fitting to His Eternity. Our eternal state necessitates

Lesson seven

that the shell of the body, which is given to us only for the purpose of work, should be temporal and worthless. For if it were to remain in eternity, then we would remain separated forever from the Source of our Life, God forbid! We have already stated (in paragraph 13) that the present form of our body, that is the will to receive for oneself alone, is not found at all in the eternal thought of creation, for there we exist in our form which pertains to state three. But we need to have a body here in this reality of state two in order to enable us to heal it. Regarding the situation of the created beings of the world other than the human, we do not need to consider them in any different way. As we shall see further on (paragraph 39), humankind is the center of creation. The other created beings help to bring the human to his and her perfection and thus go up and down together with him and her, rather than in an autonomous fashion.

19. Now we can answer the fourth question that we asked. Since it is in the nature of the Good to do good, how is it that God could create created beings that suffer and feel pain all their lives? As we have already said, all these sufferings necessarily follow from our state one, in which our complete and eternal perfection is received from our future state three. This perfection compels us either to follow the path of Torah and *mitzvot*, or the path of suffering, in order to arrive at our eternal form in state three in actuality (paragraph 15).

All these sufferings prevail only over our shell of a body, which, from its creation, was destined only for death and burial. This teaches us that the will to receive for oneself alone that is in the body was likewise only created in order for us to blot it out, remove it from the world, and transform it into the will to give. The sufferings that we undergo are simply disclosures that reveal to us the futility and damage that overlies the will to receive for oneself alone.

Let us see what it will be like when all humanity agrees unanimously to nullify and completely remove the will to receive for themselves alone that is within them, and they will then have no will other than that of giving benefit to their companions. Then all our worries, and all that is injurious to us, will vanish from the earth, and all beings will be certain of healthy and full lives, since each one of us will have a whole world looking out for us and fulfilling our needs.

Take time to contemplate and feel the beauty, hope, and promise of this statement. Allow yourself time to meditate on this incredible vision for humanity. All the damaging elements will have disappeared and everyone will have a whole world caring for and giving benefit to each person.

Can you see how it could come about? What reforms would be necessary? How would the world look in practice if we were all to act from our will to give instead of our will to receive? What would our relationships be like? Our communities? Our economic systems? Our international relations? Take these individual questions and ponder them in as detailed a way as you can manage. Try and envisage practical solutions. Write them in your journal. This is a really mind-stretching exercise!

Rabbi Yehudah Lev Ashlag himself described in detail his vision for a society that would be based on the precept of "Love your neighbor as yourself" in actual practice. According to his vision, building such a society would start with communities, either rural or urban, within which all the inhabitants would live both socially and economically, according to the principle of, "What can I give to my fellow in order that I shall be in affinity of form with my Creator?" Such a community would be a living example of the beauty and delight inherent in a life that is not based on the will to receive for oneself, but one based on the will to give to one's fellow, from the desire to cleave to the Creator. These centers would influence the wider community like waves which spread out from the center of a pool, until the whole nation would act according to the principle of "Love your neighbor as yourself," in practice. Finally all the nations of the world would come to act from this principle.

Clearly, in order to arrive at the possibility of establishing such a center, one would have to have a core number of people who are already acting from the will to give as their focus.

Introduction to the Zohar

19. *(continued)* It is from the fact that all are chasing after their own will to receive for themselves that all the sufferings and the wars, the slaughters and the holocausts, from which we have no refuge, originate. Our bodies become weakened with all kinds of illnesses and pains. Yet all the sufferings of our world are only warning lights to push us into doing this work of nullifying the evil shell of the body and receiving the perfected form of the will to give. As we have said, the way of suffering itself has the capacity to bring us to the desired form of the body.

Up until now Rabbi Ashlag has discussed the *tikkun* that we do according to the way of suffering. Now he is going to add an important fact with regard to doing our *tikkun* through the way of consciousness, the way of Torah and *mitzvot*:

Introduction to the Zohar

19. *(continued)* You should know that the commandments in the Torah that deal with the relationship of a person to his or her fellow take precedence over the *mitzvot* that are between ourselves and God, as acting benevolently towards our fellow leads us to act towards God in a similar way.

This is an extraordinary statement. So many people place their emphasis on ritual acts. This is one of the great dividers between the religious world and the so-called secular world. However, Rabbi Ashlag is clearly telling us here that we need to put our emphasis on the *mitzvot* which are between a person and his or her fellow. These consist of forgiving people, not telling lies, not slandering, not taking vengeance, not judging others, not giving way to anger, not shaming someone else, not giving way to hatred. Giving someone the benefit of the doubt. Giving charity, doing acts of loving-kindness, providing hospitality, teaching, ethics in business, and many more. These are all summed up in the phrase, "Love your neighbor as yourself."

However, the secular Jew, the religious Jew and the non-Jew all have to practise "Love your neighbor as yourself," from the need to come into affinity of form with the Creator, as we have explained at length above. That is to say, we need to operate from the principle of "Love the Lord your God." History has proven that even a society initially founded on equality, such as those of communist Russia or China, cannot maintain the high principles of their founders because of the reality of the will to receive for oneself alone. In the end, such societies are doomed to deteriorate. Thus the desire to found an equal and just society, whose basis is "Love your neighbor as yourself," has to be founded only for the purpose of serving the Creator. Without this motivation there is no incentive to persevere and ascend above our basic nature, the nature that was implanted within us, which is the will to receive for oneself alone. So we see that even societies based on humanitarian principles are condemned to fall and collapse, as we have seen with our own eyes, unless they embody love for the Creator.

One of the main differences between the *mitzvot* that are between ourselves and one's fellow, as opposed to those between ourselves and God, is that in those between ourselves and our fellows we can and do receive feedback. In the mutual relationships that exist between husband and wife, or in those that exist between friends, in our work relationships, in our relationships with neighbors, and with those who annoy us, we find the maximum potential for feedback. With the help of these *mitzvot* that we carry out between ourselves and our fellow, we can truly look at our motives, asking ourselves the questions, "Where am I acting from?" "What are my real intentions?" "Am I acting from my will to receive for oneself alone or am I acting from my will to benefit?" In the *mitzvot* which exist between oneself and God the feedback is more subtle.

Look at the *mitzvot* between a person and one's fellow. See which are the ones you keep and are important to you. List them in your journal. We shall be returning to this subject in lesson thirteen.

1. *In the Shadow of the Ladder, chapter six, One Person's Journey*
2. *Perush haSulam, Hakdamat Sefer haZohar, paragraph 236*

Ein Od Milvado!

"There is nothing other than the One!"

Lesson Eight

The essence of the soul; how desire begets needs and needs give birth to thoughts as to how to satisfy those needs; the differences between people
Paragraphs 20–24 of the Introduction to the Zohar

Introduction to the Zohar

20. In the light of what we have already explained, we have resolved our first question, which was, "What is our essence?"

Our essence, like that of all of the created world, is neither more nor less than the will to receive. However, not in the form that it manifests in state two, which is the will to receive for ourselves alone, but in its true form that exists in state one in the *Ein Sof*; in its eternal form, which is of receiving only in order to give satisfaction to our Creator. Even though we have not yet arrived in practice at the third state, and our work is still incomplete, nevertheless this does not damage our essence in any sense as the third state is already ours with complete certainty, as it is implicit in state one.

There is a principle in the Talmud that declares: If anyone is owed money that he or she is sure to collect, it is as if he or she has already collected it.[1] That this has not yet occurred in practice is considered a defect only if there is even the smallest doubt as to whether or not it will happen.

The fact that state three is not yet manifest to our consciousness would only be a problem if there were any doubt as to whether state three was going to happen or not. But since it is certainly going to come about, it is as if we had already come into the third state. Likewise, the body in its present form does not damage our essence in any way, since it and all its acquisitions will be completely nullified together with the entire framework of uncleanness that is its source. We learn [from the Talmud] that anything which is about to be burned can be considered as if it were burned already. Thus the body is considered as if it never came into being.

Look at this principle from the Talmud: "If anyone is owed money that he is sure to collect, it is as if he has already collected it." Can you see how this is a definition of faith? If we have total faith that we are going to receive the money, then we would we have the same joy as if we had already received it. If, however, there exists even the smallest iota of doubt, this would constitute a defect

Lesson eight

in our faith, as in that case we would rather have the money now. In the same way, if we have total faith that state three is already there waiting for us in total and complete perfection, we would have the same inner joy, no matter what the state two experience is. The ups and downs of the reality of this world would trouble us less, because we have confidence in the outcome of the process.

Can you feel the deep joy in knowing that our perfection already exists? Can you feel a new feeling of hope and confidence in the future, knowing that you, in your deepest essence, are already complete, as is all humanity, in the best possible way?

In the same way that we understand that there are parallel universes, we can let this parallelism penetrate our lives. We are conscious of harsh experiences and feel sorrow for ourselves and for our fellows, but there is an additional possibility, and that is to open up to the recognition that these experiences are not the whole story, but there is a parallel reality of joy and perfection.

Rabbi Baruch Shalom haLevi Ashlag wrote an article on this point in his book of essays, *Bircat Shalom*, which we shall study now. In order to understand this article we need to know one further detail: The 'right-hand line' and the 'left-hand line' refer to two basic states of consciousness upon which all the inner work rests.

The right-hand line is the state in which the state of consciousness of the person is that of faith. The person says with all his heart, "The way things are is the way they are meant to be, because the Creator is Good and does good, and the One manages the world in the best possible way." In this state of consciousness a person is in a state of joy and trust; he is happy with his lot. Even if all he has is the smallest contact with spirituality, he feels joyous, happy, and whole. In this state of consciousness the person is in affinity of form with the Creator.

The left-hand line is the state of consciousness of criticism. A person does an accounting for himself and sees the truth. He is aware of his deficiencies how, in truth, he is far from being in affinity of form with the Creator. He sees how all that he does is mixed with selfish love. This state of consciousness is one of lack; it causes him to feel sincere longing for the One, and creates the condition for true prayer to well up from the depths of his heart that God should grant his wish to become united with Him.

In order to do the inner work we need both these lines.

Lesson eight

In the following article, Rabbi Baruch Shalom haLevi Ashlag looks at how having faith in our future perfection gives us strength and joy in the present:

> The greatness of a person depends on the measure of one's faith in the future
> The holy *Zohar* states, and this is its language:
>
>> "Then Moses will sing with the children of Israel, this song to the Lord …" (Exod. 15:1).² Rabbi Abba asks, " '[Moses] *will* sing?' (Hebrew: *yashir*) and should the Scripture not have said, 'And [Moses] sang?' (Hebrew: *shar*)?" This matter depends on the future to come, that [Moses] completed [the song] both for that time and for the future to come. Israel will sing the praise of this song in the future to come."
>
> The answer that the *Zohar* gives to the question as to why the Scripture is speaking in the future tense is that the Scripture is referring to the time to come. Concerning this answer, one needs to ask, What does this have to teach us regarding our inner work?
>
> It is known that Moses is called "the faithful shepherd." My father, of blessed memory, explained that this name was given to Moses because Moses provided the children of Israel with the virtue of faith. Faith is termed *Malchut*, that is, Moses introduced the concept of *Yirat Shamayim* (the fear of being separated from God)—which is also called *Malchut Shamayim*—to the people of Israel. Thus, Moses our Teacher, peace be upon him, is called "the faithful shepherd" because of the attribute of faith, *Malchut*, which he supplied to the people. As the Scripture writes, "And they believed in God and in Moses His servant" (Exod. 14:31). This tells us that Moses is called "the faithful shepherd" because Moses brought the possibility of having faith in the One to the people.
>
> It is a known fact that a person cannot live (thrive) from a state of negativity but only from a state of positivity. That which a person receives, and enjoys receiving, is termed 'sustenance'. This is a consequence of the purpose of creation, which is the desire of the One to give pleasure to the created beings. Consequently, a person has to receive pleasure and joy so that he has something with which to please his will to receive. This is the positive state: Positivity implies fulfillment. With fulfillment the person satisfies his lacks.
>
> However, a person also needs to have a lack; otherwise, he has no place within himself to put the light of life. This lack is termed the 'vessel'. If the person has no vessels, he cannot receive anything.
>
> A lack is defined as 'desire'. That is to say, a person wants something and he feels that whatever it is he is wanting is that which he lacks. He wants to supply this lack. Both the extent to which he feels the lack, and the urgency with which

he feels the need to supply this lack, make up the degree by which the lack is measured. What defines a lack as being big or small? This depends on the extent to which the person feels the urgency for the lack to be supplied.

Sometimes a person has the feeling that he lacks something and he feels it with all his heart and soul, yet he does not have a strong will to gratify the lack. The fact that he does not have a strong will to satisfy that particular lack may have many different causes:

1) It is possible that he told his friends what he lacks and how he feels how much he needs this thing, but his friends gave him to understand that he does not have the ability to obtain that which he lacks. His friends have influenced him with their opinions that he needs to come to terms with his situation. They have weakened his power of fortitude that he could have prevailed over the obstacles preventing him from obtaining his desire. Consequently, both the lack, and the desire for it to be satisfied have weakened, because the person sees that he will never obtain that which he wants. Since he cannot see any reality that he would be able to fulfill his desire, then not obtaining his purpose causes the lack to weaken. So we see that the desire, which was originally big, lessens from despair of ever achieving it.

2) Sometimes it happens that even when the person does not tell his friends what he is yearning for, but he only overhears his friends talking, and he hears how his friends have given up hope of ever achieving their goal, then he, too, becomes influenced by their despair. He loses any enthusiasm that he may be able to reach *dvekut*, that is to say, affinity of form with the Creator, at the earliest possible opportunity, and thus he loses the power of this desire.

3) Sometimes a person thinks for himself, without any negative influence from outside, and he begins to make an accounting, and he sees that every time he wants to come closer to holiness, it actually seems the opposite—that he is going backwards and not forwards, and so he loses the power to work. We see that he is beaten down by his burden, that he has nothing with which to sustain himself because he only sees negativity and darkness. Consequently, he loses the spirit of life that he had. It is as if he has lost even the sustenance that he had previously with which he could keep his soul alive, and now he feels himself as being spiritually dead. Even though he sees the truth now, that is, he recognizes the evil which is within him, even so, this is a negative, and from this a person cannot receive any life-force. One can only sustain the will to receive through the positive.

Therefore, it is incumbent upon a person to go to the right-hand line (to the consciousness of faith) for two reasons: 1) that his will should not weaken through listening to negative talk, 2) in order to receive life-force, because this comes to a person through the positive, that is through the light, which is in a state of wholeness.

But this is hard to understand; at the very moment when a person is engaged in a critical appraisal of his way of serving God, and sees the truth, that he is really sunk in selfish love, how can you tell him to move to the right-hand line, which is the consciousness of wholeness? Wouldn't that be a complete lie? According to the best of the person's ability he is making a true self-assessment of his position.

It is known that the community and the individual are equivalent: Whatever applies to the community applies equally to the individual. With respect to the community we need to believe in the coming of the Messiah, as it is written in the prayer, "I believe in the coming of the Messiah, and even though he may tarry, nevertheless I shall wait for him, as he may come any day."[3] Therefore, it is forbidden for a person to despair and say, "I see I am not able to reach *dvekut*, affinity of form, with the One." But he should say, "Affinity of form means that I leave the exile of the nations of the world, which is the term for selfish love, and I come into the domain of holiness. Here I may correct the root of my soul and cleave to the Source of all Life."

From what we have said, it follows, that if a person believes redemption will come for the community, then perforce he must believe redemption will come to him as an individual. Thus a person needs to accept his own wholeness from the future, such that he may imagine for himself the measure of goodness, joy, and gladness he will receive when all his lacks are supplied. This will certainly give the person the spiritual satisfaction and strength to work, so he may achieve the aim he hopes for.

From what we have said, it follows, that first of all a person has to picture for himself the happiness and the delight he will have on achieving what he is looking for. But even prior to this a person has to know the purpose that he wants to achieve, and he needs to pay close attention and take great interest in the question as to what he expects out of his life. In other words he should say to himself, "I have come to know for certain what it is that I want, now that I have clarified for myself the different pleasures that one may obtain in this life. If I had the possibility to achieve my desire, then I would have the strength and understanding to say, "Now I can give thanks to the Creator of the world for the fact that He created it. Simply, I can now say with all my heart, 'Blessed be He that spoke and the world came into being.'[4] Now that I feel the goodness and joy, I can truthfully say it was worth it for me and for all created beings to have been created, so we may all receive the good and delight that I now receive from the purpose of creation, which is designated as the will to benefit the created beings."

Lesson eight

Even though the person may still be far from achieving his aim, nevertheless, if he knows, with the clearest of knowledge, from what it is that he will be able to receive his happiness in the future, then he already has the wherewithal to receive life in the present. This is what the Rabbis said: Rabbi Meir says, "Whoever occupies himself with Torah for its own sake will merit many things. Not only that, but the whole world becomes worthwhile to him. He is called 'friend,' 'beloved,' 'lover of the One,' 'a lover of all people,' 'one who gives joy to God,' 'one who gives joy to people'; he is clothed in humility and in the fear of being separated from the Creator. He is fitted to be a *Tzaddik*, a pious one, upright and faithful, keeping his fellow far from sin and bringing his fellow closer to the One. Others rejoice in his counsel and in his wisdom, in his understanding and his fortitude, as it is said, 'I have counsel and wisdom, I am understanding, I have fortitude' (Prov. 8:14). Sovereignty is given to him, governance, and resource in judgment. Secrets of the Torah are revealed to him and he becomes like an overflowing spring, like a river that does not cease. He is modest and long-suffering, forgiving those who insult him, and he is great and exalted over all God's created beings."[5]

However, without paying attention a person cannot know what is the purpose of his life, in which case he is not able to say, "It is *this* that I want."

When a person pays attention to that which he is able to achieve he feels the importance of his goal and he can imagine for himself the happiness and wholeness that will be his. So when a person feels the importance of the purpose of his life, and pictures for himself the happiness and wholeness he will achieve—and for sure, the joy and delight that he will have on its achieving cannot be estimated—then to the measure that he believes in the importance of coming to affinity of form with the Creator, and to the degree in which he believes in the principle: "Even though the Messiah tarries, nevertheless, I shall wait for him until he comes," he can receive now, in the present, the light of life, from the future, when his purpose will be fulfilled.

It is well known that there is *Or Pnimi* (inner light: the light that is actually received by the vessel) and *Or Makif* (surrounding light: the light that shines on the vessel from outside). My father, of blessed memory, taught that the *Or Pnimi* is the light received in the present, and the *Or Makif* is defined as light that will be received by the vessel in the future, but which has not yet been attained by the vessel. However, the *Or Makif* also gives a measure of light in the present according to the measure of trust the person has that he will receive it in the future.

My father told a parable about this: Once it happened that many people brought a certain type of merchandise to the market, as a result of which, this particular merchandise lost its value. All the merchants decided to sell off their stock as best they could, but there were no buyers. People were afraid to buy—they thought if they waited, maybe the price of the merchandise would go even lower. However, one man bought up all the merchandise at a very low price. When he came home and told his family what had happened at the market, they laughed at him, "What have you done? Surely all the other merchants will now want to sell off all the stocks they have in their warehouses, and the price is going to go even lower. You will find that you have wasted your money!" But the man remained adamant in his opinion. He said, "Now I am happier than ever, because I am going to make a fortune out of this merchandise! Not like usual, when I would know that I should make a profit of twenty percent, this time I shall make a profit of five hundred percent! However, I shall not sell the merchandise now, but I shall store it in the warehouse and only bring it to the market in three years' time when it will be scarce, and then I shall be able to ask any price I want for it."

So we see, that in the present, that is this year, when he prepares his accounts to see how much profit he has made, he has not made any. In the present, he has nothing to rejoice over. This is analogous to the *Or Pnimi*, which gives light to the vessel in the present. But the *Or Makif*, which gives light to the vessel in the future, also gives light in the present according to the extent that a person believes in the future, when he will receive his long-awaited reward and his joy will be complete. Now the person feels joy and is in a happy mood because of what he is going to get in the future.

This is the meaning of the above parable, regarding the merchant whom everyone laughed at because he could not find any merchandise to buy at the market other than this particular merchandise that had lost its value, and which no one wanted to buy. We find that he bought just the very thing that others had left as it did not have any value for them. He is happy and glad now, since he has total belief and feels certain that in three years time this merchandise will be scarce, and then he will get rich. We see that from what will be in the future, he gets pleasure in the present.

From what we have said it follows, that according to the measure of the person's belief in the future, plus the fact that he does not despair of ever reaching the future, as it is written, "Even though the Messiah tarries, nevertheless, I shall wait for him to come," he can take pleasure in the present moment from the future yet to come.

From the above it follows that even though a person went to the left-hand line of consciousness, that is to say, he made a self-accounting and saw that he really is in the pit of lowliness—and he saw this truth, as he did not want to deceive

Lesson eight

himself and justify his thoughts or deeds, but he sought to know the truth, and he did not care how bitter the truth is, but he really wanted to arrive at the purpose for which he was born—nonetheless, from all this truth, he cannot carry on his life, because it is impossible to live without joy, which is designated as being life-force and life. In order to live we need the light that gives life to a person, and through this life-force we have the actual possibility of working and arriving at the purpose for which we have been created.

Because of this, the person then has to move over to the right-hand line of consciousness, which is defined as wholeness. This wholeness gives the person life-force in the present moment and sustenance to his will to receive. However, this wholeness has to be based on a foundation of truth. So the question arises, how can someone receive wholeness at the same time that he sees the truth, which is that he is still sunk in selfish love from the top of his head to the soles of his feet, and that he does not have a single real spark of altruism in him? At this, he needs to say to himself, "All that I see is correct; however, this is from the perspective of the *Or Pnimi* (inner light). As regarding the present, I am sunk in selfish love, and I have nothing from which I can receive joy and life. But by means of the *Or Makif* (surrounding light) that gives light in the future, I can believe in my wholeness, as I believe in what our Sages have said, 'Even though the Messiah tarries, I shall wait for him until he comes.' Thus, I am able to draw towards me the *Or Makif*, so that it will also give light in the present." According to the measure of trust that he has in the coming of the Messiah for himself personally, he can draw life-force and joy that can give him light, now, in the present.

Thus we see that the person who is going to the right-hand line of consciousness in order to receive wholeness is actually acting in complete truth, since the *Or Makif* gives light in the present. It is actually a true path. In addition, by the fact that the person believes in the coming of the Messiah in an individual sense, he has a great virtue that through the *mitzvah* of faith he actually brings his future closer to his present in which the *Or Makif* will become *Or Pnimi*. When the *Or Makif* actually enclothes the person, in the present, then the *Or Makif* of the future becomes *Or Pnimi*.

Even though, from the rational aspect, the person sees, every time, how he gets further and further from the goal, going backwards rather than forwards, nevertheless, he overcomes his feelings of despair and goes above rationale (he goes to the consciousness of faith). Then his faith itself, his belief that in the end he will reach his goal, strengthens little by little, each time, in just the same way that small coins eventually add up to a large sum, until the person merits complete and perfect faith. This complete and eternal faith that the person merits is the light of loving-kindness with the enlightenment of wisdom (*Or d'chasadim beha'arat chochmah*), as it is written in the *Perush haSulam*.

From all that we have said, we can now understand the answer that the holy *Zohar* gives to the question as to why the Scripture writes: "Then Moses *will* sing" in the language of the future tense, which hints that in the future to come Israel will sing praise with this song. And we asked: What does this come to teach us for our inner work? Surely regarding our inner work we require to know what we need to do now in the present? If so, what can we learn from what will be in the future yet to come?

As we have explained, the matter is understood: We need to go to the consciousness of the right-hand line, which has the modality of wholeness, in order to receive life, as we cannot live from the negative. Therefore, it is good advice to feel wholeness from what will be in the future. This is why the righteous sing the song that belongs to the future. They sing it now in the present for what they will receive in the future.

According to the measure that the righteous can picture for themselves the good and the joy that they will receive in the future, so they feel this in the present. They have the faith that there is a future; that in the future, all of us will be rectified. For this they give thanks to God in the present. The measure of the praise they are able to give in the present being proportionate with their feeling.

Apart from the fact that a person now receives life from positivity, he also benefits from the fact that he views the goal of creation in general as having importance. This comes through picturing for himself the goodness and joy that is prepared for the created beings to receive. Every time he reflects on this, he sees, little by little, a bit more of what we may receive in the future; that is, he sees what is prepared for us from the perspective of the purpose of creation. Even though he sees his present situation, that there is still a huge gap separating him from his objective, he reaps the benefit of his belief in the future. However, this depends on the measure that he believes in the goal, as in the parable above. This is according to the Talmudic principle that whatever a person is sure to collect is counted as already collected.

From what we have said, we can understand the holy *Zohar*'s answer concerning why the Scripture writes in the future tense, "Then Moses will sing." It is a hint that Israel will sing this song of praise in the future yet to come. The reason we need to know this, is so that we shall be able to receive happiness and life-force now, from what will be in the future, and through this we can sing in the present as if we are already receiving now, in the present, all the good and joy. This is designated as receiving illumination from the *Or Makif*. The *Or Makif* illuminates the inner vessel from afar; so even though a person may yet

Lesson eight

be far from achieving the goodness and delight, nevertheless he or she can draw illumination from the *Or Makif* even in the present.⁶

Let us return to the beginning of paragraph 20 in the *Introduction to the Zohar* to see how this learning fits in.

Introduction to the Zohar

20. In the light of what we have already explained, we have resolved our first question, which was, "What is our essence?"

Our essence, like that of all of the created world, is neither more nor less than the will to receive. Not, however, in the form that it manifests in state two, which is the will to receive for ourselves alone, but in its true form that exists in state one in the *Ein Sof*—in its eternal form—which is that of receiving only in order to give satisfaction to our Creator. Even though we have not yet arrived in practice at the third state, and our work is still incomplete, this does not damage our essence in any sense as the third state is already ours with complete certainty, as it is implicit in state one.

There is a principle in the Talmud that declares: If anyone is owed money that he or she are sure to collect, it is as if he or she has already collected it. That this has not yet occurred in practice is considered a defect only if there is even the smallest doubt as to whether or not it will happen.

The fact that state three is not yet manifest to our consciousness would only be a problem if there were any doubt as to whether state three was going to happen or not. But since it is certainly going to come about, it is as if we had already come into the third state. Likewise, the body in its present form does not damage our essence in any way, since it, and all its acquisitions, will be completely nullified, together with the entire framework of uncleanness that is its source. We learn [from the Talmud] that anything which is about to be burned can be considered as if it were burned already. Thus the body is considered as if it never came into being.

The essence of the soul that is enclothed within the body is also that of will; however, its essence is that of the will to give. It is drawn to us from the framework of the four worlds, *Atzilut*, *Briyah*, *Yetzirah*, and *Assiyah*, of holiness. The souls exist eternally, since the form of the will to give is in complete affinity of form with the Life of all Life and is not at all exchangeable. (See paragraph 32 for completion of this discussion.)

21. You should not be led astray in this matter by the opinion of certain philosophers who say that the essence of the soul consists of the intellect, and it exists only because of the knowledge it acquires and through which it grows and has all its being. They maintain that what remains of the soul after the death of

Lesson eight

the body completely depends on the measure of intellectual learning a person achieves within his or her lifetime, to the extent that if a person lived his or her life without having acquired any intellectual learning, then nothing would survive the death of the body. This is not the view of Torah. Also, it does not speak to our hearts which intuitively know a deeper truth. Anyone who has ever tried to learn anything intellectually knows and feels that such knowledge is something acquired and not an integral part of a person's essence.

The only material that is actually **created**, whether we are dealing with spiritual entities or physical entities, is no more and no less than the will to receive. Even though we stated that the soul has solely the will to give benefit, this is true only because it is enclothed in returned light in the higher worlds from which it comes to us. The matter of this enclothing is well described in the *Petichah l'Chochmat haKabbalah*, paragraphs 13-16. (We shall study this material further on in this lesson.)

Both body and soul stem from the same root within the *Ein Sof*. This root is the vessel that is included with the light of the *Ein Sof*. It has the desire of the will to receive. As we shall learn subsequently, this desire is manifested primarily by the body, whereas the soul, which travels through the framework of holiness, acquires the will to give benefit. In the language of the Kabbalah the root vessel of the *Ein Sof* is termed 'the *Malchut* of the *Ein Sof*'.

Rabbi Ashlag describes briefly the origin and development of the body and of the soul, from their root until their manifestation, in his commentary *Or Pnimi*, part of the *Talmud Eser haSephirot*.

> And you need to know that the highest light has to emanate through four levels, until the will to receive manifests within the created being as a fixed and complete entity. The reason why the light needs to emanate through these four stages is that the will to receive is included immediately within the light as it emanates from its Root (the *Atzmut*, the essence of the One). Actually, this is how the light is designated as having left the Creator, acquiring its own name, 'light'. So long as the change of form that is the will to receive is *not* included within the light, the light is certainly designated as being in the modality of the Creator, and is not an emanation that has transformed and left the Creator. This is because in spiritual matters there cannot be pictured any differentiation between entities except through change of form.
>
> So long as there is no manifestation of this will to receive on the part of the vessel itself, it is not yet permanent in the vessel. The created being has to desire to receive the bounty; only then is the will to receive designated as being manifest

Lesson eight

by the vessel itself. This desire can only occur when the vessel lacks the bounty, because only then is it possible for the vessel to long for the bounty on its own part, such that the vessel's own will to receive now becomes apparent. Only then are the vessels of receiving completed in a permanent way.

One other thing you need to know is that every emanation of light from the Creator, just as it includes within it the modality of the will to receive, as we have said, must also include within it the modality of the will to give benefit. If this were not the case, the Creator and the created being would be in a state of opposition of form, which is complete separation from each other, God forbid; for opposition of form distances one from the other, as the East is removed from the West. Therefore, every light that emanates from the Creator also has to include within it the modality of the will to give benefit, in order that there may be closeness of form between the Creator and the created being. [7]

We may ask, How is the will to give benefit included within the created being?

Rabbi Ashlag drew our attention to the relevant section in the *Petichah l'Chochmat haKabbalah* at the end of paragraph 21 in the *Introduction to the Zohar*, where he addresses this point. However, this section of the *Petichah* is difficult to follow because he uses very concentrated language, including many terms we have not yet learned. To the best of my ability I shall explain the terms as we go along in the text itself, and I have also added definitions following this section. My suggestion to you is: First read the text from the *Petichah l'Chochmat haKabbalah* all the way through, then carry on reading the section from the *Introduction to the Zohar* that follows, and then read through the definitions. Then read the entire section from the *Petichah l'Chochmat haKabbalah* again. You may find the accompanying diagram on page 125 to be of use.

(It might take you several times. Have patience with yourself. It is worth taking pains and getting familiar with the ideas and terms, as these appear in all Kabbalah writings.)

Petichah l'Chochmat haKabbalah

The matter is as follows: Just as physical things are separated from each other through physical distance, so spiritual entities are separated from each other by the difference of form between them. You can find this also in this world. An example would consist of two people who are of like mind. They love each other, and even if they are physically far away from one another, it makes no difference to their relationship. The opposite is also true. If two people are far from each other in their way of looking at life, then they hate each other, and even if they

Lesson eight

are physically close to each other, it does not bring them any closer together. So difference of form distances them from one another and similarity of form brings them close to one another. If, for example, the nature of one person is entirely opposite from the nature of the other, then they are as far away from each other as the East is from the West.

In spirituality this applies in a similar way. All matters of distance, closeness, union, and coming together as one, which we discern in the spiritual worlds, are solely measures of difference of form. To the degree that spiritual entities are different in form they are separated from each other, and to the degree that they have affinity of form they join together.

So even that the will to receive is an intrinsic part of every created being, as it is the sole created aspect of the created being, and this is the vessel that is fit to receive the aim of the thought of creation, nevertheless, it is the cause of the created being becoming completely separated from the Creator, as there is a difference of form between it and the Creator, even to the extent of opposition of form. For the Creator's purpose is wholly to give benefit and He does not have the tiniest spark of receiving, whereas the modality of the created being is entirely receiving and he does not have the tiniest spark of giving benefit. There can be no greater difference of form than this, and it is therefore inevitable that this difference of form separates the created being from the Creator.

In order to deliver the created beings from this tremendous separation, the Creator caused the will to receive to contract, which led to the light leaving the vessel (Hebrew: *Tzimtzum*). Thus the final modality of the will to receive (the fourth modality) was separated from all the spiritual entities of holiness (*Partzufei Kedushah*), such that the greatest measure of receiving was left in the modality of an empty space, that is to say, a vessel empty of all light. (This empty space, the *Challal haPanui*, is the origin of the framework of uncleanness.)

All the spiritual entities that are in the framework of holiness emerged with the modality of a barrier, *Masach* (the ability to overcome self-gratification) erected over their vessels of receiving (*Malchut*), to prevent them from receiving light in their fourth (final) modality.

Then when the *Or Elyon* (highest light) comes to the created being, this *Masach* (barrier) rejects it, pushing it back to the Creator. It is as if the *Or Elyon* and the *Masach* are clashing with each other, and this results in the *Masach* raising *Or Chozer* (returning light) from the vessel to the Creator, that is from below to above.

This *Or Chozer* then enclothes the ten *Sephirot* (which are all the facets) of the *Or Elyon*. When the *Or Chozer* enclothes the *Or Elyon*, it itself becomes the

Lesson eight

vessel with which to receive the *Or Elyon* in place of the fourth modality (the original vessel of receiving).

Subsequently, the *Malchut* of the spiritual entity expands exactly in accordance with the measure of the *Or Chozer*, which is the light that the vessel gave back to the Creator. The *Or Chozer* then enclothes the *Or Elyon*, and thus the *Or Elyon*, together with the *Or Chozer*, emanate from above to below (from the Creator to the created being), and thus the lights become enclothed in the vessels, that is, within the framework of this *Or Chozer*. This is the inner meaning of the 'head aspect' of the spiritual entity and the 'body aspect' of the spiritual entity that exist at every stage. For the union that results from the clash between the *Or Elyon* and the *Masach* raises the *Or Chozer* from below to above, and enclothes the ten *Sephirot* of the *Or Elyon* as ten *Sephirot* of the head of the spiritual entity. This is only a potential vessel, because in the head aspect of the spiritual entity actual enclothing cannot take place.

After this, when the *Malchut* subsequently expands, according to the measure of the *Or Chozer* as it emanates from above to below, then the *Or Chozer* becomes a vessel for the *Or Elyon*, and the light is enclothed in actuality in the vessel, and this is called 'the body of the spiritual entity'; the term 'body' implying a completed vessel (that is a vessel which receives the light in actuality).

So now, after the *Tzimtzum*, new vessels have been made within the spiritual entities of the framework of holiness, which are used instead of the fourth modality of the vessels. These are made from the *Or Chozer* (returned light) that resulted from the clash of the *Or Elyon* (highest light) with the *Masach* and the subsequent union. However, we need to understand how this *Or Chozer* (returned light) became a vessel with which to receive light. After all, primarily, it is light that was pushed back by the *Masach* when the vessel overcame its desire to receive. It seems to be operating here in a role that is opposite to its very nature!

I shall explain this to you by taking an example from this world: It is in the nature of a person to value and hold dear the quality of giving benefit, and to be repulsed by and despise the quality of taking from one's fellow. Therefore, if we were to take the case that somebody comes to another person's house and the host asks him to eat, even though he may be very hungry he refuses to eat, as taking a gift from his fellow is despicable and lowly in his view. However, if the host beseeches the guest repeatedly to join him in a meal, to such a measure that it becomes obvious to him that he will be doing the host a great favor if he eats his food, then he is agreeable and eats with him. He no longer feels he is receiving a gift and the host is giving to him, rather, he feels the opposite. He now feels

The flow of the *Or Elyon* (Highest Light) and its interaction with the *Malchut* (vessel of the *Ein Sof*) as described in the *Petichah l'Chochmat haKabbalah*:

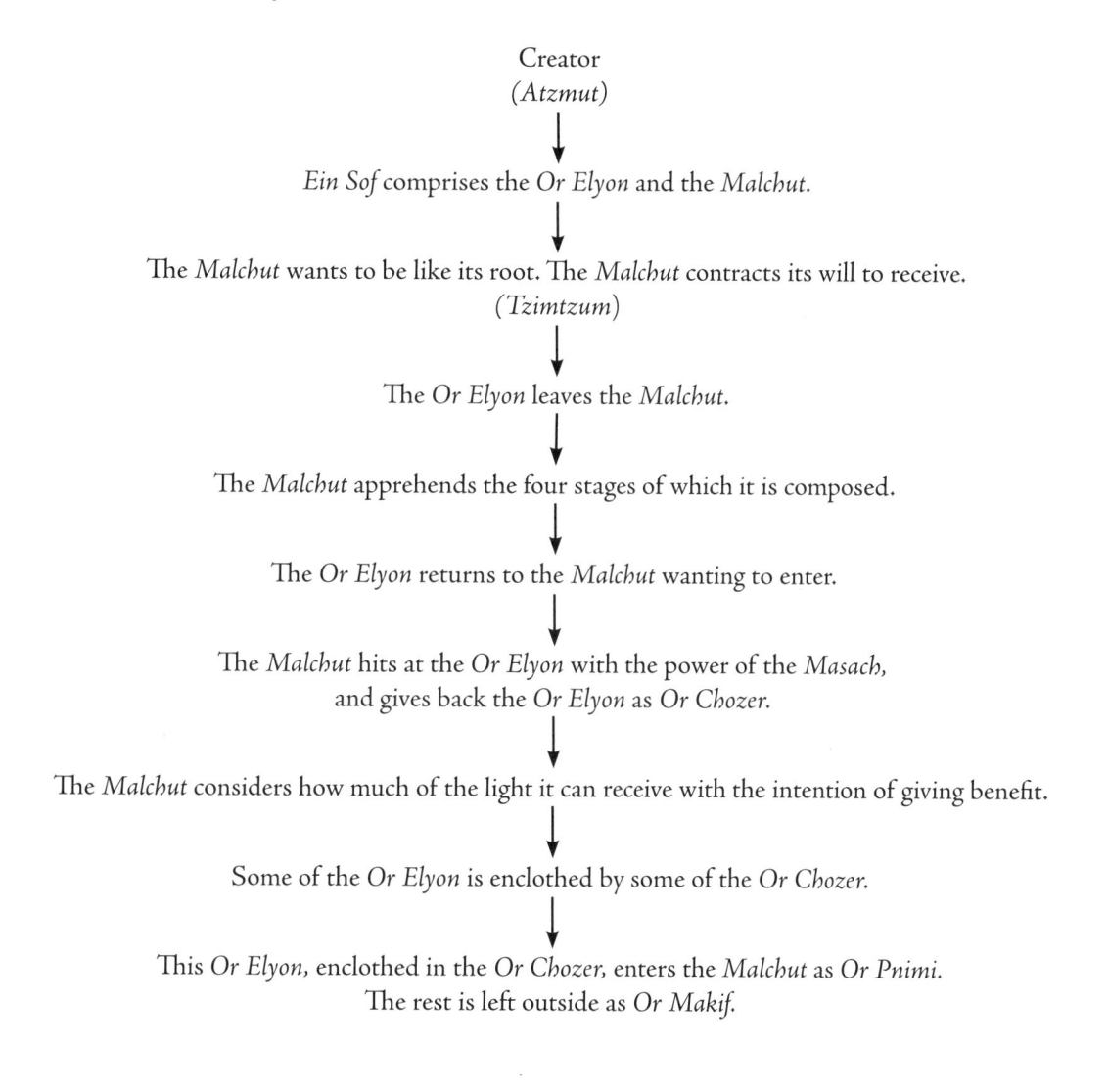

Creator
(*Atzmut*)
↓
Ein Sof comprises the *Or Elyon* and the *Malchut*.
↓
The *Malchut* wants to be like its root. The *Malchut* contracts its will to receive.
(*Tzimtzum*)
↓
The *Or Elyon* leaves the *Malchut*.
↓
The *Malchut* apprehends the four stages of which it is composed.
↓
The *Or Elyon* returns to the *Malchut* wanting to enter.
↓
The *Malchut* hits at the *Or Elyon* with the power of the *Masach*,
and gives back the *Or Elyon* as *Or Chozer*.
↓
The *Malchut* considers how much of the light it can receive with the intention of giving benefit.
↓
Some of the *Or Elyon* is enclothed by some of the *Or Chozer*.
↓
This *Or Elyon*, enclothed in the *Or Chozer*, enters the *Malchut* as *Or Pnimi*.
The rest is left outside as *Or Makif*.

Lesson eight

that he is the giver and he is the one who is doing the host a favour by accepting the meal.

So here we see, that even though hunger and appetite are the particular vessels for receiving food, and this man had sufficient hunger and appetite to receive his host's meal, nevertheless, he was unable to taste even the smallest thing in his friend's house on account of his feelings of shame. However, when the host began to entreat him, and he began to refuse, there began to form within him new vessels for receiving the meal. The power of the host's entreaties and the power of the guest's refusals grew stronger, until in the end they grew to a sufficient measure as to transform the guest's quality of receiving to a quality of giving, to the extent that the guest was able to believe that he was doing a favor and bringing great satisfaction to his host by virtue of his eating. Thus new vessels for receiving his host's meal were formed. It transpires that the force of the guest's refusal became the main vessel for receiving the meal in place of the hunger and the appetite, even though these are truly the customary vessels.

From this above analogy of the host and his guest, we can understand the matter of the union that results from the clash between the *Or Elyon* and the *Masach*, and the matter of the *Or Chozer* returned by the *Masach*, which forms a new vessel for receiving the highest light, instead of the fourth modality of the vessel.

One can compare the clash of the *Or Elyon*, which hits the *Masach* because it wants to emanate into the fourth modality of the vessel, to the pleading of the host with his guest to eat with him. Just as the host so ardently desires his friend to receive the good meal he has prepared, so does the highest light want to give to the vessel. Similarly, one can compare the *Masach* hitting at the *Or Elyon* and returning it, to the rejection and refusal of the guest to eat the host's meal. He pushes the bounty away. We see that it is just the very refusal and pushing away that actually creates the correct vessel for receiving the host's meal.

This is analogous to the *Or Chozer* that goes up to the Creator, following the clash of the *Or Elyon* on the *Masach* and its subsequent rejection of the *Or Elyon*. The *Or Chozer* becomes the new vessel for receiving the *Or Elyon* in place of the fourth modality of the vessel, which was the actual vessel of receiving before the *Tzimtzum*. However, this *Masach* is installed only in the spiritual entities of the worlds of *Atzilut*, *Briyah*, *Yetzirah*, and *Assiyah* that belong to the framework of holiness. This *Masach* is not rectified for the spiritual entities that belong to the *klipot* (shells), or that belong to this world. In these worlds it is the fourth modality of the vessel itself that is used as the vessel for receiving. This causes the spiritual entities of these worlds to be separated from the *Or Elyon*, because the antipathy of form that is inherent

Lesson eight

in the fourth modality of the vessel with respect to the *Or Elyon* separates these spiritual entities from the *Or Elyon*. Thus the *klipot*, and the wicked, are considered as 'dead' because they are separated from the Life of all Lives by their will to receive for themselves alone.

Go into this deeply because it is impossible to explain it further.[8]

Rabbi Ashlag explains to us here that although the essential desire of the soul at its source in the *Ein Sof* is indeed the will to receive, it uses the will to give benefit as it descends through the spiritual worlds in the framework of holiness. This takes the form of the *Masach* and the *Or Chozer* (returned light). Thus we read in the *Introduction to the Zohar*:

Introduction to the Zohar

21. (*continued*) The only material that is actually **created**, whether we are dealing with spiritual entities or physical entities, is no more and no less than the will to receive. Even though we stated that the soul has solely the will to give benefit, this is true only because it is enclothed in returned light in the higher worlds from which it comes to us. The matter of this enclothing is well described in the *Petichah l'Chochmat haKabbalah* paragraphs 13-16, as above.

Terms which appear in the above paragraphs:
Tzimtzum—The first event in the evolving chain of the worlds
In the *Ein Sof*, the *Or Elyon* (the highest light) and the *Malchut* of the *Ein Sof*, (the vessel of the *Ein Sof*) are in simple union, according to the inner meaning of the phrase, "He and His Name are One." 'He', referring to the light and 'His Name', referring to the vessel.

However, the *Malchut* of the *Ein Sof* desired additional affinity of form (*dvekut*) with the *Or Elyon*, not because of any lack in their unity, which was already present, but because every branch wants to be like its root. This is a spiritual law. The vessel, being a branch of the light, wants to be giving just as the light is giving. Therefore, the *Malchut* contracted (*tzimtzema*) its will to receive in order to lessen its difference of form with the light.

There is no compulsion in spirituality, and all actions depend upon desire. Therefore, as a consequence of the *Tzimtzum*, the *Or Elyon* left the *Malchut*, and the *Malchut* became empty of light. In this way a space for the evolution of the worlds was formed.

(Don't be misled into thinking we are talking about material space, God forbid. A 'space' in the language of the Kabbalah means a potential area of consciousness.)

Lesson eight

Parzuf (spiritual entity)
A complete spiritual entity is one that includes both a head aspect and a body aspect. The 'head' represents the potential of the vessel, wherein the vessel makes a calculation of how much light it can receive with the intention of giving and how much it must reject. The 'body' represents the part of the vessel that receives the light in actuality.

Again be careful to note that we are talking about consciousness and not spatial images.

Kedushah (holiness)
Whatever is in affinity of form with the Creator, whether it is a complete framework, or one spiritual entity, is designated as being in holiness.

Fourth modality of the vessel
The final and most complete form of the will to receive. This is the vessel itself. It comes into expression in the consciousness of this world as the will to receive for oneself alone, or, as it is sometimes called, the will to receive for the sake of receiving. These two terms are synonymous.

The complete rectification of the fourth modality of the vessel is the will to receive for the sake of giving benefit.

Challal Panui (empty space)
The source of the will to receive for oneself alone. The *Malchut* of the *Ein Sof* gives rise to the *Challal Panui* following the *Tzimtzum*. This is the part of the vessel that, as yet, cannot receive with the intention of giving benefit, as it is not yet rectified. It is the source of the framework of uncleanness.

Masach
This is the power of prevailing that the vessel exerts over its lack. The *Masach* represents the action of the vessel, when, despite the lack it feels, it prefers to return the light rather than receive it for itself. It chooses affinity of form (*dvekut*).

Tzimzum and *Masach*
After the *Malchut* of the *Ein Sof* chose more *dvekut* and the light left it, the *Malchut* remained empty. We say that the *Malchut* is in *tzimtzum*, which implies that the lack is not supplied. The process of *tzimtzum* lessens the difference of

form that exists between the *Malchut* and the light, in that the *Malchut* is not receiving, but it does not give rise to complete affinity of form with the light. This is because the light has the active desire to give benefit.

The light awakens the desire in the *Malchut* that it should receive from it. The light "hits" the *Malchut*, which persists in its refusal to accept it, until it perceives that by its acceptance it would cause great pleasure to the Creator.

This refusal to accept the light, unless it is for the purpose of giving, is carried out by the *Masach* of the *Malchut*, as the vessel's desire for affinity of form with the light prevails over its own desire to receive the light. Only with the *Malchut*'s acceptance of the light is it possible for the Creator to actually carry out the original thought of creation, which is to give pleasure to the created beings. So we see that the light and the vessel arrive at a compromise. The part of the light that the vessel is able to receive for the sake of giving benefit, it receives; this light is called *Or Pnimi*, 'inner light'. The part of the light that the vessel is not able to receive with the intention of giving benefit it rejects via the *Masach*. This light remains outside the vessel and is called *Or Makif* 'surrounding light'. The action of the compromise, taken altogether, is called the *Zivug d'Haca'ah*. (The word *zivug* (union) refers to the part of the compromise wherein the *Masach* allows light into the vessel; *haca'ah* (hitting) refers to the part of the compromise wherein most of the light is kept out, as the *Malchut* "hits" the light back towards the Creator in order to retain its affinity of form.)

Haca'ah (hitting, or clashing with)
In the language of the Kabbalah two opposing opinions are referred to as 'hitting at each other'. The opinion of the light is that it should enter the vessel. The opinion of the vessel is not to allow the light to enter.

Zivug (union)
When it is enclothed in the *Or Chozer*, the *Or Elyon* can enter the vessel. This entry of light into the vessel is called *zivug* (union).

Zivug d'Haca'ah (The entry of the light into the spiritual entity)
This term describes the action which takes place between the *Masach* and the *Or Elyon*. The *Masach* first of all pushes the light back towards the Creator as *Or Chozer*, and only afterwards does the *Masach* allow a certain amount of light into the vessel, according to its intention of giving benefit.

Or Elyon (highest light), also called *Or Yashar* (straight light)
This is the light that comes directly from the Creator in accordance with the purpose of creation. Its direction is termed 'from above to below'.

The ten *Sephirot* of the highest light
These are the subtlest vessels for the *Or Elyon*, that, following the *Tzimtzum*, are revealed as being the components of the *Malchut*. They contain impressions of the light they had when they were filled with light in the *Ein Sof* and are therefore called *Sephirot*, which means "shining ones." They function as channels for the *Or Elyon* at every level. We shall learn their details in due course.

Or Chozer (returned light)
This is the light which the *Masach* gives back as its first action when the *Or Elyon* hits it. Subsequently, a part of the *Or Chozer* becomes the 'returned light that enclothes the *Or Elyon*', in accordance with the calculation of the vessel, which decides how much it can receive with the intention of giving benefit.

From Below to Above
The direction of the *Or Chozer*, from the created being to the Creator, is termed from 'below to above'. This light gives the vessel affinity of form with the Creator.

Enclothing
The term 'enclothing' in the Kabbalah refers to a lower spiritual entity that provides a framework or support for a higher spiritual entity. In order to do so, the highest, purest aspect of the supporting entity has to be in affinity of form with the lowest aspect of the higher, more inner spiritual entity.

The term 'the *Or Chozer* that enclothes the *Or Elyon*', means that the *Or Chozer* provides a framework, or a new vessel, through which the *Malchut* can receive the *Or Elyon*, instead of receiving with the fourth modality of the vessel. The *Or Chozer* is in affinity of form with the *Or Elyon*, thus allowing the *Or Elyon* to be received with the intention of giving benefit.

Here ends the list of the definitions and terms. It is worth going over this whole section again, but if you don't fully understand it, or the process learned, don't get stuck and feel unable to move forward. In Kabbalah the same ideas are repeated many times in different ways. If you don't understand it this time, you

Lesson eight

will have other opportunities subsequently. This also teaches us to let go of the feeling we need to "control" our learning. The truth is in fact the opposite. It is a privilege to have any contact with this learning at all, and the answers, understandings, and insights come for each person naturally and at their own pace.

Rabbi Ashlag continues in the *Introduction to the Zohar*:

Introduction to the Zohar

21. *(continued)* The way we discriminate between one entity and another is only via its will alone. The will that is in every entity gives birth to needs, and needs give birth to thoughts and to intellectual considerations in the appropriate measure required to bring about the satisfaction of these needs, all of which are generated by the will to receive.

So we see that the change of form that exists between the soul and the body is expressed in practice by the difference that exists between their wills. The will of the soul is to give benefit, and the will of the body is to receive. So we see that desire, whether it is to receive or to give, is the prime mover for the whole of the spiritual and physical cosmos. Thus will begets needs, which produce thoughts and actions.

Take a few moments to consider the unique expression of your soul. How does the desire of your soul manifest itself? Can we become more practised at paying attention to the soul's desire so that we are more willing to act on it? Write in your journal on these questions.

Introduction to the Zohar

21. *(continued)* Insofar as people's desires differ from one another, so do their needs, their thoughts and their intellectual worlds differ from each other.

Take time to contemplate this. What a beautiful, non-judgmental way this is of defining the differences between people. Write in your journal ways in which you perceive members of your family as differing from you. Write how these differences enrich your life. Do the same for your friends.

Rabbi Ashlag continues this theme:

Introduction to the Zohar

21. *(continued)* For example, there are those whose will to receive is limited to animal lusts alone. As a result, their needs, their thoughts and even their intellectual worlds are devoted to gratifying this animal will. Even though they are

Lesson eight

using their intellect and their experience as human beings, nevertheless these are subjugated to the purpose of supplying their animal needs.

As we noted earlier, satisfying one's basic needs for existence such as sufficient food, a roof over our heads, basic security, and so forth, even though these are needs we have in common with the animal kingdom, does not separate us from the Creator. These basic needs are not what Rabbi Ashlag is defining here as animal lusts. Rather, the definition of animal lusts implies going beyond the physical necessity of reasonable living, longing instead for luxuries that appertain to the material world.

Take a moment to jot down a few examples from your own life where you act predominantly to gratify your will to receive for yourself alone at this animal level.

Introduction to the Zohar
21. *(continued)* Other people's will to receive predominantly takes the form of human appetites which are, for example, issues of honor or of control over others, which are not desires found within the animal species. All their needs, thoughts and intellectual designs are dedicated to gratifying this will in every possible way.

Dominance for the sake of maintaining the best chances of survival of the group, or for the fertilization of the females with the most potent seed is certainly demonstrated in the higher animal species. However, this dominance, or desire for control, is actually a means to fulfill the underlying desire of survival, which is a desire all life forms share. In this paragraph Rabbi Ashlag is referring to the will for honor or for power over others as desires in themselves, which are purely human appetites.

Now find examples of the will to dominate or receive honor for oneself alone within yourself. Jot the examples down in your journal.

Introduction to the Zohar
21. *(continued)* Then there are people whose will to receive is directed towards scholarship and acquiring intellectual knowledge. Their needs, thoughts and intellectual world are directed towards satisfying this end.

Jot down examples of these wills to receive from your own life.

Introduction to the Zohar

22. These three types of will are to be found, for the most part, in varying degrees throughout the entire human species, but combined in each person in differing amounts, which thus accounts for the variations that exist between one person and another. From this consideration of materialistic attributes, one can extrapolate to a like consideration of the attributes of spiritual entities according to their spiritual value.

23. One can also regard the human soul in this way. Human souls are spiritual entities which, through the garments of the specific type of light they receive from the higher spiritual worlds from which they have come, have only the will to give pleasure to God. This will is the essential nature of the soul. Thus, when the soul is enclothed within the body of the human being, it begets within the person needs, thoughts and intellectual designs which are directed towards fulfilling its will to give benefit to its full capacity, in other words, according to the measure of the will within that particular soul.

It is worthwhile to take time to consider the desires of the soul. For the most part we are not as conscious of the will of the soul as we are of the ego or of the body. The voice of the soul is quieter, less strident in its demands. It has different ways of expressing itself, which vary from one individual to another. The desires of the soul may be experienced as a whisper of an inner voice, a flash of intuition, or stirrings of conscience. Likewise, the fulfillment of its desires also differs from person to person according to the unique qualities of the individual. One person may express the will to give via creativity, another through voluntary work in the community. Yet another may express his or her giving benefit primarily within the family, while another may express giving benefit through work in education. There are myriad expressions to giving benefit. Do you have one way or several ways of giving benefit that are characteristic of you?

Introduction to the Zohar

24. The substance and essence of the body is only the will to receive for itself alone. All that happens to it and its acquisitions are only fulfillments of this defective will to receive. It was only created right from the start in order for us to remove it entirely from the world so that we may come to the third state, a state of perfection that manifests at the end of the time of healing. Therefore the body, together with all its acquisitions, is mortal, transitory, and worthless, like a passing shadow that leaves no trace behind it. In contrast, the being and essence of the soul consists only of the will to give. All that happens to it and its acquisitions are fulfillments of that will to give that already exists in the first eternal state, and in the third state that has yet to come. Therefore, it is not at all

Lesson eight

mortal or exchangeable; it itself and all that it has acquired exist forever in life eternal. At the time of the death of the body, no lack occurs to the soul and all it has acquired. On the contrary, the absence of the body in its defective form strengthens the soul greatly and enables it to then ascend to the higher spiritual worlds, to the Garden of Eden.

The acquisitions of the soul are thus all the unconditional love, compassion and kindness that the soul has managed to give, to others and to God, during its sojourn on earth. Together with the soul itself *these* acquisitions are eternal.

Introduction to the Zohar

24. (continued). Now we have properly explained that the immortality of the soul is in no way dependent on what knowledge it acquired, as those philosophers suggested. On the contrary, its immortality is part of its very essence, which is the will to give. The knowledge that it acquires is its reward, not its essence.

1. Gemorrah, Yevamot 38b
2. Zohar, Perush haSulam, Parashat b'Shalach, paragraph 216. The Scripture quoted from Exodus is usually translated "then Moses sang" but if translated literally the Hebrew does say "then Moses will sing", as the Zohar points out.
3. One of the thirteen principles of faith as formulated by Maimonides. Recited as part of the morning prayers.
4. Prayer Book, Morning Prayer
5. Pirkei Avot, chapter six
6. Bircat Shalom, volume two, year 5747, article nine
7. Talmud Eser haSephirot part one, chapter one, paragraph 50
8. Petichah l'Chochmat haKabbalah paragraphs 13–16

Ein Od Milvado!

"There is nothing other than the One!"

Lesson Nine

The language of the branches; the revival of the dead; the true goal and fulfillment of the will to receive
Paragraphs 25–28 of the Introduction to the Zohar

During this lesson we shall have the opportunity to learn another small piece translated from the *Zohar*. However, before we can get directly to it we first need to understand the nature of the language of the *Zohar* and of the other books of Kabbalah. They were written in a code called the "language of the branches" as described by Rabbi Ashlag in his commentary on the *Etz Chayim* of the Ari, the *Talmud Eser haSephirot*. Here follows his description:

> First of all we need to know that when we want to talk about spiritual entities that are beyond space, time, and movement, and even more so when we refer to Divinity, we do not have the words available with which we can express ourselves or with which we can even think about such matters. All of our vocabulary is extrapolated from the world as it relates to our senses. So how can we use words taken from our everyday vocabulary in an area that cannot be experienced by the senses or even imagined by the imagination? For example, if we consider a delicate word such as "lights," even that is used in an imaginary way as borrowed from the light of the sun or the light felt by satisfaction. So how can we use these words to express ourselves when dealing with matters of Divinity? The use of such a word will certainly not give the reader a true sense of what is actually being talked about.
>
> This is even more so in the case where we are using words to reveal in writing a complex discussion of the wisdom of Kabbalah on the printed page, in a manner similar to that of researchers in any other discipline. Then, if we were to err in our understanding of the precise meaning of even one word that is used inaccurately, the reader would become completely confused and would not understand the whole discussion.
>
> For this reason, the masters of Kabbalah chose a special language that can be called "the language of the branches." It is based on the premise that **there is no entity or pattern of behavior in this world that is not drawn from its root in the spiritual worlds.** On the contrary, the beginning of every entity in this world is in the upper worlds, and only subsequently does it evolve down into this world.

Lesson nine

Thus the Sages found a ready-made language at their disposal which they could use to communicate their perception of the upper worlds, both orally between each other, and in writing across generations. **They simply took the names of the branches that appear in this world, such that each name, being self-explanatory, points, as with a finger, to its spiritual root in the system of the higher worlds.**

This adequately explains the fact that there are to be found in most books of Kabbalah expressions that are astonishing and that sometimes appear alien to the human spirit. Once the Sages had chosen this language of the branches with which to express themselves, they could not omit any one of the branches because of its lowliness and thus suppress any particular concept, seeing there is no other branch in this world that they could substitute instead. They could not exchange one branch for another, for, just as two hairs do not sprout from one single pore, so two branches never come from the same root. It is inconceivable to omit one essential element of wisdom because of the lowliness of its expression. Moreover, such an omission would cause a defect and great confusion in the entire exposition of the wisdom. This is because we have no other wisdom, amongst all the worldly wisdoms, like that of the Kabbalah, wherein the issues are so interwoven with each other through prime mover and sequel, or cause and effect; where the issues are joined and connected one to another from beginning to end in one long chain. Therefore, one is not free to exchange or convert one term for another, or exchange a lowly expression for a higher one. On the contrary, we are obliged to always use the appropriate branch, which points, as with a finger, to its root in the higher world. Then we must explain the term, giving an exact definition that can be understood by students.

While people's eyes have not yet opened to directly perceive spiritual phenomena, and they lack proficiency in the knowledge of how the branches in this world relate to their roots in the higher worlds, they are like blind men feeling their way along a wall, as they are not able to understand even one word in its true meaning. Every word is the name of a certain branch that relates to its root. Therefore, the only possibility of understanding is for them to receive an explanation from a master Kabbalist, who, when he explains a concept, is really translating from one language to another—from the language of the branches to the colloquial spoken language—and thus he is able to explain a spiritual concept to some degree.

And this is the matter over which I have labored in this explanation, to explain the ten *Sephirot* in the way that the great and godly Sage, the Ari, taught, according to their spiritual purity, they being abstract from all tangible apprehension. In this way, even the beginner can approach this wisdom without stumbling on

Lesson nine

any materialization or mistake. By understanding these ten *Sephirot* the door will be opened to look and know how to understand all other matters in this wisdom.[1]

The language used in the Kabbalah is a most important aspect of its study, and it is really worthwhile spending time on this point. Firstly, it is due to the fact that this basic understanding of the language of the *Zohar* was lacking for generations that so many misunderstandings have grown up around the nature of the Kabbalah that persist to this day. Secondly, we can see from this discussion how important it is for us to take the trouble to learn the language and the terms of the Kabbalah as precisely as we possibly can, just as we would any other body of knowledge that we wish to learn, like zoology or computer science. Similarly, in the realm of Kabbalah, only through the fact that there are terms and definitions of words can we understand the material precisely. In addition, only a common understanding of these terms enables accurate communication between people about the subject being discussed. In his work, the *Talmud Eser haSephirot*, Rabbi Ashlag includes what amounts to a dictionary of the "language of the branches," in which he elucidates the exact meanings of the terms used by the Ari in his work the *Etz Chayim*. These definitions also apply to other works of the Kabbalah, including the *Zohar*.

The concept behind the language of the branches is not complex. Imagine an upside-down tree, with the roots in the spiritual worlds and the branches in this world. By indicating a word normally applied to a particular branch in this world, the Sage actually intended the spiritual root from which this particular branch sprang. However, unless one has a clear perception of the relationships that exist between the branches as they appear in this world and their corresponding roots in the higher worlds, one would not know how to decipher this language. This is the great work that Rabbi Ashlag did. By deciphering this language for us, and translating its terms and definitions into our spoken language, he opened up the possibility for ordinary men and women, who do not possess such insight, to, nonetheless, study the Kabbalah, and thus benefit themselves and others.

Now that the idea of the language of the branches is understood we can continue with our study of the *Introduction of the Zohar*:

Introduction to the Zohar

25. Now we can offer a complete solution to our fifth inquiry (paragraph 3) in which we asked the following question: Seeing that the body is so defective that

139

the soul cannot manifest its full purity until the body has completely disintegrated, why then, does the body have to return in the revival of the dead? The question is compounded by the statement of the Sages, which tells us that when the bodies will return to life they will have all the blemishes that they acquired during their lifetimes, so that no one will be able to claim that this is someone else.

Zohar
Come and see: So shall it be when they awaken from the dust at the resurrection of the dead. As they went into the grave, so will they get up. If they were limping or blind when they went in, so they will be limping or blind when they get up, that is to say, in the same garment (which is the body). They should not say that this is some other body that has been awakened for revival. After that, the Holy Blessed One will heal them and they will be whole before Him. Then the world will be completely whole, and on that day God will be One and His Name, One.[2]

Let us translate this passage from the language in which it is written, the language of the branches, into our regular spoken language:

Language of the Branches	Spoken Language
dust	inactive
dead	the wicked, who are in opposition of form with respect to the Creator
limping or **blind**	uncorrected defects in the vessel that is using its will to receive for oneself alone
body	the will to receive for oneself alone
heal	the rectification of the will to receive, giving it the intention of giving benefit
whole	the will to receive is complete, both with respect to the *tikkun* of creation and with respect to the purpose of creation; the will to receive with the intention of giving benefit
day	direct revelation of the Creator
God	light that emanates from the essence of the Creator
His Name	the rectified vessel in the *Ein Sof*
One	in *dvekut*, affinity of form

Lesson nine

Now the above paragraph from the *Zohar* when written in spoken language would read as follows:

"Come and see: So shall it be when the wicked awaken; that is, the wills to receive become active after being inactive, at the resurrection of the wicked. In the same way that they were put aside, so will they get up. If they were using a particular will to receive for oneself alone, which went into disuse, so they will be using the identical will to receive for oneself alone when it becomes active. One could not say that this is some other will to receive that has been awakened for revival. After that the Holy Blessed One will rectify the wills to receive for oneself alone, and they will be transformed into the wills to receive in order to give benefit. Then both the individual, and the general consciousness, will only operate according to the will to receive for giving benefit. On that day God will be One and His Name, One. There will be a direct revelation of the light of the One together with the rectified will to receive, which will all be in affinity of form."

Introduction to the Zohar

25. (continued) We can understand this very well in the light of the thought of creation, that is, from state one. Since the thought of creation is to give pleasure to created beings, this, of necessity, requires the creation of a massive will to receive all the bounty that is contained in the thought of creation. Immense pleasure and immense will to receive the pleasure go together. We have already said that this immense will to receive is the only raw material of creation. One needs nothing more in order to fulfill the thought of creation. The nature of a perfect Creator implies that nothing superfluous would be created. As it is said in the Song of Unity, "In all Your work, You have forgotten nothing. You did nothing less than what was necessary and nothing more."

This prodigious will to receive was removed from the framework of holiness and was given over to the framework of uncleanness from which springs the existence of the bodies, their sustenance, and their acquisitions in this world.

This is the case until a person reaches thirteen years of age. Then, through the practice of Torah, he or she begins to attain a soul of holiness, which then gets its sustenance from the framework of the worlds of holiness, according to the measure of the holy soul which he or she has attained.

We have also said above, that no healing comes for the body during the course of the period of the world's existence which is given to us for the work of Torah and *mitzvot*. That is to say, no healing comes to this massive will to receive that is contained within the body. All healing that comes through our work only affects the soul, which ascends, through this healing, to higher levels of holiness and purity, ever increasing the soul's will to give. It is for this reason that the destiny of the body is to die, to be buried, and to disintegrate, as it itself receives no healing.

However, it cannot remain like this, because, in the final analysis, if this massive will to receive were to be permanently lost from the world, the thought of creation could not be carried out. The purpose of creation is that we should receive all the great delights with which God planned to give joy to His created beings. Great will to receive and great pleasure go together. If the will to receive were to be reduced in any measure, then in accordance with that reduced measure, the joy and pleasure received would be correspondingly lessened.

26. Now, we have already seen that state one absolutely obliges that state three should issue forth in all the full measure of the thought of creation, just as it is in state one, with not even the smallest detail missing. Therefore it is state one which necessitates the resurrection of the dead bodies. That is to say, it necessitates the resurrection of the body's prodigious will to receive for oneself, which has already been wiped out, lost, and rotted in state two, and must then come and be revived again in all its most exaggerated measure with no straits placed upon it, in other words, with all the blemishes that it had. Then the work begins anew of transforming this enormous will to receive, so that it will only be used as the will to receive in order to give benefit.

From this we profit in two ways: Firstly, we now have a vessel of sufficient capacity to receive all the good, the delight and the tenderness that is implied in the thought of creation, inasmuch as we already have a body with a fantastically large desire to receive those pleasures, and the measure of the desire and the measure of the pleasure received go together. Secondly, since our receiving in this manner will only occur according to the measure with which we can give satisfaction to our Creator, and, furthermore, this type of receiving is considered as complete giving, we find that we have also come to complete affinity of form, which is oneness with God. This is our form in state three. Thus we can see that state one definitely requires the revival of the dead.

27. The revival of the dead can only come about close to the end of the healing process, which is to say, near the completion of state two. For once we have merited to negate our prodigious will to receive for ourselves and received the will only of giving benefit, and once we have merited all the wonderful degrees of the soul, which are called *Nefesh, Ruach, Neshamah, Chayah,* and *Yechidah,* through our work in negating this will to receive, we shall then have reached a most supreme perfection. At this point, it is possible to revive the body, with all its prodigious will to receive, but now we are no longer damaged by it, as it does

not separate us from our unity with God. On the contrary, we overcome it and give to it the form of giving benefit.

Actually, this is the accepted way of dealing with any personal negative trait we wish to work on. At first, we need to completely disassociate from it to the absolute extreme, so that nothing is left of it at all. Afterwards, we can allow it to come back when we can then accept it and deal with it in the middle way. But so long as we have not first removed it from ourselves, it is not at all possible to deal with it in the desired and balanced manner.

28. We have already seen that the Sages said that in the future the dead will come back to life with all their blemishes, and after that they will be healed. What this means is that in the first instance, the body, which is the prodigious will to receive, is revived without any limits at all. It re-appears exactly in the way it grew while under the subjugation of the worlds of uncleanness, before we merited to purify it somewhat through the practice of Torah and *mitzvot*. This is what is meant by the expression, "with all its blemishes."

At this point, we begin a new work, which is to bring all this massive will to receive into the form of the will to give. Then the will to receive will be healed, as it, too, will have attained affinity of form with God. The Sages' remark, "that no one should say that it is another," means that the will to receive should not manifest in any form other than that which it takes in the thought of creation. For there it stands, this enormous will to receive, ready to receive all the good that is implied in the thought of creation, except that in the meantime, it has been given to the *klipot* (shells, framework of uncleanness) and then given over for purification. But in the final analysis, it may not be a different will to receive, because if it were to exist in any lesser measure, it would be considered as other than itself, and not fitting at all for use as a vessel for all the good that is implied in the thought of creation. Indeed it is already receiving there in the aspect of state one. Understand this well.

So here we have a very different view of what the "revival of the dead" means, other than meaning the physical revival of the body. The "dead" as spoken of here, are not the physical bones and sinews with which we live out our lives, only for them to be placed in the grave and rot. Here the "dead" are the wills to receive for oneself alone, which each one of us has in forms unique to each person. These wills to receive will revive at the end of the healing time with all their particular characteristics, because ultimately they constitute the vessels with which we may receive all that God wants to give us.

Lesson nine

The word 'dead' in the language of the branches means the wicked, who use their will to receive for themselves alone and are thus cut off from their Source of all Life. So the dead which will be revived are the untransformed wills to receive for oneself alone. However, in state three, these will come under the domination of the will to give, in which case they will no longer damage us, but on the contrary, they will be the perfected will to receive, for the sake of which all this incredible creation came into being.

However, what is true in the macrocosm is also true for each individual, and is true at all times. Each one of us has wounds and hurts deep within us. They cause us to separate from our souls because they make us feel bad. We get angry when we look at what has happened to us and feel ourselves to be victims. We may blame the Creator and not consider the One as being good. However, we can look at our wounds as though they are wills to receive that have been put aside, as during our everyday life we force them into our subconscious. But they did not disappear. During therapy these wounds resurface in forms that are as painful as they were when we first experienced them. This is equivalent to the revival of the dead for the individual. Now, with our more objective perspective, we can receive these wounds with compassion and forgiveness and let them go, as they receive their appropriate *tikkun*.

This is just one example of the resurrection of the dead as it manifests in our everyday lives. See if you can find others. Write them down.

To complete this lesson we shall read from the *Talmud Eser haSephirot*. We start with a piece from the writings of the Ari, the *Etz Chayim*, and continue with the corresponding commentary written by Rabbi Ashlag, the *Or Pnimi*:

> *Etz Chayim*
> And subsequently there arose, within His undifferentiated will, [the desire] to create the worlds and to bring forth the created beings, in order to bring to light the perfection of His works, His Names, and His attributes, since this was the reason for the creation of the worlds.[3]

> *Or Pnimi*
> You already know the inner meaning of the phrase, "He (the light) and His Name (the vessel) are One," that even though the will to receive, which is included in the *Ein Sof*, has a difference of form as compared to the light of the *Ein Sof*, may the One be blessed, nevertheless, this does not separate it from the highest light, but they are in simple unity. Although this is the case, this matter of

the potential difference of form between the light and the vessel does constitute the cause for the creation of the worlds, which were created in order to bring forth the perfection of His works, His Names, and His attributes, according to the words of the Ari, above. It is the creation of the worlds, and their evolution down until this world, that provide the possibility of practising Torah and *mitzvot*, not for the sake of receiving, but only for the sake of giving satisfaction to the Creator. Thus the souls are able to transform their inherent form of receiving, which separates them from the Creator, to the form of giving benefit, that is to say, receiving from the Creator in order to give pleasure to the One, since this is what the One wants. This constitutes affinity of form with the Creator, which is designated as being *dvekut* and unity, as the souls have been stripped of their will to receive with the intention of receiving, and have acquired the intention of giving benefit, which is the form of desire of the Creator Himself. Since, as you know, affinity of form unites spiritual entities, so the worlds then return to their original state, as we have explained.[4]

The *Tzimtzum* took place only according to the inner meaning of the words, "And subsequently there arose, within His undifferentiated will, [the desire] to create the worlds and to bring forth the created beings, in order to bring to light the perfection of His works, His Names, and His attributes, since this was the reason for the creation of the worlds." (*Etz Chayim*)

This means that the part of God, which is the vessel, desired the same affinity of form that is destined to be revealed in the future through the creation of the worlds; that is to say, it desired the form of the will to receive in order to give pleasure to the Creator. This form of the vessel has a most superior value: On the one hand it is purely giving, because its entire desire only consists of giving pleasure to its Source without consideration of its will to receive for itself at all. Therefore its form is in complete affinity with the highest light of God, and it cleaves to God with ultimate unity. On the other hand, it can also deepen and enlarge its capacity for receiving to an infinite measure, as now the form of receiving no longer causes antipathy of form, because this form of receiving comes only from a desire of giving benefit.[5]

---

1. *Histaclut Pnimit, Talmud Eser haSephirot*, part one
2. *Zohar, Perush HaSulam, Parshat Emor*, paragraph 51
3. *Talmud Eser haSephirot*, part one, chapter one, paragraph 2
4. *Talmud Eser haSephirot*, part one, chapter one, *Or Pnimi*, paragraph 40
5. *Talmud Eser haSephirot*, part one, chapter one, *Or Pnimi*, paragraph 90

Ein Od Milvado!

"There is nothing other than the One!"

Lesson Ten

The work of our lives; further concerning the framework of uncleanness

Paragraphs 29–32 of the Introduction to the Zohar

Introduction to the Zohar

29. Now the door has been opened for us to settle the second question that we asked above (paragraph 1). We wanted to know, "What is our role in the long chain of reality of which we constitute but tiny links during our short lives?"

You should know that the work of the years of our life is divided into four parts:

Part one: In this period a person attains the massive will to receive in its full measure, without limits placed on its spoiled nature, under the influence of the framework of the four worlds of uncleanness. If we were not to have this spoiled will to receive within us, we would not be able to heal it in any way, as we cannot heal anything that is not within us. The measure of the will to receive that is inherent in our bodies, simply by virtue of being born into this world, is not sufficiently large, so the will to receive needs to be a vehicle for the unclean *klipot* ("shells"—lights which sustain the framework of uncleanness) for at least thirteen years. During this period, the *klipot* dominate it and give it satisfaction from their lights. But the effect of these lights is to keep increasing and amplifying the will to receive, because the satisfaction that the *klipot* supply to the will to receive only serves to amplify its demands.

For example, when a person is born, he only desires one unit and no more. But when the *sitra achra* (the evil side) supplies this unit, this promptly enlarges his will to receive so that now the desire has grown to two hundred units. Then, when the *sitra achra* satisfies these two hundred units, the will to receive expands once again, and now the desire is for four hundred units. If he fails to deal with this process through practising Torah and *mitzvot* and thus purifying the will to receive and transforming it into the will to give, then the will to receive just carries on expanding throughout the person's life until he dies with half of his cravings unfulfilled. In this case, all the person's life was lived within the domain of the *klipot* whose function is to increase and expand the will to receive and to amplify it beyond any limits. The purpose of the framework of the *klipot* is to provide a person with all the raw material he needs to work on, in order to correct it.

Lesson ten

This is the paradox with which we live. On the one hand, we are born with a nature which requires fulfillment and satisfaction; on the other hand, if we run to fulfill this desire we are separated from the Creator.

Here is a piece of writing translated from Rabbi Ashlag's work, *haHakdamah l'Panim Meirot uMasbirot* (The Introduction to Welcoming and Illuminating Revelations):

> And this is what the Sages have said, "This is the evil inclination, this is the Satan, this is the angel of death, who goes down and seduces, then goes up and accuses and comes and takes one's soul."[1]
>
> Two main damaging consequences occurred due to the sin of the Tree of Knowledge. The first damaging consequence is implied in the phrase "goes up and accuses."
>
> After Eve was enticed and Adam and Eve both ate from the Tree of Knowledge, they acquired within their body makeup the vessels of receiving, consisting of the will to receive for themselves alone. (These stem from the *Challal haPanui* (empty space) following the *Tzimtzum*.) Thus, hatred and separation occurred between the eternal soul, which God had breathed into the nostrils of Adam, and the body of Adam.
>
> This is similar to the Sages' teaching, "Whoever is filled with pride, says the Holy Blessed One, he and I cannot dwell in the same dwelling."[2] Pride stems from the vessels of receiving for oneself alone that originate in the *Challal haPanui* from which the highest light had already separated itself from the time of the *Tzimtzum* and onwards. We know from what is written in the Holy *Zohar*, that the Holy Blessed One hates (is in opposition of form with respect to) the bodies, which are entirely made up of wills to receive for themselves alone. Thus the eternal soul left Adam. This was the first evil consequence.
>
> The second damaging consequence of the sin of the Tree of Knowledge was the descent into the framework of uncleanness of the two hundred and eighty-eight sparks of light that were left following the shattering of the vessels. These had previously been redeemed and had joined with the framework of holiness (from whence they maintained the Garden of Eden), but now, in order that the world would not be destroyed, they descended and were handed over to the framework of uncleanness and the *klipot* (shells). Due to the opposition of form that separates the framework of holiness from the vessels of receiving for oneself alone, the framework of holiness was no longer able to support and sustain Adam and the rest of humankind, since Adam and Eve's makeup was now composed of the vessels of receiving for oneself alone. So the two hundred

and eighty-eight sparks were handed over to the framework of uncleanness to provide sustenance to humankind and to support the existence of the world throughout the time that the souls incarnate in the bodies. Six hundred thousand souls for each generation, and to the thousandth generation until the end of the *tikkun*.

From this you may understand why the *klipot* are called '*klipot*' (shells). It is because they act like the shell of a fruit whose hard shell covers and protects it from all dirt or damage until it is ripe for eating, and without which the fruit would be destroyed and not come to fulfill its purpose. Similarly, the two hundred and eighty-eight sparks were handed to the *klipot* in order to sustain and prepare reality until the time when the souls will join with each other and achieve the desired purpose of creation.

But this second evil consequence "comes and takes a person's soul"! What I want to say is, that even the tiny fragment of soul that is left to the human, which is only like a drop of sweat in comparison to the former eternal soul, is oppressed by the *sitra achra* by its very giving to it! The *sitra achra* gives to the soul from the two hundred and eighty-eight sparks which fell to the lot of the framework of uncleanness. In order to understand this we need to depict the *sitra achra* exactly, in order that you will become wise to its ways.

Now I have already pointed out in my book *Panim Meirot uMasbirot* that all the parts of reality in this lowest world are branches which come from roots in the higher worlds, as an imprint is formed from a template. This is the way that each world relates to the world higher than it. You should know that the only distinction that exists between the branches of one world and their roots in the corresponding higher world consists of the type of material involved. That is to say, the materials in this world are physical, whereas in the world of *Yetzirah* they are spiritual; likewise, for each and every world, according to its aspect. However, regarding the happenings and processes that are within the worlds, when comparing the branch with its root, they are as equivalent as two drops of water. Thus the imprint is entirely equivalent to the template with which it has been stamped. Consequently, by investigating the branch of the *sitra achra* in this world, you may know its root in the higher world. For example, we find in the *Zohar* of the weekly portion *Tazriah*, that the infections which occur in the body of the human being are branches of the corresponding higher *sitra achra*.

If we investigate the animal kingdom, we find that the flow, which arises in the body of the animal through the achieving of pleasure, is that which multiplies and fertilizes life. Therefore, the Divine Providence stamped the smallest created beings with such a nature that wherever they look they find satisfaction and pleasure from even the most insignificant things, since the state of the smallest

Lesson ten

created beings requires that they need to multiply life the most, in order that there should be satisfaction sufficient for growth. Thus we see that pleasure is the father of life.

However, this rule only applies when the pleasure is given to the entity as a whole. But when the pleasure is collected and received by only one separate aspect of the entity of the animal, we find that an opposite rule applies, that is to say, the pleasure of separation. If, for example, an animal has an ulcer on its skin that makes it want to scratch and rub, we find that the scratching itself brings its own reward. On the one hand, the animal experiences intense pleasure so that it cannot refrain from scratching. But the pleasure itself has the drug of death connected with it, such that if the animal is not restrained, it will pay the consequence. The more pleasure it obtains from the scratching, the more the ulcer deepens, and then the pleasure turns to pain. At the beginning, it begins to heal over, but again the temptation to scratch occurs even more than previously. If the animal does not restrain itself, then again, the scratching will exact its price, and the ulcer will get bigger. This goes on until the bitter drop, which is the final consequence, when the blood becomes poisoned in the animal. Thus the animal dies through the pleasure it received, because its pleasure was the pleasure of separation, which is received only by **part** of the entity. Thus death comes to the entity. This is in contradistinction to the case where pleasure is received by the **whole** entity.

Now we can thoroughly understand the nature of the *sitra achra* in its spiritual form, such that it consists of the will to receive for oneself alone, not giving benefit to anything other than itself. This is analogous to the characteristic of the itching caused by the ulcer that demands to be scratched, without reference at all to the general health of the entire animal. The *sitra achra*, in actuality, is thus a form of demand that can never be paid off, in that it increases its demand for payment, ever increasing the debt and the damage to the maximum, just as the scratching gives pleasure to the animal, as we said above. And the latter part of the *sitra achra* is the drop of the drug of death that oppresses the person and separates him, even from the last spark of life that is left to him. This is similar to the drop of the drug of death that poisons all the blood in the entity of the animal. And this is what the Sages said, that the *sitra achra* finally comes and takes a person's soul. The Sages have said that the angel of death waits with a drawn sword with a drop of poison on the end of the sword, and when the person opens his mouth he throws in the drop and then the person dies; such that the sword of the angel of death is the consequence of the *sitra achra*. This ultimate consequence is termed a sword, by reason of the separation that gets larger the more the person receives for himself alone, and then the separation destroys him. Now the person inevitably opens his mouth, as he must obtain his sustenance from the *sitra achra*, until he gets the last drop of poison that is at the end of the sword, which then completely separates him from the last spark of his life.

From its inception, the make-up of the human body was built with incredible exactitude to receive the bounty required for its existence from the framework of holiness. For every action that is assured and permanent has its parts guarded against excess or deficit of any sort whatsoever. However, any action that is not assured has an innate impermanence that is caused by its parts lacking harmony. Thus we find within it deficit or excess.

It says in the Song of Unity, "Concerning all your work You did not forget anything, You caused neither excess nor deficit." It is an obligatory principle that from the Perfect Creator can only come a perfect work. However, when the human moved over from the framework of holiness to the framework of the *sitra achra*, because of the added component in his makeup that came about by reason of the eating from the Tree of Knowledge, there were already present many parts in the body that are either in excess, or present unnecessarily, which do not receive anything from the bounty provided by the *sitra achra* that is necessary to sustain existence. Therefore, a person is obliged to receive sustenance into the body in excess of what is actually needed, since these excess parts join in every demand the body makes, and therefore the body receives for them also. But these excess parts cannot in fact use that which the body receives for them, and thus we are left with excess and with waste which the body is subsequently obliged to expel. So we find that the vessels for food and digestion labor for these excess parts unnecessarily and they get worn out. Their end is predetermined, as it is in any work that lacks harmony of its parts, and in the end they disintegrate. Thus you find that the death of the body is predetermined as a consequence of the eating from the Tree of Knowledge.

Now we have learned that there are two diametrically opposed parameters conducting our existence. The management of the maintenance and sustenance of existence immediately moved over from the framework of holiness to the framework of uncleanness because of the appendage—the immense will to receive for oneself alone that attached itself to the people of this world through the eating of the fruit of the Tree of Knowledge. This appendage caused separation, opposition of form, and hatred between the framework of holiness and the bodies of the people of this world. This means that the framework of holiness can no longer sustain people or nourish them from its high table. So, in order that the world would not be utterly destroyed, and in order to provide people with the process of their *tikkun*, the framework of holiness handed over

Lesson ten

the main bounty necessary for the existence of the world to the framework of the *sitra achra*. This consists of the two hundred and eighty-eight sparks of light that resulted from the shattering of the vessels (an early event in the evolution of the spiritual worlds), and which originally belonged to the framework of holiness. These were handed over by the framework of holiness to the framework of the *sitra achra*, so that they may sustain the people of the world during the time of their *tikkun*.

But this has caused the order of existence to became very confused, as from something that is intrinsically evil, only evil can ensue. Whichever way you look at it the matter is problematic. For if the bounty given to the people of the world were to be reduced, this would certainly bring about destruction and suffering. On the other hand, if the bounty for the world were to be increased, then this would bring about an increase in the power of separation, as people receive the bounty for themselves alone! This is in accordance with what the Sages have said, "If a person has one portion, then they want two hundred; if they have two hundred, then they want four hundred." This is an exact analogy to the pleasure of separation that the flesh receives when scratching the ulcer; the degree of pleasure increases the separation and the disease. Thus we find that increasing the bounty to the world serves to increase the selfish love of those who receive it, until a person swallows his or her friend up alive. Even a person's physical life becomes shortened, because, through the increased amount of receiving one arrives faster at that last drop of bitterness. Wherever one turns, people just see the worst.[3]

This is a phenomenon that we all experience in our own lives. We want something, but when we acquire it, it loses its flavor after a relatively short period and we find we are craving or wanting something else! Look at this process firstly in material terms: You can see it very clearly with entertainment these days. First we want the video, then we want the computer games, then we want the internet, then the DVD, and so it goes on … .

Write in your journal about a time when you really wanted something material only to find that a short time after you got it, it had lost its meaning and you wanted something else in its stead.

Now look at this process in terms of our will to receive for oneself alone in emotional terms. Have you noticed that indulgence in anger only makes us quicker to get angry next time? Or indulging in feelings of self-pity when we receive the "light" associated with them only serves to make us more self-pitying the next time, or makes it that much harder to get out of those feelings?

Lesson ten

See if you can pinpoint some aspect of your emotional will to receive for oneself alone which tends to enlarge the more it receives its light. If you can, write about it in your own way.

Up until now we have considered the will to receive for oneself alone as it expresses itself in terms of this physical world. This constitutes the first of the four stages which make up our lives. Rabbi Ashlag goes on to explain the development of the will to receive in the realm of spirituality, which forms the content of the second part of our lives.

Introduction to the Zohar

30. Part two: This takes place from the age of thirteen years and onwards, when strength is given to a point within the person's heart, the hitherto inactive part of the *Nefesh* of holiness (the smallest of the lights pertaining to the soul). This point, which was enclothed within the will to receive at the time of birth, only begins to awaken from the age of thirteen years. From this time onwards, the person begins to enter into the domain of the framework of the worlds of holiness, according to the degree with which he involves himself with Torah and *mitzvot*.

A person's main purpose during this period is to attain and enlarge his spiritual will to receive. From birth until the age of thirteen years, he acquires a will to receive which relates only to the physical world. Therefore, even though the person has acquired a massive will to receive before the age of thirteen, this does not in fact spell the end of the growth of his will to receive. Actually, the major part of the will to receive becomes manifest when it is applied to the realm of spirituality.

For example, the will to receive before the age of thirteen desires to swallow up all the riches and glory that exist in this physical world, when it is obvious to all that this world is only temporary, like a shadow that passes and leaves no trace. But when a person acquires the enormous will to receive that appertains to spirituality, then he wants to swallow up all the good and richness of the next world for his own pleasure. The person wants to acquire an everlasting possession. He wants to acquire eternity!

So the major part of the massive will to receive only becomes complete when the person acquires a will to receive in spirituality.

We see here that the will to receive for oneself alone in the realm of spirituality actually constitutes the chief measure of the will to receive for oneself alone. This starts to develop at bar mitzvah or bat mitzvah, and this is the importance of this age.

Lesson ten

In our days the development of the spiritual will to receive for oneself alone takes different expressions. The "New Age" of our days mirrors a tremendous expansion of the will to receive for oneself alone into the realm of spirituality. Channelling, personal development, healing are just some of its expressions. (I do not intend to say that everyone who is involved with the spiritual expressions of the "New Age" is acting necessarily out of the will to receive for oneself alone, but the *initial* motive of a person setting out on a spiritual path always stems from the will to receive for oneself alone, because this is the default consciousness we all have. However, if his overall intention is actually to give benefit, then the person can purify his intention as he works.) The traditional road leading to the development of the will to receive in the realm of spirituality is that of the work of Torah and *mitzvot*, which the son or daughter takes on, at age twelve for a girl, thirteen for a boy.

Rabbi Ashlag continues by explaining the beginning of the expansion of the will to receive in spirituality, how it affects one and its importance. A piece of information we require here is that the practice of Torah, *mitzvot*, and good deeds which is carried out with the intention of giving benefit is called 'Torah for its own sake'. The practice of Torah, *mitzvot*, and good deeds in which our motives are mixed, including those that are self-serving, is called 'Torah that is practised not for its own sake'.

Introduction to the Zohar

31. The *Zohar* comments on the Scripture, "The leech has two daughters crying, 'Give! Give!'" (Prov. 30:15) as follows:

The meaning of "the leech" is hell. The wicked who are trapped in this hell are crying, "Give! Give! Give me this world! Give me the world to come!" [4]

Still, despite this, part two of a person's life is inestimably more important than part one. Not only is it the stage where the person acquires the true measure of the will to receive, giving him or her all the material that is needed to work with, but it is the step that brings the person to practise Torah and *mitzvot* for its own sake. As the Sages taught, "A person should practise Torah and *mitzvot*, even if it is not for its own sake, because through practising not for its own sake he will eventually come to practise for its own sake." [5]

Therefore, this part that develops after the age of thirteen is nonetheless considered as belonging to the realm of holiness, according to the inner meaning of the phrase, "The holy maidservant who serves her Mistress" (Prov. 30:23), the Mistress here being a metaphor for the *Shechinah*. For it is the maidservant (who represents the practice of Torah **not** for its own sake) who brings a person to the practice of Torah **for its own sake,** thus enabling him or her to merit the inspirational presence of the *Shechinah*.

However, a person must use all the necessary means in focusing his or her intention to come to the stage of practising Torah for its own sake. If this effort is not made, then the person will not come to the stage of practising Torah for its own sake, but will fall straight into the trap of the unclean maidservant, who is the opposite number to the maidservant of the side of holiness. The purpose of the unclean maidservant is to confuse a person, so the work of Torah that is practised not for its own sake will never lead them to Torah that is practised for its own sake. About this maidservant it is said, "And the maidservant will disinherit her Mistress" (Prov. 30:23). She will not allow the person to get close to the Mistress, to the Holy *Shechinah*.

Let us look now at a piece from the *Zohar* that compares the maidservant with the Mistress, the holy *Shechinah*. The maidservant represents the practice of the Torah that is **not** for its own sake, and the *Shechinah* represents the practice of the Torah that **is** for its own sake.

The practice of Torah that is not for its own sake, in which the intention of receiving for oneself alone is mixed in, is also referred to as 'the practice of Torah in order to receive a prize'. Likewise, the practice of Torah for its own sake is also called 'the practice of Torah, not in order to receive a prize':

> The second *mitzvah*: "And God said, 'Let there be light,' and there was light" (Gen. 1:3). This is love; the love of loving-kindness.
>
> As it is said, "With eternal love I have loved you, therefore I have drawn lovingkindness to you" (Jer. 31:2). And concerning this it is written, "Do not stir up nor awaken My love, until it will please" (Song of Sol. 2:7).
>
> The fear of being separated from God is considered as the rectified left-hand side. (The state in which the person does not want to be in separation from the Creator and therefore refrains from receiving for himself.)
>
> The love of God is considered as the right-hand side. (The state in which the person wants to give benefit to the Creator.)
>
> There is (true) fear of God and there is (false) fear of God.
>
> There is (true) love of God and there is (false) love of God.
>
> If a person fears God so that he should not become poor, or so that his children should not die in his lifetime, this is not a true fear of God, because, if it transpired that he did become poor, or his children did die within his lifetime, then he would not fear Him. Similarly, with regard to the love of God. Such fear of God or love of God are not true.

Lesson ten

True love of God and true fear of God occur when a person loves the One and fears to be separate from the One without any conditions, whether things go well or go badly. The other types are designated as love and fear only in order to get a prize.

Therefore, the Holy Blessed One said: "I charge you, O daughters of Jerusalem, by the hinds and the gazelles in the field. Do not stir up nor awaken My love, until it will please" (Song of Sol. 2:7). This is love that is without a prize and does not expect a prize.

The fear of God and the love of God that are practised for the sake of receiving a prize belong to the maidservant, as it is written, "For three things the earth is angered, and for four it cannot bear; for a slave when he becomes king, and a fool when he is filled with food, for an unloved woman who is married, and a maidservant who disinherits her mistress" (Prov. 30:21). [6]

Rabbi Ashlag explains the above passage from the *Zohar* in his work the *Hakdamah l'Talmud Eser haSephirot*:

Now we shall begin our explanation of this passage from the *Zohar* at its end. It tells us that the fear and the love that a person has when he practises Torah and *mitzvot* with the intention of getting something out of it personally, has the aspect of being the maidservant, about which it is written, "The earth is angered … when a maidservant disinherits her mistress." It is difficult for us to understand this. We have learned the principle that a person should always engage himself in Torah and *mitzvot* even when practising Torah not for its own sake. So why should the earth be angered? We further need to understand the relationship between practising Torah not for its own sake and the position of a maidservant. We also have to understand the phrase, "the maidservant who disinherits her mistress." What kind of inheritance is referred to here?

You may understand this matter by considering all that we have explained so far in this *Introduction [to the Talmud Eser HaSephirot]*, that the Sages only permitted the practice of Torah not for its own sake, on the condition that through such practice one would come to the state of practising Torah for its own sake via the light within it that transforms one. Therefore, involvement in Torah which is not for its own sake is considered as a maidservant who helps and does the menial jobs for her Mistress, the holy *Shechinah*. After all, the end result is to come to the practice of Torah for its own sake, thus meriting to give life-force to the *Shechinah*. Then this maidservant, which is the aspect of practising Torah not for its own sake, is yet considered to be a holy maidservant, in that she helps and prepares the way for holiness. She is called "the maidservant of the holy world of *Assiyah*."

However, if a person's faith is not complete, and he does not practise Torah and *mitzvot* solely because he feels that God is commanding him to do so [but he mixes in his self-serving motives], then, as we have previously seen, such practice of Torah and *mitzvot* will in no way help to reveal the light within Torah. The person's eyes are defective and they transform the light within Torah into darkness … .This type of work in Torah is no longer in the category of the holy maidservant because through such practice of Torah a person cannot come to the practice of Torah for its own sake. Therefore, such work comes into the domain of the maidservant of the *klipot*, who inherits this work in Torah and exploits it for her own benefit. This causes the earth to be angry. That is to say, the holy *Shechinah*, which is called 'earth', is angry because the Torah and spiritual work that should have come to her, as her possession, have been exploited by the maidservant of the *klipot* who brings them down into the possession of the framework of evil. Thus the maidservant disinherits her Mistress, God forbid.[7]

Rabbi Ashlag cautions us here that the expansion of the will to receive in spirituality only brings a person to holiness if he is careful about his intention. Since all of us are born bearing the intrinsic nature of the will to receive for oneself alone we have no choice other than to begin our spiritual practice by receiving for ourselves alone. Unless we are careful to ask for help in purifying our motives we are liable to arrive at an even greater separation than if we only dealt with the physical world alone!

The final part of this stage of a person's life, which constitutes the expansion of the will to receive in the realm of spirituality, is explained by Rabbi Ashlag in the continuation of the *Introduction to the Zohar*:

Introduction to the Zohar

31. (continued) The final level of this second part is that a person should fall in love with God with a great lust similar to the way a man of large appetite lusts after something in the physical world. This desire should grow in the person until it never leaves his or her awareness, by day or by night. Just as the poet says, "When I remember Him, I just cannot sleep." Then, it is said of such a person, "Desire fulfilled is a Tree of Life" (Prov. 13:13), the Tree of Life here being a metaphor for the five levels of the soul, which are described below.

Desire is the vessel for the light. The greater the desire, the greater is the light that one day will come into the vessel. The expansion of the will to receive in the realm of spirituality is the main part of the vessel with which the purpose of creation may be fulfilled, and it constitutes a much greater will to receive than that pertaining to the physical world. Therefore the expansion of the will to receive into the realm of spirituality has great value. However, the light cannot enter the vessel while the vessel is in opposition of form to it. Therefore the vessel still requires transformation.

In the next part of a person's life, the work consists of leaving aside the will to receive for oneself alone completely, turning one's attention solely to the will to give. This change of focus by the individual requires tremendous effort and a lot of help from Above.

Introduction to the Zohar

32. Part three: This part applies to the work with Torah and *mitzvot* which is done for its own sake, that is, in order to give pleasure to God and not for the sake of a reward. This work purifies the will to receive for oneself alone and transforms it into the will to give, whereby, according to the measure of purification of the will to receive, it now becomes a suitable and fitting vessel to receive the five parts of the soul, which are called, '*Nefesh*', '*Ruach*', '*Neshamah*', '*Chayah*', and '*Yechidah*' (see paragraph 42).

These aspects, which belong to the will to give, cannot be enclothed within a person's body so long as the will to receive for oneself alone dominates it, as the soul is in opposition of form to the body. Even if it is in some difference of form, the soul still cannot be enclothed within the body. For the light to be enclothed within a vessel, there must be affinity of form between them, for enclothing of the light within the vessel and affinity of form go hand in hand with each other.

At the very moment when the person merits to be wholly concerned only with the will to give and has no aspect left of the will to receive for oneself, then the person is in complete affinity of form with the five parts of the soul, the *Nefesh*, *Ruach*, *Neshamah*, *Chayah*, and *Yechidah*. These originate in their source in the *Ein Sof* in state one, come through the worlds of holiness and are immediately drawn to the person, who enclothes them one by one.

This part of a person's life, in which he occupies himself with Torah for its own sake, is one in which the person achieves the state of *dvekut*. It is the stage in which a person is able to give with the sole intention of giving benefit, that is without receiving at all. Such a person is called a '*Tzaddik*', a righteous person. However, he is still considered as an intermediate or unfinished *Tzaddik*, since there is one further aspect of development necessary before he would be able to fulfill the purpose of creation, as described below:

Introduction to the Zohar

32. *(continued)* Part four: This part applies to the work we do after the revival of the dead. The will to receive, after it had already disappeared through death and burial, now returns and comes back to life in its most prodigious form. This is the inner meaning of the saying of the Sages, "In the future the dead will come to life again with all their blemishes." At this stage, we transform the will to receive for oneself alone into the will to receive in order to give, and thus fulfill the purpose of creation and the purpose for which we ourselves were created. However, there are a few special people who are already doing this work during their lives in this world.

We see that the will to receive with the intention of giving benefit is the most perfect form of the vessel. It has achieved both affinity of form with the light, as in part three *and* it is fulfilling the purpose of creation. Thus it constitutes a vessel for receiving that is suited to receive all the good that God wants to give.

We shall enlarge on this subject by studying an article on the inner work taken from the *Bircat Shalom* of Rabbi Baruch Shalom haLevi Ashlag. To understand the article we need to know that the Hebrew word *zachut* means purity, clarity or transparency; it also means merit. It implies affinity of form with the Creator. We also need to know that the term 'nations', as used in the language of the branches, means those aspects of our personality that are concerned with receiving for oneself alone (aspects of the ego). Furthermore, the term 'Israel' relates to the soul that is within us and its desire to give unconditionally.

The article opens with a description of a phenomenon that occurred in the First Temple. When the Children of Israel offered a sacrifice, there would appear in the smoke above the sacrifice either the shape of a lion eating its prey or the shape of a dog. If the sacrifice was made in a true spirit of giving benefit then the lion appeared. If the sacrifice had self-serving motives mixed in, then the dog appeared. Thus the people had instant feedback from Above on their intentions: [8]

> Article 14
> We may explain what is written in the *Zohar*:
>
>> The Sages established: If, when offering up a sacrifice, Israel had *zachut*, a lion of fire would come down to eat the sacrifices. If they did not have *zachut* the likeness of a dog of fire would come down." [9]

Lesson ten

It is known that a lion implies *chesed*, (loving-kindness), which is the right-hand line of Ezekiel's chariot. If Israel had *zachut*, which is pure, which is giving benefit, then from Above they were shown the corresponding attribute that came in the likeness of a lion. Then the attribute of *chesed* would spread out to the created beings and there would be more bounty available for the created beings.

If they did not have *zachut*, that is, they were not giving benefit but were involved in selfish love, then from Above they would draw to themselves an aspect of a dog. The characteristic of a dog is hinted at by what is written in the *Zohar*, "... and the leech has two daughters saying, 'Give! Give!' (Prov. 30:15) (Hebrew: *Huv! Huv!*). This is the way a dog barks, *Huv! Huv!* Give! Give! Give me the wealth of this world! Give me the wealth of the next world!" We see that the dog is concerned with receiving and not with giving benefit. Therefore if we are pre-occupied with egoistic selfish love and not with giving benefit, then from Above they show us that we cannot give bounty to our fellows. This follows from the principle that what one gives out is what one receives back. So from Above they sent the likeness of a dog.

It follows from this that our main work is to merit and obtain vessels suitable for receiving the bounty. These are the vessels of giving benefit. Therefore, a person needs to concentrate all of his labor on just one thing, the vessels of giving benefit. The acquisition of these vessels is the only reward that the person wants to receive from the practice of Torah and *mitzvot*, that through this he will come to *dvekut* with God—this being the purpose of a person, to merit *dvekut* with God.

Likewise, we see in the words of the *Zohar* that the Sages explained the Scripture, "... the loving-kindness of nations is sinful" (Prov. 14:34), as meaning that everything the nations do, they do for themselves alone.[10] This means that even the acts of loving-kindness that they do, even their acts of giving, do not have the intention of giving benefit, but their intention in giving is to receive for themselves alone. In other words, they need to receive a reward; otherwise, they are not able to do acts of giving. This is not so regarding Israel, who are able to do acts of altruistic giving.

We need to understand why the people of Israel are capable of doing acts of giving benefit. Furthermore, we need to understand the reason why we hear from people who have begun their spiritual work of keeping Torah and *mitzvot*, that before they began they were much more able to do acts with the intention of giving benefit, but now that they have started their spiritual work it is harder for them to do such acts.

In order to understand the above, we need to remember the general rule that the human is termed a created being only because he has within him the will to receive; because it is this that determines the created being as created, *yesh m'ayin*. We see that from his nature a person is actually unable to do any act of giving benefit unless he were to receive from it some reward. However, the reward does not have to be something material that the person receives for his trouble, but it could be that he receives some comfort. In other words, if there were to arise within him some feeling of compassion for his fellow, and his conscience does not let him rest unless he helps the other person, then this is also designated as being recompense. But simply to do something for the other one so that the other person will have pleasure, then the person says to himself or to herself, "What will I gain from this?"

This is not, however, the case regarding the people of Israel. Due to the unique quality of Torah and *mitzvot*, they are able to obtain a second nature, that is to say, instead of the nature they were born with, which consists of the will to receive, they now receive a different nature with which they can now do acts of giving benefit. This they obtain through the practice of Torah and *mitzvot*, which they carry out because the Creator gave them sparks of giving benefit that bring people to the feeling that they want to be like their root.

This cannot occur without Torah and *mitzvot*. Without Torah and *mitzvot* a person is unable to leave his will to receive for himself alone and cannot do any act of giving without receiving something in exchange.

From this we can understand what those who come to the spiritual path report: Before they took on a religious way of life they actually had more strength to do acts of giving than after they began to keep Torah and *mitzvot*; now they feel it is actually more difficult for them to do acts of giving!

The reason for this follows from what we learn in the *Introduction to the Zohar*:

> From birth until the age of thirteen years, a person acquires a will to receive which relates only to the physical world. Therefore, even though one has acquired a massive will to receive before the age of thirteen, this does not in fact spell the end of the growth of one's will to receive. Actually, the major part of the will to receive becomes manifest when it is applied to the realm of spirituality.
>
> For example, the will to receive before the age of thirteen desires to swallow up all the riches and glory that exist in this physical world when it is obvious to all that this world is only temporary, like a shadow that passes and leaves no trace. But when a person acquires the enormous will to receive that pertains to spirituality, then he wants to swallow up all the good and richness of the next world for his or her own pleasure. The person wants to acquire an everlasting possession. He or she desires to acquire eternity!

Lesson ten

So the major part of the massive will to receive only becomes complete when the person acquires a will to receive in spirituality.

It follows from this that before the person entered the spiritual life of Torah and *mitzvot* he had a will to receive for himself alone that related to the material; but this was not so big, and therefore he had more strength to do acts of giving. This is not the case now that he has entered the religious life, as his will to receive has grown together with his will to receive in spirituality. This makes it harder for him to overcome his will to receive for himself alone for the reason that now it has a greater power than it had when it was just the will to receive in the material aspect of existence. Before he became spiritual he had some power to do acts of giving; but this is not the case now that he has started to keep Torah and *mitzvot*, as he has acquired the will to receive in spirituality.

The question is asked: Can one say that he has thus grown worse? Or can one say that those who practise Torah and *mitzvot* are worse than others because it is harder for them to do acts of giving?

Answer: The will to receive has got bigger, as we have said; therefore it is harder to overcome it. One can give as an analogy that prior to acquiring a will to receive in spirituality the evil within a person was only thirty percent, but when the person acquired a will to receive in spirituality the evil within him increased by another seventy percent. Therefore the person needs greater power to overcome it.

However, it would not be true to say that in this new situation the person has gone backwards; the contrary is the case, but now he needs special help in overcoming the powers of evil that he has acquired. The requisite aid is the practice of Torah and *mitzvot* with the intention that the light within the Torah will bring him back to the good way.

We see that in fact the person progressed and acquired more evil in order to rectify it. But all beginnings are difficult, so he thinks he has grown worse! However, a person needs to know that each time he progresses they give him (from Above) some more evil so that he can rectify it until he merits to rectify it all.

Article 15: Additional Explanation to the Previous Article

Further to article 14, this article concerns the matter that the will to receive in the material world is only half of the stage of the will to receive. When a person receives the will to receive in the realm of spirituality, then he has a complete will to receive.

Accordingly, it follows that when a person only has a will to receive in the material realm then he is not all that bad. So what does he need to receive the will to receive in spirituality for? So that he will get worse? The person says, "It is better to simply stay with the material will to receive. Why should I strive to reach the stage of the will to receive in the realm of spirituality by which I may become more wicked? Why should I get myself into danger? Maybe I will not manage to correct my will to receive for myself alone? If that were to happen it would certainly be better just to stay with the material will to receive for myself so that all my desires will be confined to material objects and not to start hankering after spirituality at all."

However, it is written in the *Introduction to the Zohar*:

> 29. You should know that the work of the years of our life is divided into four parts:
>
> Part one: In this period a person attains the massive will to receive in its full measure, without limits placed on its spoiled nature under the influence of the framework of the four worlds of uncleanness. If we were not to have this spoiled will to receive within us, we would not be able to heal it in any way as we cannot heal anything that is not within us.

So we see that really we have no choice but to act in ways that will bring us the acquisition of the will to receive in spirituality. However, this is not so easy to acquire, because the will to receive in spirituality depends on faith. A person first has to believe that there is such a thing as spirituality and that it is more important than all material delights, such that is it is better to give up on material delights in order to acquire spiritual delights. Therefore one has to work hard to attain even this stage, and not everyone gets there without a huge effort. Even so, the will to receive that the person thus acquires is, nonetheless, considered as evil, in that this will to receive is still defective.

This is the matter of, "from Torah that is practised not for its own sake comes Torah that is practised for its own sake." That is, first of all a person needs to reach the stage that he practises Torah and *mitzvot* not for its own sake. Only after that can the person correct his practice such that it should be for its own sake. One cannot give intention if there is no action. Only once there is an action is it possible to try to have the intention that the action should go on the right path. This is designated as doing the action for the sake of heaven.

According to the above, it follows that there are, generally speaking, four categories in the work of a person that are needed in order to reach the perfection for which we were created.

These are:
+ receiving with the intention of receiving,
+ giving benefit with the intention of receiving,

Lesson ten

- giving benefit with the intention of giving benefit,
- receiving with the intention of giving benefit.

Receiving with the intention of receiving: This is the first stage. All created beings are born with this. That is to say that at this stage they do not understand any way of being other than that of selfish love. They do not have any interest in doing anything for someone else, but they are sunk in the nature with which they were born, which is receiving for themselves alone. This is the general consciousness of the world, and one person is no different from another in this respect.

Second stage: **Giving with the intention of receiving.** This is a stage in which a person has left the general consciousness of the world in which he used to act just in order to receive, and now does acts of giving benefit. But the person needs an excuse to do so: Why does he want to be different from the rest of the world? Why does he want to act in ways that are opposite from those which his innate nature dictates? So the person tells his body (will to receive), "Know that by doing this act of giving benefit you will get a greater delight afterwards." He lets the body understand that the work involved in doing this act is worthwhile for it, that it is profitable for it. If his body (will to receive) believes him, then it will let him do the act of giving, according to the measure that it believes that it is to its advantage to cancel an act of receiving for itself alone (like resting) in order to do an act of giving.

This stage is designated as: "from practising Torah not for its own sake we can come to practise Torah for its own sake." It is a springboard with which we can jump from one stage to the next; that is, from the stage of the practice of Torah not for its own sake, to the practice of Torah for its own sake. This is because, with regard to the action itself, these two states are equal. There is nothing further we need add to the action itself in order to come to the state of the practice of Torah for its own sake. Therefore, since from the perspective of the action alone these two states are equivalent, we see that one need add no further physical action. Only with respect to the **intention** of the action is there further work to be done. This means that a person needs now only to consider whether the action he is performing is really for the sake of fulfilling a *mitzvah* of God; that it is God who commanded us to do *mitzvot*, and we want to uphold the *mitzvot* of the One, because for us it is a great merit (*zachut*) to serve Him. Furthermore, the One also let us know how we can we can serve Him.

Then comes the work of clarification of our intention: Is this really true? Is it really true that the person, in his practice of Torah and *mitzvot*, only has the intention of giving pleasure to the Creator, or does he have other considerations involved? Is he fulfilling Torah and *mitzvot* from reasons more concerned with selfish love?

When the person sees just how removed he is from the state in which all his actions are done just for the sake of heaven, then he needs to clarify his intentions on a true basis.

There are many people who have not done this clarification with integrity, but really think they are working for the sake of heaven. Even if they have some awareness that their work is not one hundred percent for the sake of heaven, nevertheless, they consider themselves as practising Torah for its own sake for the most part, just that they have a little bit more to add with respect to "for its own sake." But in fact they lack a true assessment of their situation, either from their nature, or because they lack a good teacher who could show them how not to deceive themselves. Thus they are not actually able to come to practise Torah for its own sake.

The practice of Torah for its own sake is designated as truth; the practice of Torah that is not for its own sake is designated as a lie. There needs to be some intermediate stage between the lie and the truth, such that there can be a springboard for one to move from the lie to the truth. This intermediate stage is to know that the lie really is a lie. If the person considers the lie as being the truth, then it follows that he is misled and is really treading a false path. However, if the person knows that the path he is on is really a lie, then he can use this knowledge as a springboard to get to the truth.

It is the case that so long as the person does not know that the path he is pursuing is really a lie, he has no reason to change his path in order to follow a different path; he lacks the clarity to realize that he is following a false path. Only when the person realizes that he is really involved in a lie is he able to change his way and go on a true path.

If a person is already on a true path, that is to say, he is already trying to practise Torah for its own sake, but has not yet achieved this as a spiritual stage, what may this be likened to? It may be likened to a person who wants to travel to Jerusalem, who therefore gets on the bus marked to Jerusalem. Even when he has travelled eighty or ninety percent of the way to Jerusalem, one cannot say that he has arrived in Jerusalem. Only when the person has arrived in actuality in Jerusalem can one say that he is in Jerusalem.

It is the same in spirituality: If we were to say, for example, that Jerusalem represents the truth, that is to say the practice of Torah for its own sake, then we have to say that the person travelling to it is still in the lie, since he is still practicing Torah not for its own sake, which is designated as a lie. It maybe that the person has nearly arrived, and is standing by the gate that is designated as truth,

Lesson ten

which is the practice of Torah for its own sake; nevertheless he is outside. From this we can see that it is impossible for a person to know when he has arrived at the spiritual stage wherein one is practising Torah for its own sake before he has merited the full stage of this practice.

So when can a person know that he has actually achieved the stage of the practice of Torah for its own sake? What is the sign by which he may know that now he has reached the stage of the truth?

We find the answer to this, in the *Hakdamah l'Talmud Eser haSephirot*:

> By this you may understand what the Sages implied when they asked, "What constitutes *teshuvah* (repentance)?" (actually arriving at the stage of Torah for its own sake) and answered, "when God Himself testifies that the person will never again return to his foolishness." This is a surprising definition, as who is going to go up to heaven to hear God's testimony? What is more, to whom is God expected to give this testimony? Is it not enough that God Himself knows that the man or woman has repented with all their heart and will not sin (use the will to receive for oneself alone) anymore?
>
> Yet from what we have already clarified, the matter is quite simple. In truth, a person can never be completely certain that he will not sin again unless he has already merited the comprehension of God's Providence, which is that the One acts with cause and effect. This is the revelation of God's face. This direct revelation of God's face, coming as it does as a grace from God, is termed 'testimony', as it is God's grace itself that enables a person to attain this perception of cause and effect which ensures that he will not sin again. Thus we can say that it is God Himself who testifies for the person. [11]

(In order to understand the above we need to know that the term "revelation of God's face" refers to the state of consciousness in which a person has already achieved *dvekut* with God and affinity of form. The person knows and sees that God works according to His Name, which is that the One is Good and does good. He has also grasped the evolution of the events of his own life from the aspect of cause and effect, such that the person sees and knows that every positive action of a *mitzvah* that is done with the intention of giving benefit causes unity with the Creator, and the negative action of a sin causes separation from the Creator.)

Article 15 *(continued)*
It follows from this that when a person arrives at the spiritual stage of giving benefit he merits the revelation of God's face from God Himself, may the One

be blessed, and this is termed that the One, who knows all secrets, testifies for the person that he has attained the spiritual stage of practising Torah for its own sake.

This is designated as being the third stage in spirituality, that is, **giving benefit with the intention of giving benefit**. This means that the person has already arrived at the practice of Torah for its own sake as a spiritual stage. He has reached the stage of truth. This came to the person through the springboard of the practice of Torah not for its own sake leading to the practice of Torah for its own sake. The person fulfilled all the necessary conditions not to stay stuck at the stage of the practice of Torah that is not for its own sake.

After one has finished the spiritual stage of being a giver with the intention of giving benefit, then comes the fourth stage of **receiving with the intention of giving benefit**. This is the stage of perfection. That is to say, the person has reached the stage at which he says, "I want to receive joy and delight" because he knows for himself that he wants to fulfill the purpose of creation. The Creator created the creation for the reason that it is His will to give good to His created beings. Therefore, the person wants to receive from God all the good and delight because this is His will, may the One be blessed. But to receive from the One just to fulfill egoistic selfish love, the person has neither will nor desire, since he has already reached the spiritual stage of giving for the sake of giving benefit, which is affinity of form with the Creator. Therefore the person now wants only to fulfill the will of God, which is the desire to benefit all created beings.

We need to know that there exists both the purpose of creation and the *tikkun* of the creation. The purpose of the creation is that the Creator wants to give good to the created beings. This implies that the created beings should receive goodness and joy. The more pleasure they receive, the greater the joy of the Creator. Therefore, whoever is at the stage of perfection continually wants to increase his or her receiving of joy and pleasure, as this is the purpose of creation which, as we have explained, is to give good to the created beings.

This is not the case concerning the stage of one who has reached the spiritual stage of giving with the intention of giving benefit, which is designated as being unity and affinity of form. This is only the *tikkun* of the creation.

Creation needs to come to the stage in which the created beings will receive goodness and joy, but still be left, after receiving all the joy, with the intention of giving benefit. This is designated as 'receiving with the intention of giving benefit', which is the ultimate aim of the creation.[12]

1. *Talmud, Bava Batra 17*
2. *Talmud, Bava Batra 98a*

Lesson ten

3. *Hakdamah l'Panim Meirot uMasbirot, paragraphs 19 and 20*

4. *Tikkunei haZohar (a part of the Zohar), Tikkunim Chadashim 97b*

5. *Talmud, Pesachim 50b*

6. *Tikkunei haZohar (Tikkun 30)*

7. *Hakdamah l'Talmud Eser haSephirot paragraphs 32–33*

8. *One may be surprised at the animals chosen to represent giving and receiving by the Zohar. After all, one would not want to trust oneself to the tender mercies of a lion, and many dogs give friendship and loyalty to their human companions. However, all becomes clear when we consider the way they relate to food. A lion will only eat what he needs and then leaves the rest to the lioness and the cubs. He hunts, or the lioness hunts, only when hungry. A dog, however, will eat at any time of day or night, whether hungry or not.*

9. *Zohar, Perush haSulam, Parshat Pinchas, paragraph 218*

10. *Tikkunei haZohar, Sixth Tikkun*

11. *Hakdamah l'Talmud Eser haSephirot, paragraph 56*

12. *Bircat Shalom Sefer haMa'amerim, volume one, article 14*

Ein Od Milvado!

"There is nothing other than the One!"

Lesson Eleven

The purpose of the higher worlds; the final state of the souls; the development of the wills to receive
Paragraphs 33–39 of the Introduction to the Zohar

Introduction to the Zohar

33. Now all that is left for us to explain is the sixth inquiry. Its subject was the statement of the Sages that all the worlds—the higher worlds as well as the lower worlds—were only created for the sake of the human. On the surface, it seems to be rather astonishing that for the sake of this little human, the Creator, blessed be the One, should create all this!

When one compares the value of a man or a woman with the whole of the reality of this world, not to mention the higher spiritual worlds, one cannot say that he or she has the value of even a tiny hair! Yet God created all this for us.

An even more astonishing question is: What need does the human being have for all these many and splendid spiritual worlds?

Now you need to know that all the satisfaction God has in giving pleasure to His created beings depends upon the measure that the created beings can feel that it is God who is their benefactor and it is God who gives them their enjoyment. Then God takes great delight in them, like a father who delights in playing with his dear child. His pleasure increases according to the degree that the child can feel and recognize the greatness and the noble qualities of the father. Then the child's father shows the child all the treasure houses that he has prepared for the child. Just as Scripture says, "'What a dear son Ephraim is! He is my darling child! For whenever I speak of him, I earnestly remember him. My compassion is stirred for him. I shall surely have mercy on him,' says the Lord" (Jer. 31:19). Look carefully at this sentence and you will understand and know the great delight that God enjoys with those people who have reached their wholeness. They have merited to sense His presence and to recognize His greatness in all the ways that He has prepared for them. God relates to them as a father relates to his dear child, as a father with the child of his delight. As we meditate on this description, we can understand that for the sake of the pleasure and delight God takes in these people, who have come to their wholeness, it was worth it to God to create all these worlds, the upper as well as the lower, as we shall further explain.

Lesson eleven

This paragraph, written as it is in an illustrative style, contains a few statements that at first may seem to be a little surprising or confusing. Let's take it slowly:

> "Now you need to know that all the satisfaction God has in giving pleasure to His created beings depends upon the measure that the created beings can feel that it is God who is their benefactor and it is God who gives them their enjoyment."

The satisfaction that the One has in giving pleasure to His creatures can only come to fruition according to the measure that the created beings have acquired affinity of form with the Creator. As we know, the light that God wants to give the created beings can only enter the vessel when there is affinity of form between the vessel and the light.

> "Then God takes great delight in them, like a father who delights in playing with his dear child. His pleasure increases according to the degree that the child can feel and recognize the greatness and the noble qualities of the father."

"God's pleasure increases," implies that the greater the affinity of form between the created being and God, the greater the flow of light.

We see that within this paragraph from the *Introduction to the Zohar* there are several issues we may discuss: 1) A person reaches the stage wherein he recognizes and feels that it is the One who is the Giver and who has brought him or her to the stage of being able to receive, solely with the intention of giving benefit. 2) The One has great pleasure in that He is able to give of His bounty to the righteous who have reached their wholeness. 3) The creation of all the worlds, the higher and the lower, was only for the sake of the human being.

Regarding the first issue, we may ask, does the One have a need for us to recognize Him as the Giver? The answer to this question is, of course not. The One has no lack. If so, what is the importance of recognizing the greatness and exaltedness of the Creator, of acknowledging that He is the benefactor? To go into this issue let us look at two excerpts from Rabbi Baruch Shalom Halevi Ashlag's *Bircat Shalom*:

> From the article: "The land of Israel belongs to God"
> When a person begins to do the holy work, that is, to direct his intention so that all his work should be for the sake of the One, then the battles begin between

the two desires, the desire to receive for oneself alone and the desire to give benefit. The person, through great effort, may merit to prevail, and in this way he wins the war, and then the will to give benefit to God dominates his heart. But then the person is liable to say, "my strength and the power of my hand have done this valor for me" (Deut. 8:17), meaning that it was only through his hard work that he succeeded in conquering the heart (now referred to as 'the land of Israel', because now his intention is directed only towards God). Therefore, the Scripture continues and says, "When you come into the land **which the Lord your God gives you** as an estate, then you shall inherit it and dwell on it" (Deut. 26:1). That is to say, that it was not you who conquered your heart with your own strength, but it was the Lord your God who gave it to you.

Once a person has put in the requisite labor necessary to conquer the heart through the continual battles that he had with his inner nations of the world and has overcome them, and he has inherited the heart, designated as being the land of Israel, not the land of the other nations, the person needs to believe that it was not he himself who conquered the land, but "**the Lord your God gives you,**" and not "my strength and the power of my hand have done this valor for me!"[1]

Excerpt from the article: "We have no King but You"
There are people who have achieved the spiritual stage of the fear of being separated from God for its own sake. That is to say, they recognize that the One is abundant in loving-kindness and the Source of all. They recognize the great merit they have in serving the King, moreover, this is their reward; they do not need any other recompense for their work. They negate their own self, that is, they are not interested in looking out for their own self-interest; their only concern is how to give pleasure to the Creator. Since this is a concern that the body does not find acceptable, as it consists of the will to receive for oneself alone, it opposes this work. Therefore, it is just when a person really wants to work in order to serve, that all the ups and downs begin.

In the work of serving we find that reward and punishment are defined in a totally different way than the usual way we define them when we work for some personal gain. When a person feels there is a purpose to his service, and he feels that he has some aspect of coming closer to the One, this is his reward. Punishment is now defined as those times when the person does not feel there is any point in his work; this becomes the worst punishment a person could possibly get, that he has lost any enthusiasm for his work. Then a person needs to say that surely this distance that he feels is because he is far away (in opposition of form) from the One. A person understands that if he were close to

Lesson eleven

God, then he should be feeling a different feeling from that which he is now experiencing. It is written, "Splendor and pleasantness are in His place" (Chron. I 1:27). This implies that when a person feels himself as being in a conscious state of holiness—and since regarding holiness it is written "splendor and pleasantness"—he should be experiencing feelings that are consonant with splendor and pleasantness. But now the person feels that he even lacks life-force; he sees everything as being black, and he feels that he simply cannot get out of his present situation. For a person who wants to reach the stage of serving God only for the sake of the One, this is the worst punishment of all. The person judges himself by his feeling and concludes that he is not in the consciousness of holiness after all. The person wants to overcome the state that he is in, but he sees he has no possibility of coming to affinity of form with God. Sometimes he may fall into despair; he wants to run away from the battleground and he comes to the conclusion that there does not exist even the faintest possibility that he could come to the stage of spirituality wherein a person does not care about himself but only cares for God.

The question is asked: What is the truth? Is the person wrong? Is it possible to come to the state wherein all one's deeds are done only for the sake of heaven? Or not? Does trying to overcome one's situation help? That is to say, does the person have it within his power that he could come to do all his deeds for the sake of Heaven?

The answer, as we say in the prayers of *Rosh haShanah* (the Jewish New Year), is, "We have no King but You." We do not have the strength within us to overcome the will to receive for oneself alone, such that we would be able to undertake the task that You should be our King and we would serve You only because of the importance of the King; and as for ourselves we would not do any action excepting those that would give You pleasure. Only You can give us this strength, only You can give us a new nature, namely that of a will to give. Therefore, as we say in the *Rosh haShanah* prayers, "Our Father, our King, we have sinned before You."

A person cannot simply say, "We have no King besides You," meaning that he acknowledges that only the Creator can give the strength to overcome the will to receive for oneself alone, because from where does a person know that this is not in his power? Therefore, first of all the person has to do everything he possibly can in order to reach the consciousness of the will to give, as it is written, "Whatever your hand can find that is in your power to do, do" (Eccles. 9:10). Then a person comes to the state in which he feels how far away he is from God; he feels he has no power do anything for God. The person feels that even though he keeps Torah and *mitzvot*, nevertheless, he feels he is a sinner because he sees he does not work for the sake of heaven. Therefore a person has to say first of all, "Our Father, our King, we have sinned before You." That even though he keeps Torah and *mitzvot*, nevertheless, he feels himself to be a sinner because he sees he is not doing anything solely for the sake of heaven. After this the person says with all his heart, "Our Father, our King, we have no King but You," that is, he now knows that only the Creator can help us reach the stage where the One is our King, and we serve Him only for the sake of serving the King.

And this will be our reward, that we have the merit to serve the King. Only then is it within our power to do all we can for the sake of Heaven. That is to say, if the Creator does not give a person this power of understanding, such that he feels that he has a great King, then the person has no power of his own to serve God for the sake of Heaven. The will to receive for oneself alone maintains: What will I gain from this, that I give to God? So long as the will to receive for oneself rules, a person has no recourse other than to obey it. There are even times when the person may go so far as to question the whole basis of his work and say, "Now I see that all the work I put in was for nothing, and I did not gain anything from the effort that I made." Now the person actually sees that all the effort he made really was for nothing (that is, he cannot gain a new nature as a direct result of his efforts only). Therefore, when the Creator helps the person and gives him the will to give, then he feels he has a great King. This only the Creator can give. Only now does the person have it in his power to withstand the questions his will to receive raises. Now he can say, "Our Father, our King, we have no King but You," because only You can give us the feeling that we have a great King, and that it is worthwhile to serve the One, to give the One satisfaction.[2]

The next excerpt we are going to study comes from the *Perush haSulam* on the *Zohar* and tells us that all our deeds are actually caused by the Creator.

When you read this excerpt remember that in the Kabbalah the expression 'reward and punishment' implies that the consequence of a person's action is either positive, that is to say the deed causes affinity of form with the Creator, and that is the person's reward; or is negative, which implies that it causes separation from the Creator, and that is the punishment.

And know that the only difference that there is between this world as it is before the *tikkun* is complete, and as it will be at the end of the *tikkun* is as follows:

Before the end of the *tikkun*, the *Malchut* is known as "The Tree of Knowledge of Good and Evil." This is the way that God operates in this world: So long as the souls have not come into their wholeness, wherein they can receive the whole of the goodness that the One thought to give them according to the purpose of creation, there is no choice but for this Providence to act according to the modality of good and evil. This gives rise to reward and punishment, for our vessels of receiving are still dirty with receiving for oneself alone, which leads them to be extremely contracted in size, and separates us from the Creator, may the One be blessed.

The complete goodness, in the great measure that the One purposed to give us, is not available to us unless the vessel is operating in the modality of receiving with the intention of giving benefit, which allows joy without any limit or contraction. This is not the case for the vessel that receives for oneself alone; it is limited and very contracted indeed, as its satisfaction extinguishes the joy immediately.

This is the inner meaning of the Scripture, "All that God worked is for His sake" (Prov. 16:4). That is to say, all the actions that take place in the world were only created in the first place in order to give the One satisfaction. It follows that all the people are using the ways of the world in completely the opposite way from that which was intended at their creation. The Holy Blessed One says: The whole world was created for Me, that is to say, "All that God worked is for His sake," also, "Everything is called in My Name, for My glory I have created it, I have formed it, even made it" (Isa. 43:7). But we say the exact opposite, going to the other extreme. We say, the whole world was only created for us, and we want to swallow all the good in the world into our belly for our enjoyment and for our glory. Therefore, it is not surprising that we are not yet fit to receive His complete goodness; consequently, we experience the Divine Providence as operating in the mode of good and evil, according to reward and punishment—the reward and punishment being consequent on good and evil. Since we are using the vessels of receiving in exactly the opposite way intended at their creation, inevitably we shall experience some of the actions of the Divine Providence as being bad for us.

It is a law that a created being can never receive anything that is actually evil from God. If a created being were to apprehend God as working evil, this would constitute a defect, God forbid, in His glory, because this is not compatible with the perfect creator. Therefore, when a person feels bad, in like measure he is pervaded with denial of the Divine Providence. The Creator is hidden from him, and this is the greatest punishment of all. The feeling of good and evil that stems from the way we experience the Divine Providence causes the experience of reward and punishment. If the person makes the effort not to be separated from his faith in God, may the One be blessed, even though he may subjectively experience the Divine Providence as bad, nevertheless, he receives his reward. But if, God forbid, he is not able to make this effort, then he is punished, because he has separated from his faith in the Creator. We find that even though He alone did, does, and will do all the deeds, this fact remains hidden from all who feel good and bad. Because when a person is feeling bad, power is given to the *sitra achra* to conceal both His Providence and the person's own faith from himself, and so he comes to the great punishment of separation. He becomes filled with thoughts of denial of God. Yet when he comes back to himself, we see that he receives his reward and can once again be in affinity of form with the Creator.

So from the power of reward and punishment itself, God prepared that finally we may merit, even through this means, to come to the end of the *tikkun*, that is, all the human beings will receive the rectified vessels of receiving in order to give benefit to their Creator, according to the measure of the Scripture, "All that God works is for His own sake," as was created from the outset. And then the great light of the end of the *tikkun* will be revealed, in which we shall come to return to the One from love. Even all the arrogant acts will transform into meritorious acts, and all the evils we suffered will transform into great good. Then His Divine Providence will be revealed to the whole world. All will see that He alone did, does, and will do all the deeds and acts which preceded this final *tikkun*.

For now that the evil and the punishment have transformed into great good and merits, it will be possible for all to actually apprehend their Worker, because all will now be fitting to the work of His hands, may the One be blessed. Now all will praise and bless Him for what seemed to be evils and punishments at the time. And this is the main focus of this article. Because until now, we thought that the *tikkun* was in our hands, for it is on this we receive reward or punishment. However, when the great union of light at the end of the *tikkun* will happen, then we shall see that the *tikkunim* themselves, and even the punishments, were all the work of His hands. And thus it is written, "And the firmament tells the work of His hands" (Ps. 19:2), because the great union of light, which will come at the end of the *tikkun*, will tell that all is the work of His hands, and He alone did, does, and will do all the acts, all of them.[3]

These two ideas: 1) that the Creator is the author of all acts, and 2) that the One has great joy when He can fulfill the purpose of creation, which is to give the created beings pleasure, appear frequently, both in the writings of Rabbi Ashlag and of those of his son, Rabbi Baruch Shalom haLevi Ashlag, in many different ways.

Lesson eleven

Rabbi Ashlag continues in the *Introduction to the Zohar* to further delineate the development of the vessel, which is designated as the will to receive.

Introduction to the Zohar

34. In order to prepare His created beings, so that they would be able to reach this high and elevated state, God works through four stages, which develop naturally one from the other, and which are called: the **inanimate**, the **plant**, the **animal**, and the **speaking**. These are actually four levels of the will to receive. Every single world amongst all the higher worlds (and also our physical world) is divided into these four categories. The greatest aspect of desire is contained in the fourth level of the will to receive, but it is not possible for this fourth level to emerge without the prior existence of the three previous levels. The will to receive is revealed and developed gradually through the three previous levels before reaching its completed form in the fourth level.

The root of everything in our world is to be found in the higher worlds. These higher worlds develop and cascade down, one from another, in a way similar to the way a template transfers its image to the wax stamped with it. The four levels of development, the inanimate, plant, animal, and speaking, are to be found in the higher worlds; they originate in the higher worlds and cascade down to our world where they take on a physical form. Thus, this world is also built out of four modalities, which develop one from another, and are inanimate, plant, animal, and human.

In just the same way that these four components of the physical world develop, the plant from the inanimate, the animal from the plant, and so on, likewise the will to receive for oneself alone develops according to these four components within the framework of uncleanness. Similarly the *nefesh* also develops according to these four components within the worlds of holiness.

Rabbi Ashlag continues with a description of the determining characteristic of each component. He also describes the development of the will to receive for oneself alone as it develops these four components, through the worlds of uncleanness:

Introduction to the Zohar

35. The first level of the will to receive is called **inanimate**. It is the beginning of the manifestation of the will to receive in this physical world. The inanimate is characterized by having only a general capacity for movement. Individual objects within the realm of the inanimate have no perceptible capacity to move of their own. The will to receive gives birth to needs, and these needs give birth to movements sufficient to attain these needs. Since here the will to receive is

very minimal, its effect is only apparent as causing a general movement, but its effect is not apparent on the individual parts.

Examples of the inanimate in the physical world are the stones, planets, sun, earth. Consider how their will to receive manifests itself. Do you understand what is meant by a general movement rather than individual? If not, this will become clear when comparing the inanimate with the other levels of the will to receive.

Introduction to the Zohar

36. The next and second aspect of the will to receive is the **plant** modality. This is already a much greater manifestation of the will to receive than is attributed to the inanimate. Here the will to receive influences each and every individual separately. As we see in the plant world, each individual has its own particular capacity for movement. Plants turn and move to face the sun. Plants, too, can "eat" and "drink" and rid themselves of waste products. This is a capacity that each individual plant has. However, plants do not have any capacity for free motion in a way that is peculiar to each individual plant.

37. Now we can add the **animal** kingdom, which is the third aspect of the will to receive. This is a much more advanced level of the will to receive. Here, the will to receive endows every single animal with the capacity of feeling itself to be an individual. Each animal has its own particular life, different from that of other animals. However, animals, generally speaking, lack the capacity to feel the feelings of other animals. They have no capacity to feel the pain of their fellow animals' misfortune or to rejoice in their fellow animals' happiness and suchlike.

This is a generalization describing the overall characteristic of the animal kingdom. Of course, in many individual instances we know that certain of the higher animals do help each other and share certain emotions. Rabbi Ashlag's point becomes clearer in the next paragraph:

Introduction to the Zohar

38. Finally we come to the speaking, which is the fourth level of the will to receive. This is the will to receive in its completed and final form. At this human level of the will to receive, the capacity exists to feel the pain of others as well as our own.

If you want to know exactly how great the difference is between the third level of the will to receive, the animal level, and the fourth level of the will to receive, the human level, I tell you that it is exactly that of one element of creation as compared to the totality of creation! The will to receive as it exists in the animal

Lesson eleven

kingdom, lacking the capacity to feel the other's feelings, is only able to give birth to the lacks and needs of that one individual animal. This is not so in the human kingdom in which the capacity to feel other people's feelings gives rise to lacks that were not originally the person's own, but are born from seeing that which his fellow possesses. The person fills with jealousy and he desires to own everything that another owns. A person's wants and needs become greatly multiplied until he wants to swallow up the substance of the whole world.

In our un-transformed state, our capacity to feel each other's feelings leads to jealousy and envy, greatly multiplying our will to receive for ourselves alone. Many of our economic systems stem from this capacity for jealousy and envy. Part of the drive for globalization and so-called free markets, wherein the rich get richer and the poor, poorer, stems from the ability of the human being to see what his or her fellow has and to desire that too.

Here is a piece from the *Petichah l'Chochmat haKabbalah* that describes the development of the will to receive, starting from the higher worlds until its final manifestation in this world:

> As we have said, the will to receive is inevitably included immediately in the thought of creation—with all the many orders that are in it—together with the great bounty that God planned to bestow in order to give pleasure to the created beings.
>
> You should know that this is the inner meaning of the words 'light' and 'vessel' as we discern them in the upper worlds. For they come inevitably bound together and cascade down together from stage to stage.
>
> According to the measure that the stages descend from the direct revelation of God's light, becoming estranged from the Blessed One, so is the measure of materialization of the will to receive that is included within the bounty. It is also possible to say the opposite, that according to the measure of materialization of the will to receive that is included within the bounty, so does it descend from stage to stage, until it reaches the lowest place of all, in which the will to receive has materialized to its most appropriate measure. This stage is designated by the name of the world of *Assiyah*, and the will to receive is designated as the body of a person. The bounty that the body receives within it is designated as the dimension of life force that is in the body.
>
> Similarly, this process holds for all the other created beings of this world. The distinction between the upper worlds and this world is that while the will to receive that is included within God's bounty has not yet materialized into its

Lesson eleven

final form, it is designated as still being in the spiritual worlds, which are higher than this world. Once the will to receive has materialized into its final form, it is designated as being already within this world.

The order by which the will to receive cascades down through the higher worlds, until it achieves its final form in this world, occurs according to the arrangement of the four modalities represented by the letters of the four-letter Name of the One. For these four letters, י'ה'ו'ה' (*Yud, Hay, Vav, Hay*), which make up the Name, include the whole of reality without even the tiniest exception. Generally speaking, they are described by the ten *Sephirot*: *Chochmah, Binah, Tiferet, Malchut*, and their root. These comprise ten *Sephirot*, because the *Sephirah Tiferet* includes within itself the six *Sephirot* called: *Chesed, Gevurah, Tiferet, Netzach, Hod*, and *Yesod*. The root of the *Sephirot* is called *Keter*. However, in their essence, the ten *Sephirot* are called *Chochmah, Binah, Tiferet*, and *Malchut*. Remember this! These are the four worlds, that are called *Atzilut, Briyah, Yetzirah*, and *Assiyah*. *Assiyah* includes this world within it.

There is no created being in this world that did not originate from the *Ein Sof*, that is to say, that did not stem from the purpose of creation—which is to give pleasure to His created beings as we stated above. The created being therefore includes together the light and vessel; that is to say, it consists of a certain measure of bounty together with the will sufficient to receive this bounty. The measure of bounty emanates from the One's essence, *yesh m'yesh*, whereas the will to receive the bounty is created anew, *yesh m'ayin*, as we have explained. In order that the will to receive may come into its final form, it must cascade down, together with the bounty that is in it, through the four worlds, *Atzilut, Briyah, Yetzirah*, and *Assiyah*. Then the created being is finished with respect to its light and vessel, which are then designated as the body and its incumbent life-force.[4]

Let us return to the *Introduction to the Zohar*:

Introduction to the Zohar

39. Now it has been explained that the desired purpose of the Creator in carrying out the creation is only to give pleasure to His created beings in order that His created beings should recognize His truth and His greatness. They should receive from Him all the good and the pleasantness that He has prepared for them. Its measure is indicated in the quotation, "'What a dear son Ephraim is! He is my darling child! For whenever I speak of him, I earnestly remember him. My compassion is stirred for him. I shall surely have mercy on him,' says the Lord" (Jer. 31:19).

It is clear that this purpose cannot be fulfilled by the inanimate realm, not even by the great spheres, the earth, the moon, or the sun, no matter how brightly

Lesson eleven

they shine. Nor can it be fulfilled by the plant or the animal kingdoms, which lack the capacity to feel the feelings of the other, even those of one from the same species. How could they possibly feel appreciation for the Divine and His Goodness? **Only human beings have the required potential to appreciate God through their capacity to feel the feelings of their fellow human beings.**

What a beautiful paragraph! Take the time to simply breathe it in and enjoy it. Here the will to receive, multiplied millions of times through our capacity to feel each other's feelings, is in its transformed state. We feel compassion and love for each other, and happiness in each other's joy. This leads us to affinity of form with God and the capacity to appreciate the Source of all life.

Remember a time when you sincerely and altruistically felt joy for someone else and their joy became yours. When you write about it, use the present tense. Relive that joy and know that we are always capable of feeling joy for each other. Then recall a moment of shared joy when you were part of a team or a community and experienced together a shared relief or achievement. Write about it in the present, as you recall that precious uplift of spirit.

Introduction to the Zohar

39. *(continued)* Once a human being completes his or her work in Torah and *mitzvot* and transmutes the will to receive for oneself into the will to give to others, then he comes into affinity of form with the Creator. The person then receives all the levels that are prepared for him in the upper worlds, which are called *Nefesh, Ruach, Neshamah, Chayah,* and *Yechidah,* through which he becomes fitted to receive all the content implicit in the thought of creation. Thus we see that all the worlds were only created for the sake of the human being.

Thus we see that the measure and quality of light received is dependent on the measure and stature of the appropriate spiritual vessel. We shall look more deeply into this point in this passage from the *Talmud Eser haSephirot*:

We need to know, first of all, what the essence of a spiritual vessel is. Since the created being is receiving the bounty of its life-force from the Creator, it has to be the case that it has the will and desire to receive this very bounty from Him, may the One be blessed. And know that it is the dimension of this will and this desire that comprises the entire matter of the created being, such that all that is within the created being, aside from this material, is not ascribed to this material, but is attributed to the bounty that the created being receives from the Creator. And not only that, but this material, that is the will to receive, sets the measure of magnitude and stature of every created being, every spiritual entity, and every *Sephirah*.

For the emanation of the highest light from the Creator is certainly without measure or dimension, only the created being itself setting a measure to the bounty, since it receives no more and no less than the measure of its desire and will to receive. This is the criterion (of how much light a vessel may receive) which operates in spirituality, because compulsion is not practised there, and everything depends on will. Therefore, we designate this 'will to receive' as being the vessel for receiving of the created being. This vessel is defined as the created being's material aspect, by virtue of which the created being came forth from being included within the Creator to become a separate entity. This separate entity is named a created being since it is defined by this matter, which is not to be found at all within the Creator. The will to receive certainly does not operate within the Creator, as from whom could the One receive? Understand this well.

Further on we shall learn that in this material there are four levels, from the smallest measure of receiving to the largest measure of receiving. It is the fourth level that consists of the largest measure of receiving. [5]

To conclude let us review paragraph 34 of the *Introduction to the Zohar*:

Introduction to the Zohar

34. In order to prepare His created beings, so that they would be able to reach this high and elevated state, God works through four stages which develop naturally one from the other and which are called the inanimate, the plant, the animal, and the speaking. These are actually four levels of the will to receive. Every single world amongst all the higher worlds is divided into these four categories. The greatest aspect of desire is contained in the fourth level of the will to receive, but it is not possible for this fourth level to emerge without the prior existence of the three previous levels. The will to receive is revealed and developed gradually through the three previous levels before reaching its final completed form in the fourth level.

1. Bircat Shalom, Sefer haMa'amarim, volume one article twenty-four
2. Bircat Shalom, Sefer haMa'amerim, volume four article one
3. Perush haSulam, Hakdamat Sefer haZohar, Leila d'Kalah, paragraph 139
4. Petichah l'Chochmat haKabbalah, paragraphs 2 and 3
5. Talmud Eser haSephirot, part one, chapter one, Or Pnimi, paragraph 6

Ein Od Milvado!

"There is nothing other than the One!"

Lesson Twelve

The perception of the person who splits the shell of the will to receive for oneself alone
Paragraphs 39–42 of the Introduction to the Zohar

We shall start again from paragraph 39 of the *Introduction to the Zohar*:

Introduction to the Zohar

39. Now it has been explained that the desired purpose of the Creator in carrying out the creation is only to give pleasure to His created beings in order that His created beings should recognize His truth and His greatness. They should receive from Him all the good and the pleasantness that He has prepared for them. Its measure is indicated in the quotation, "'What a dear son Ephraim is! He is my darling child! For whenever I speak of him, I earnestly remember him. My compassion is stirred for him. I shall surely have mercy on him,' says the Lord" (Jer. 31:19).

It is clear that this purpose cannot be fulfilled by the inanimate realm, not even by the great spheres, the earth, the moon, or the sun, no matter how brightly they shine. Nor can it be fulfilled by the plant or the animal kingdoms, which lack the capacity to feel the feelings of the other, even those of one from the same species. How could they possibly feel appreciation for the Divine and His Goodness? Only the human species has the required potential to appreciate God through the capacity to feel the feelings of one's fellow human beings.

40. I know that this view is not acceptable to some philosophers who believe that human beings are so negligible and worthless that they could not possibly lie at the center of such a great and exalted creation. But they, the philosophers, are like a worm that is born in a radish, which sits there and thinks that the whole of God's world is dark, bitter and small, just like the radish within which it was born. But the moment that the worm breaks through the skin of the radish and looks outside it, it is astonished and says, "I thought that the whole world was just like the radish in which I was born. But now I see before me a big, bright, and wondrously beautiful world."

It is the same with people who are immersed in the *klipot* of the will to receive with which they were born and who have never tried to use the special healing spices, which are the practical work in Torah and *mitzvot*, which have the power to penetrate this hard shell, transforming it into the will of giving pleasure to

Lesson twelve

one's Creator. Such a person, just like the worm in the radish, would have no choice but to believe that human life is empty and meaningless because this is his or her perceived reality. He or she would not be able to entertain even the thought that the whole universe was created for them. But if such a person would practise Torah and *mitzvot* with the intention of giving pleasure to God in all purity, then he would split the shell of the will to receive for oneself alone with which they were born. In place of this the person would receive the will to give. Immediately, his eyes would be opened to see and he would attain for himself all the stages of wisdom, understanding, and clear intimate knowledge that await him in the spiritual worlds, and which are delightful to such a degree that the soul loses itself in ecstasy. Then such a person would himself say, as in the words of the Sages, "What does a good guest say? He says that all the trouble which the Master of the house took, he took for me!" [1]

Rabbi Ashlag points out that the sole use of the will to receive for oneself alone leads to a very contracted and limited view of the world and of ourselves, causing us to devalue ourselves. We see that the will to receive for oneself alone is the root of the low self-esteem which characterizes our generation. This defective view corrects itself as we pay more attention to giving benefit, which we do through the healing spice of our practice of Torah and *mitzvot*.

Look closely at the above paragraphs and see how Rabbi Ashlag makes it abundantly clear that we are in fact creatures of immense value. Have you ever had the experience of having released some aspect of the ego and then being able to see the world with a newer vision? If you have, write about it in your journal.

Introduction to the Zohar

41. Yet we still have not got completely to the bottom of the question as to why the human being needs all these higher worlds that God created for him and for her?

In the *Introduction to the Zohar*, Rabbi Ashlag goes on to discuss the spiritual worlds from the perspective of this question. However, he prefaces it with a short description of the make-up of the spiritual worlds, looking at general categories of vessels, lights, and *Sephirot*. The *Sephirot* are the most subtle vessels through which the created beings can receive the Divine light.

Introduction to the Zohar

41. *(continued)* You must know that the whole spiritual universe is divided, generally speaking, into five worlds which are called 1) *Adam Kadmon*, 2) *Atzilut*,

Lesson twelve

3) *Briyah*, 4) *Yetzirah*, and 5) *Assiyah*; each one of them being composed of endless sub-worlds. These worlds correspond to the five principle *Sephirot* (see table 1, page 188). The world of *Adam Kadmon* corresponds to the *Sephirah Keter*. The world of *Atzilut* corresponds to the *Sephirah Chochmah*. The world of *Briyah* corresponds to the *Sephirah Binah*. The world of *Yetzirah* corresponds to the *Sephirah Tiferet*, and the world of *Assiyah* corresponds to the *Sephirah Malchut*. The lights that are enclothed within these five worlds are called *Yechidah, Chayah, Neshamah, Ruach*, and *Nefesh*. The light of *Yechidah* shines in the world of *Adam Kadmon*. The light of *Chayah* shines in the world of *Atzilut*. The light of *Neshamah* shines in the world of *Briyah*. The light of *Ruach* shines in the world of *Yetzirah*, and the light of *Nefesh* shines in the world of *Assiyah*. All these worlds, and everything in them, are implied in the holy four-letter Name of God, which is 'י'ה'ו'ה, (Y-H-V-H, the Hebrew letters of which are *Yud, Hay, Vav, Hay*), together with the tip of the first letter 'י. (See table 1.)

We have no way to apprehend the first world of *Adam Kadmon* on account of its elevation, so we only hint at it through the tip of the 'י (the *Yud*) of the four-letter Name. This realm being so exalted, we often do not mention it at all and refer only to the four worlds of *Atzilut, Briyah, Yetzirah*, and *Assiyah*. The letter 'י (*Yud*) itself connotes the world of *Atzilut*. The first 'ה (*Hay*) signifies the world of *Briyah*. The 'ו (*Vav*) connotes the world of *Yetzirah*, and the final 'ה (*Hay*) refers to the world of *Assiyah*.

Before we carry on, let us look at some other writings of Rabbi Ashlag that describe the worlds, vessels, lights, and *Sephirot*. Here follow two excerpts taken from the *Mavo l'Zohar* (Prologue to the *Zohar*):

> Initially, you should know that everything that is discussed in the *Zohar*, even in its narrative passages, consists of arrays or combinations of arrangements of the ten *Sephirot*, which are called *Keter, Chochmah, Binah, Chesed, Gevurah, Tiferet, Netzach, Hod, Yesod*, and *Malchut*. Just as the various combinations of the twenty-two letters of the Hebrew language are sufficient for us to reveal every object and wisdom, likewise, the arrangements and combinations of the orders of the ten *Sephirot* are sufficient to reveal every wisdom in this heavenly book.[2]

> The *Zohar* compares these ten *Sephirot*, of which the main ones are four, namely, *Chochmah, Binah, Tiferet*, and *Malchut*, to four colors. White for the *Sephirah Chochmah*, red for the *Sephirah Binah*, green for the *Sephirah Tiferet*, and black for the *Sephirah Malchut*. This may be explained by the analogy of a looking glass that has four glass panes, each one colored with one of these four colors.

Table 1

Worlds	Sephirot	Lights	God's Name	*Tikkun* of the wills to receive for themselves alone
Adam Kadmon	*Keter*	*Yechidah*	tip of *Yud* י	
Atzilut	*Chochmah*	*Chayah*	*Yud* י	speaking
Briyah	*Binah*	*Neshamah*	*Hay* ה	animal
Yetzirah	*Tiferet*	*Ruach*	*Vav* ו	plant
Assiyah	*Malchut*	*Nefesh*	*Hay* ה	inanimate

Even though the light that is within it is uniform, nevertheless when the light passes through the glass panes, it becomes colored and becomes one of these four lights: white light, red light, green light, or black light.

Similarly, the light that is in all the *Sephirot* pertains to the One and is a simple unity, from the beginning of [the world of] *Atzilut* to the bottom of [the world of] *Assiyah*. The division of the light into the ten *Sephirot: Chochmah, Binah, Tiferet,* and *Malchut,* occurs by reason of the vessels that are called, *Chochmah, Binah, Tiferet,* and *Malchut,* in that each vessel is like a fine barrier through which the Divine light passes to the spiritual entities that receive it. Therefore, it is as if each vessel gives the light another color.

The vessel of *Chochmah* that is in the world of *Atzilut* transmits white light, that is to say, colorless light, because the vessel of *Atzilut* is like the light itself, and in passing through it the Divine light undergoes no change. This is the inner meaning of what is said in the *Zohar* concerning the world of *Atzilut,* "The One, the light and the vessels are one."[3] Therefore, the light of *Atzilut* is considered to be white light. This is not the case with respect to the vessels of the worlds of *Briyah, Yetzirah,* and *Assiyah.* The light that goes through these vessels undergoes a change and opacity on the way to its receivers. This is what is meant by the association of red light with *Binah,* which is the *Sephirah* connected to the world of *Briyah,* green light with *Tiferet,* which is the *Sephirah* connected to the world of *Yetzirah,* and black light with the *Sephirah Malchut,* which is the *Sephirah* connected to the world of *Assiyah.*[4]

Now we shall look at a further excerpt from the writings of Rabbi Ashlag on the *Sephirot,* this time from the *Petichah l'Perush haSulam* (The Gateway to the *Perush haSulam*):

(This next excerpt contains Names of God. We do not pronounce them, we read them with our eyes only.)

First of all we need to know the names of the ten *Sephirot:* These are *Keter, Chochmah, Binah, Chesed, Gevurah, Tiferet, Netzach, Hod, Yesod,* and *Malchut.* They are ten covers of the light of the One that were rectified in order that the lower created beings could receive the light of the One. This is analogous to the light of the sun, which is impossible to look at except through a smoked glass that limits the sunlight and adjusts it in accordance to the capacity of the eyes. Similarly the lower created beings would not be able to grasp the light of the One if it were not covered with these ten coverings, which are termed ten '*Sephirot*' (shining ones). The lower the *Sephirah,* the more it covers the light.

Lesson twelve

> These ten *Sephirot* are implied by the ten holy Names of God that are in the Torah. The Name E-H-Y-H is the *Sephirah Keter*, the Name Y-H is the *Sephirah Chochmah*, the Name Y-H-V-H with the vowel sounds of E-L-O-H-I-M is the *Sephirah Binah*, the Name E-L is the *Sephirah Chesed*, the Name E-L-O-H-I-M is the *Sephirah Gevurah*, the Name Y-H-V-H with the vowel sound of A-DO-NAI is the *Sephirah Tiferet*, the Name TZ-VA-OT is both the *Sephirah Netzach* and the *Sephirah Hod*, the Name SHA-DAI is the *Sephirah Yesod*, and the Name A-DO-NAI is the *Sephirah Malchut*.
>
> Even though we number ten *Sephirot*, there are in fact no more than five modalities, that are called: *Keter, Chochmah, Binah, Tiferet,* and *Malchut*. Their content is described well in the *Petichah l'Chochmat haKabbalah* in the first chapter. [5]

Here follows the section from the *Petichah l'Chochmat haKabbalah* suggested in the excerpt above. Although we have learned some paragraphs of this chapter before in different contexts, here is an opportunity to learn this whole section as a continuous piece, this time concentrating on the content of the ten *Sephirot*.

> Rabbi Chananiah ben Akashia said, "The Holy Blessed One wanted to give merit to Israel, therefore He gave them much Torah and *mitzvot*, as it is written, 'God desires for the sake of His righteousness to magnify the Torah and make it glorious'" (Isa. 42:21). [6]
>
> It is known that to merit (Hebrew: *l'zachot*) has the root meaning of 'to purify' (Hebrew: *hizdachachut*). This is in accordance with what is written, "*Mitzvot* were only given in order to purify the created beings through them." [7]
>
> We need to understand the nature of this purification that we achieve through Torah and *mitzvot*. Also: What is the impurity within us that we need to purify through Torah and *mitzvot*?
>
> I have already discussed this in my books, *Panim Me'irot* and *Talmud Eser haSephirot* but I shall repeat this briefly here:
>
> The purpose of creation is that God wants to give pleasure to the created beings, according to the gift of His ample hand, may the One be blessed. As a consequence, there was imprinted in the souls a will and great desire to receive God's plenty; for the will to receive is the vessel for the measure of delight that is to be had in the bounty. For, according to the size and urgency of the will to receive that bounty, so corresponds the measure of delight and pleasure to be had in the bounty—no less and no more. The will to receive the bounty, and the bounty itself, are so intimately connected together that they can only be separated in the sense that the pleasure is associated with the flow of giving benefit, and the will to receive it is associated with the created being who receives. Both

Lesson twelve

the bounty itself and the will to receive it come from the Creator and stem necessarily from the thought of creation. However, we distinguish between them, as we mentioned above, in that the bounty stems from God's essence, may the One be blessed, which is to say that the bounty is light, *yesh m'yesh* ('is-ness'), which emanates from God's essence, whereas the will to receive, which is included within the bounty, is the root of all created beings. That is to say, the will to receive is the root of new creation, *yesh m'ayin*, which implies something that did not have prior existence.

It is certain that there is no aspect of the will to receive in the essence of the Blessed One. Therefore it follows that the said will to receive is the sole material of creation, from its beginning to its end. All the myriad variety of created beings, all their happenings, of which there is no measure, and their behaviors, those that have already come into being and those that will manifest in the future, are only different measures and arrays of the will to receive.

Everything that exists within these created beings, that is to say, all that is received within the will to receive, stamped as it is within the created beings, is drawn from God's essence, *yesh m'yesh*, may the One be blessed. This light does not have any aspect of new creation, *yesh m'ayin*, as it is not created at all but is drawn from God's eternity, *yesh m'yesh*.[3]

As we have said, the will to receive is inevitably included immediately in the thought of creation—with all the many orders that are in it—together with the great bounty that God planned to bestow, in order to give pleasure to the created beings.

You should know that this is the inner meaning of the words 'light' and 'vessel', as we discern them in the upper worlds. For they come inevitably bound together and cascade down together from stage to stage.

According to the measure that the stages descend from the direct revelation of God's light, becoming estranged from the Blessed One, so is the measure of materialization of the will to receive that is included within the bounty. It is also possible to say the opposite, that according to the measure of materialization of the will to receive that is included within the bounty, so does it descend from stage to stage, until it reaches the lowest place of all in which the will to receive has materialized to its most appropriate measure. This stage is designated by the name of the world of *Assiyah*, and the will to receive is designated as the body of a person. The bounty that the body receives within it is designated as the dimension of life-force that is in the body.

Similarly, this process holds for all the other created beings of this world. The distinction between the upper worlds and this world is that so long as the will to

Lesson twelve

receive, which is included within God's bounty, has not yet materialized into its final form, it is designated as still being in the spiritual worlds, which are higher than this world. Once the will to receive has materialized into its final form, it is designated as being already within this world.

The order by which the will to receive cascades down through the higher worlds until it achieves its final form in this world, occurs according to the arrangement of the four modalities represented by the letters of the four-letter Name of the One. For these four letters, י'ה'ו'ה (Y-H-V-H), which make up the Name, include the whole of reality without even the tiniest exception. Generally speaking, they are described by the ten *Sephirot*: *Chochmah, Binah, Tiferet, Malchut*, and their root. These comprise ten *Sephirot*, because *Tiferet* includes within itself the six *Sephirot* called: *Chesed, Gevurah, Tiferet, Netzach, Hod*, and *Yesod*. The root of the *Sephirot* is called *Keter*. However, in their essence, the ten *Sephirot* are called *Chochmah, Binah, Tiferet*, and *Malchut*. Remember this! These correspond to the four worlds, which are called *Atzilut, Briyah, Yetzirah*, and *Assiyah*. *Assiyah* includes this world within it.

There is no created being in this world that did not originate from the *Ein Sof*—the purpose of creation, which is to give pleasure to His created beings—as we stated above. The created being therefore is made up immediately from both the light and vessel; that is to say, it consists of a certain measure of bounty together with the will sufficient to receive this bounty. The measure of bounty emanates from the One's essence, *yesh m'yesh*, whereas the will to receive the bounty is created anew, *yesh m'ayin*, as we have explained. In order that the will to receive may come into its final form it must cascade down, together with the bounty that is in it, through the four worlds, *Atzilut, Briyah, Yetzirah*, and *Assiyah*. Then the created being is finished with respect to its light and vessel, which are then designated as the body and its incumbent life-force.

The need for the will to receive to unfold through these four levels of *Atzilut, Briyah, Yetzirah*, and *Assiyah* stems from there being a very important principle as regards the vessels, in that a vessel becomes fit for its task through first being filled with light and then through the light leaving it. So long as the vessel has not separated from its light at least once, it is included in the light and is nullified before it, as is a candle in the presence of a burning torch.

This nullification occurs because there is an extreme opposition of form between the light and the vessel. The light is the bounty that is drawn *yesh m'yesh* from God's essence. According to the thought of creation that is in the *Ein Sof*, the desire of the light is entirely giving and has no element of desire to receive whatsoever. Opposite to it is the vessel, which is the great will to receive

Lesson twelve

the bounty, and is the root of every new created being. It has no aspect of giving benefit whatsoever. Therefore, when they are bound together with one another, the will to receive is insubstantial with respect to the light that is in it and thus cannot determine its final form until the light has left it at least once. After the light has left, the vessel begins to yearn for it very much. It is this yearning that determines and decides the most appropriate form of the will to receive. Subsequently, when the light returns and is enclothed in the vessel, it is designated from now on as being two distinct entities, vessel and light, or body and life-force. Pay great attention to this point as it is unfathomably deep.

Therefore, the four modalities that are in the Name י' ה' ו' ה' (Y-H-V-H), which are known as *Chochmah*, *Binah*, *Tiferet*, and *Malchut*, are required. The first modality, which is called *Chochmah*, is actually the entire created being, comprising the light and the vessel together. In it is included the great will to receive, together with the totality of the light. This light is called the light of *Chochmah* or the light of *Chayah* (Life), for it is all the light of the life that is in the created being, enclothed by its vessel. However, this first modality is designated as being made up entirely of light, with the vessel within it being hardly recognized, for it is mixed with the light and nullified within it as is a candle beside a torch.

After it comes the second modality, which comes about because at the final stage of the vessel of *Chochmah* the vessel prevails over its own will to receive, preferring to be in affinity of form with the light within it. That is to say, there awakens within the vessel a desire to give bounty to the Creator. This desire of the vessel is just like that of the light that is within it, whose only desire is to give benefit. Then through this will that has awakened, the vessel draws to itself a new light from the Creator that is called the light of *Chassadim* (the light of loving-kindness). The vessel is nearly completely separated from the light of *Chochmah* which the Creator gave it, because the light of *Chochmah* can only be received within the vessel for *Chochmah*, which is the will to receive in all its great measure. In this way, the light and the vessel of the second modality are completely different from those of the first modality. The vessel of the second modality is the will to give bounty, and the light within it is designated as the light of *Chassadim*, which implies light that is drawn from the Creator through the *dvekut* of the created being with the Creator. For the will to give causes affinity of form with the Creator, and affinity of form in spirituality is defined as *dvekut*, as will be explained further on.

After this comes the third modality of the vessel. This comes about because the light in the vessel has been reduced to the light of *Chassadim* without any *Chochmah* at all. But the light of *Chochmah* is the essence of the life-force of the created being. So the vessel at the end of the second modality awakens and draws within itself a measure of the light of *Chochmah* to illuminate its light of *Chassadim*. This awakening stimulates anew a certain measure of the will to receive, which constitutes the form of a new vessel called the third modality or *Tiferet*. Its light is called 'the light of *Chassadim* with illumination of *Chochmah*', for the main part of this light is the light of *Chassadim* with only an illumination from the light of *Chochmah*.

After this comes the fourth modality of the vessel. This comes about because at the end of the third modality, the vessel awakens and draws forth the light of *Chochmah* in its full measure, as in the first modality of the vessel. We find that this awakening of the vessel has a measure of desire equal to that of the first modality of the vessel. Actually, it has an even greater measure of desire because now it is completely separated from its light. Now it does not have the light of *Chochmah* enclothed within it, but it longs for it. This measure of longing determines the complete form of the will to receive. Only after the emanation of the light together with the vessel, followed by the light leaving the vessel, may the vessel be determined. When the vessel will again receive the light, we see that the vessel precedes the light. Therefore this fourth modality of the vessel is the final vessel and is called '*Malchut*'.

These four aspects of the vessel constitute the inner meaning of the ten *Sephirot*, which can be discerned in all created beings and in every vessel, whether of the macrocosm, which are the four worlds, or of the tiniest particle in existence. The first modality is called *Chochmah*, or the world of *Atzilut*. The second modality is called *Binah*, or the world of *Briyah*. The third modality is called *Tiferet*, or the world of *Yetzirah*, and the fourth modality is called *Malchut*, or the world of *Assiyah*.

Now we shall explain the four modalities of the vessel as they pertain within every soul. For when the soul comes forth from the *Ein Sof*, blessed be the One, and comes to the world of *Atzilut*, this is the first modality of the soul. Yet it is still not known by the name 'soul' because the name 'soul' would indicate some degree of separation from the Creator, that through this separation the soul left the modality of the *Ein Sof* and came to some degree of manifestation as an independent entity. So long as it does not have the form of a vessel there is nothing to separate it from God's essence to the extent that it would be proper to call it by its own name.

As we already know, the vessel in its first modality is not recognized as a vessel at all, being entirely nullified with respect to the light. This is the inner meaning of what is said concerning the world of *Atzilut*, that it is completely divine, according to the inner meaning of the phrase in the *Zohar*, "The One, the light and the vessels are one." Even the souls of animals, when they pass through the world of *Atzilut*, are considered as still being in *dvekut* with the essence of the One.

In the world of *Briyah*, the second modality of the vessel already dominates. This is the modality of the vessel that expresses its will as that of giving benefit. Therefore, when the soul cascades down and comes into the world of *Briyah* and attains the modality of the vessel that is there, then it is designated by the name '*Neshamah*'. That is to say, it has already gone forth and become separated from the essence of God, and has achieved a name in its own right, so that it can be called '*Neshamah*'. However, this vessel is very pure, as it is in affinity of form with the Creator and is considered as being entirely spiritual.

In the world of *Yetzirah*, the third modality of the vessel is dominant, which is made up of a little measure of the will to receive. Therefore, when the soul cascades down as far as the world of *Yetzirah* and attains this vessel, it has gone forth from the spiritual modality of *Neshamah* and is called by the name '*Ruach*'. Here the vessel is already mixed with a little opacity, which refers to the small amount of will to receive that is within it. However, the vessel is still considered as spiritual, for this level of impurity is not sufficient to completely separate it from God's essence, such that it may be designated as a body that has its own independent existence.

In the world of *Assiyah*, the fourth modality of the vessel dominates. This is the completion of the vessel of the massive will to receive that we discussed above. Here the soul attains a body that is completely separate and differentiated from God's essence, and stands as an independently existing entity. Its light is called '*Nefesh*', which indicates light that has no movement of its own.

You should know that there is not a single object in existence that does not have, as part of its make-up, all four modalities of the vessel, namely, *Atzilut*, *Briyah*, *Yetzirah*, and *Assiyah*.

Now you can see how this *Nefesh*, which is the light of life enclothed in the body, is drawn, *yesh m'yesh*, from God's essence itself. As it passes through the four worlds, *Atzilut*, *Briyah*, *Yetzirah*, and *Assiyah*, it becomes increasingly distant from the direct experience of God's light, until it comes into the vessel destined for it, which is called 'the body'. The vessel is now considered as having reached its intended final form. Even though the light within it is now so diminished that one can no longer recognize the root of its origin, nevertheless, through the practice of Torah and *mitzvot* in order to give pleasure to the Creator, a person

Lesson twelve

may increasingly purify his vessel, called a 'body', until it is fit to receive the great bounty, in all the measure that makes up the thought of creation, as it did when the thought of creation created it. This is what Rabbi Chananiah ben Akashia means when he says, "The Holy Blessed One, wanted to give merit to Israel, therefore he multiplied Torah and *mitzvot* for them." [8]

In this above piece from the *Petichah l'Chochmah haKabbalah*, Rabbi Ashlag describes the way in which the soul descends from world to world, from its origin in the *Ein Sof* until its arrival in this world.

In the *Introduction to the Zohar* he is now is going on to consider the composition of each of the spiritual worlds.

Introduction to the Zohar

42. These five worlds contain all the spiritual reality originating at the level of the *Ein Sof* and continuing right down to this world. Now each is included within the others, such that each world contains within it all the aspects of each of the five worlds. Thus, the five *Sephirot*, *Keter*, *Chochmah*, *Binah*, *Tiferet*, and *Malchut*, in which are enclothed the lights, *Yechidah*, *Chayah*, *Neshamah*, *Ruach*, and *Nefesh*, which relate to each of the five worlds respectively, are also to be found within every world.

Besides the five *Sephirot*, *Keter*, *Chochmah*, *Binah*, *Tiferet*, and *Malchut*, that are present in every world, there are also to be found the four modalities of the spiritual will to receive—inanimate, plant, animal, and speaking—in each world. The speaking modality of the will to receive in these worlds is the soul of the human. The animal modalities of each world are the angels of that particular world. The plant modalities of each world are called its garments, and the inanimate modalities of the spiritual will to receive are called its houses.

These modalities enclothe one another. The speaking modality of the will to receive, being the soul of the human being, enclothes the *Sephirot*, *Keter*, *Chochmah*, *Binah*, *Tiferet*, and *Malchut*, which are the godliness of each world. The animal modalities, the angels, enclothe the souls of the human being. The plant modalities, being the garments, enclothe the angels, and the inanimate aspects, the houses, enclothe and surround all of them. (See table 2, page 196.) The concept of 'enclothing' means that when one modality enclothes another it serves and supports it and allows the development of one modality into another, just as we explained regarding the inanimate, plant, animal, and speaking components of this physical world.

Table 2
The different modalities of the spiritual will to receive and the way they enclothe each other

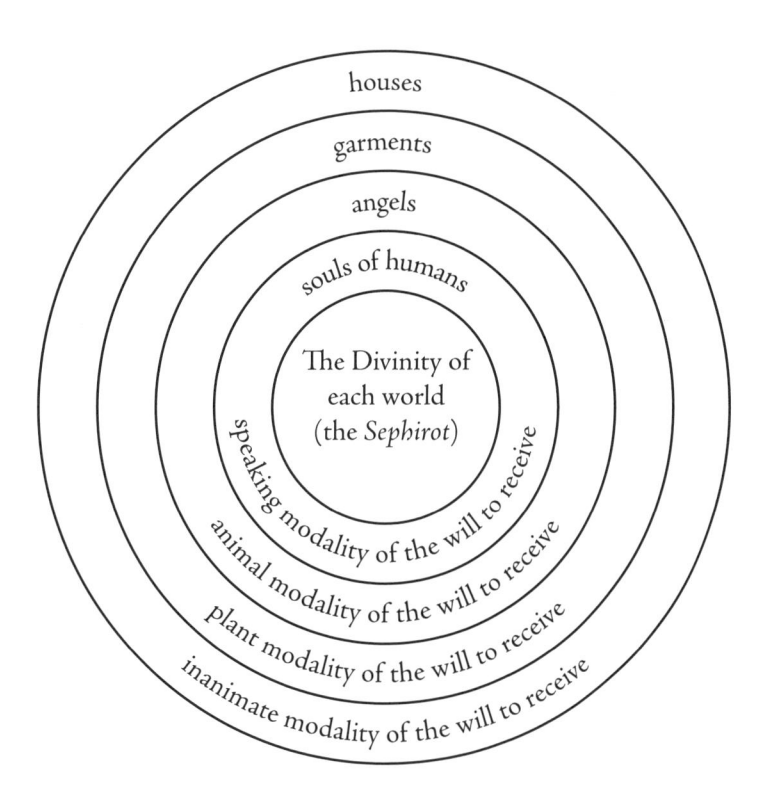

- houses
- garments
- angels
- souls of humans
- The Divinity of each world (the *Sephirot*)
- speaking modality of the will to receive
- animal modality of the will to receive
- plant modality of the will to receive
- inanimate modality of the will to receive

Lesson twelve

The term 'enclothing' implies that the purest aspect of a lower modality is in affinity of form with the lowest aspect of the higher modality. The higher modality is always the innermost element; the purpose of the outer elements being to support and serve the inner elements.

In our world, the holy *Nefesh* of the human being, which starts as a point in the heart, is enclothed by its animal aspect, called in Hebrew the *Nefesh Behamit* (the animal soul), which is characterized by its will to receive for oneself alone.

So we see that it is precisely those parts of ourselves which, comprised of sin or ego, separate us from God, yet, acting as *klipot*, enclothe our divine *Nefesh*, support her, and enhance her development. Just as the shell of a fruit protects it from harm until the fruit is ripe.

How can this be? It stems from the very purpose of creation wherein the will to receive for oneself, in its transformed state, will be the very vessel to receive all the good that the Creator wants to bestow upon us. The untransformed ego is the very same material out of which our transformed state is made.

Let us take an example: stubbornness in a four-year old is the material from which determination is born in the adult. Without the stubbornness of the child, the determination to overcome obstacles in the adult would not have been possible.

With regard to ourselves, seeing the value, even in our negative qualities, is not always easy for us. Our sins and ego tend either to blind us or to make us feel ashamed or guilty. One strategy is to learn to be objective about oneself. Viewing one's good points and one's negative aspects dispassionately can help us enormously on the spiritual path. This takes time and patience with oneself. One way to learn how to do this, as recommended by the Sages, is to practise a daily review. Going over the events of the day, in our mind or in our journal, and considering how we responded to them, helps us become objective and dispassionate about ourselves. Everything comes from the Creator—events we feel good about and events we feel badly about— to which we respond in either positive or negative ways.

Ask yourself, "What happened today?" When you have a list of five events examine your response to these events. A dispassionate review helps us learn that even from our negative qualities much good may subsequently ensue.

Introduction to the Zohar

42. *(continued)* This is just the same, by analogy, as occurs in the relationship of the inanimate, plant, animal, and human to each other in this physical world. We have already pointed out how the inanimate, plant, and animal kingdoms on the physical plane did not come into existence for themselves, but rather, their

purpose was to open up and expand the fourth modality of the will to receive, the speaking modality, which is the human species. Their only purpose, therefore, is to serve and help humankind. This is also true of all the spiritual worlds. The three modalities of inanimate, plant, and animal in the spiritual worlds are only there to serve and assist the speaking modality in the spiritual worlds, which is the human soul. Therefore, they all enclothe the soul of the human for the person's benefit.

Rabbi Ashlag expands on these ideas in the *Mavo l'Zohar* (Prologue to the *Zohar*) as below:

> Even though the *Zohar* deals with every world, both from the perspective of the *Sephirot*, which comprise the godliness that illumines each particular world, and from the perspective of all the inanimate, plant, animal, and speaking vessels that constitute the created beings of that world, nevertheless the main intention of the *Zohar* is focused specifically on the modality of the speaking vessels of each particular world.
>
> I shall explain this with the help of an example from this world: It has been explained (*Introduction to the Zohar* paragraph 42) that the inanimate, plant, animal, and speaking modalities that are to be found in each and every world, even in this world, are the four modalities of the will to receive. Within each one of these categories there exist all of the four modalities, namely the inanimate, plant, animal, and speaking.
>
> A person in this world needs to receive nourishment and develop through all the modalities of the will to receive for oneself alone, namely the inanimate, plant, animal, and speaking that pertain to this world. For the nourishment of the human has within it these four modalities, which come from the four modalities of the inanimate, plant, animal, and speaking that comprise the human will to receive for oneself alone. These are: *a)* the inanimate, which is the will to receive that which is needed for survival; *b)* the plant modality, which consists of a will to receive beyond that which is needed simply for survival, that is a desire for luxuries, but limited to animal lusts alone; *c)* the animal modality, which consists of a longing for specifically human appetites, such as honor and power; *d)* the speaking modality which consists of a thirst for knowledge.
>
> The will to receive that which is needed for survival is the inanimate modality of the will to receive. The will for animal-like desires is the plant modality of the will to receive for oneself alone, as these desires come only to give growth and pleasure to the person's vessel, which consists of the flesh of his or her body. The desire for human-type lusts is the animal modality of the will to receive for

oneself alone, as the desire for honor, power, and so forth increase a person's spirit. The desire for knowledge is the speaking modality of the will to receive for oneself alone.

You find that regarding the first modality of the will to receive, which is the measure of the will to survive, and the second modality, which is the will to receive animal lusts for oneself alone that are over and above those of survival, the person has these wills to receive fulfilled and nourished by entities that are lower than him, namely by the inanimate, the plant, and the animal. But as regards the third modality, which is that of human lusts, such as honor or power, a person has these desires fulfilled and nourished by his or her colleagues, who are at the same level as himself or herself. Regarding the fourth level of nourishment, which is knowledge, a person receives and is nourished by a modality above himself, that is, from the essence of wisdom and intelligence, which are spiritual modalities.

A similar process applies in the orders of the upper spiritual worlds. For the worlds are templates for each other, with a higher world acting as a template for the world lower than it. Every modality of inanimate, plant, animal, and speaking in the world of *Briyah* imprints itself in the world of *Yetzirah*, and from the inanimate, plant, animal, and speaking modalities of *Yetzirah* are stamped the inanimate, plant, animal, and speaking modalities of *Assiyah*. Similarly, from the inanimate, plant, animal, and speaking modalities of *Assiyah* are stamped the inanimate, plant, animal, and speaking modalities of this world. As we explained above (in the *Introduction to the Zohar*, paragraph 42), the inanimate entities in the spiritual worlds are called 'temples'. The plant entities are called 'garments'. The animal entities are called 'angels'. The speaking modality is the human souls of each world. The ten *Sephirot* in every world are its Divinity. Study this carefully.

The human souls are the center of every world, and they are nourished from the entire spiritual reality of that world, just as a physical human being is nourished by the entire physical reality of this world. A person receives the first modality of the will to receive, which is the basic will to receive necessary for survival, from the illumination which emanates from the houses and the garments of this world.

The second modality of the will to receive for oneself alone, which comprises desire for physical luxuries that increase the physical will to receive, a person receives from the modality of the angels in the world. They give him spiritual lights over and above those needed for survival. These are important, as they increase the spiritual vessel available for his soul to be enclothed therein.

Lesson twelve

> Regarding both the first and the second modalities of his will to receive for himself alone, a person receives nourishment from aspects of the world that are lower than himself, namely the temples, garments, and angels that are there, which are below the souls of humankind.
>
> The third modality of the will to receive for oneself alone, which is that of human desires that amplify the *Ruach* of a person, is received from other people in this world. We find that also in the spiritual worlds a person receives this third modality from all the souls that are in that world, through whom the illumination of the *Ruach* of the person's soul is enlarged.
>
> A person receives the fourth modality of the will to receive for oneself alone, which is the desire for knowledge, from the *Sephirot* pertaining to that world, from which he receives the aspects of *Chochmah*, *Binah*, and *Da'at* for his soul.
>
> So we see that the soul of the human, which is found in every world, needs to grow and be perfected through all the modalities that are to be found in that world.
>
> We need to know that all the words of the *Zohar* concerning any component in the upper worlds that is under discussion, whichever category it belongs to —*Sephirot*, souls, angels, garments, or temples—are primarily directed to the degree that the soul of the human in that world receives from them and is nourished by them, such that all the words of the *Zohar* are focused on the needs of the soul. If you are diligent in keeping to this line of thought, then you will understand this wisdom and succeed in all your ways.[9]

Give examples in your journal from your own experience of the different modalities of the wills to receive that you find within yourself: inanimate, plant, animal, and human, according to the above definitions. Look at the will to receive for oneself alone and look at the will to give benefit according to each of the above categories.

Then look at how these are supported by your environment: physical, emotional, and spiritual. Consider which part of your environment supports and nourishes which modality of the will to receive for oneself alone. Then consider which aspects of your environment support which modality of the will to give benefit.

Rabbi Ashlag emphasizes again and again the importance of the company we keep, the friends we surround ourselves with, the books we read, and the media we watch because of their influence on our spiritual development for good or for evil. We have freedom of choice and the capacity to influence our own development by choosing our physical, mental, and spiritual environment.

Here is an excerpt from his work *Matan Torah* (the Gift of the Torah):

> The Environment as a Cause
>
> One can always add to our spiritual environment, which consists of our friends, our books, our teachers, and so on. This can be likened to one who has inherited a small measure of seed grain from his father, and could produce from this small measure a large quantity of wheat, just by choosing a suitable environment for the seed. The required environment is a fertile ground, that contains all the minerals and raw materials with which to support the wheat in plenitude. Just as the work consists of improving the environmental conditions so they will suit the needs for germination and growth, so the wise person will act with intelligence and chose the best conditions and find blessing, whereas the fool just takes what there is to hand and so turns the sowing of his seed to a curse instead of a blessing.
>
> It follows that the superior quality and profitability of the wheat depends entirely on the environment in which the seed was sown. However, once it has been sown in its chosen environment, the outcome of the wheat has already been determined according to the measure that the environment is able to give to it. ...
>
> We have the freedom to choose our environment, our books, and our teachers, who can give us good intelligent wisdom. If a person does not do this but is prepared to come into any opportune environment or read any available book, then he is bound to fall into a bad environment or waste his time with books that have no value, which are many and more convenient. From this, he is bound to come to hold worthless or even evil views which lead him into sin and wickedness.
>
> Therefore, one who makes the effort in his life and chooses, each time, a better environment, is destined for improvement and reward. This is awarded to the person, not by reason of his thoughts or good deeds, which come to him without his choice, but from the effort he made to find a good environment which brings him to these thoughts and deeds. Thus Rabbi Joshua Ben Perchia said, "Make for yourself a *Rav* (teacher), acquire for yourself a friend." [10] [11]

Rabbi Baruch Shalom haLevi Ashlag spoke much about the influence of community on the individual and the necessity we all have to be helped in our spiritual work by friends who hold the values we would like to adopt.

Here follows an excerpt from one of his many articles on the subject, taken from *Bircat Shalom*:

Lesson twelve

Purpose of the Group

It being the case that a person is created with a vessel called 'selfish love' (egoism), it follows that if he cannot see that as a result of a particular action he will gain something for himself, then he does not have the motive to do even the slightest thing. Yet without nullifying this selfish love, one cannot come to *dvekut* with God, which means affinity of form. Since this is against our nature, we need a group, the members of which will all be able to work together to nullify the will to receive for oneself alone. The will to receive for oneself alone is designated as being evil, since it is that which prevents us from coming to the purpose for which the human was created.

Therefore, the group needs to be composed of individuals who are all of the opinion that we need to transform the will to receive for oneself alone to the will to give benefit. All these individuals form one big power that each individual member of the group can use to fight his or her own will to receive for oneself alone. This is the case, because every person's will is made up of the wills of all of the others of the group. We see that in this way, each one obtains a great and firmly based will for transforming the will to receive. In order that this should come about, each person has to nullify himself with respect to the other, and this is achieved by looking at the virtues of one's friends and not at their deficiencies.[12]

1. *Berachot 58a*
2. *Mavo l'Zohar, paragraph 2*
3. *Hakdamah l'Tikkunei haZohar, Ma'alot haSulam, paragraph 69*
4. *Mavo l'Zohar, paragraph 7*
5. *Petichah l'Perush haSulam, paragraphs 1 and 3*
6. *Makot 23b*
7. *Bereshit Raba, beginning chapter forty-four*
8. *Petichah l'Chochmat haKabbalah chapter one, paragraphs 1–10*
9. *Mavo l'Zohar, paragraphs 19–21*
10. *Ethics of the Fathers, chapter one, mishnah six*
11. *Ma'amar haCherut, edition Or haGanuz, page 116*
12. *Bircat Shalom, Sefer haMa'amarim, volume one, article one*

Ein Od Milvado!

"There is nothing other than the One!"

Lesson Thirteen

The relationship of the soul with the higher worlds; the *mitzvot*
Paragraphs 43–44 of the Introduction to the Zohar

Introduction to the Zohar

43. A person, the moment he or she is born, has a soul of holiness. But this is not a realized soul. It is, rather, an inactive soul, or a soul in potential; the least aspect of the soul. Since it is still small, this aspect of soul is considered as a point, which is enclothed within a person's heart, that is to say, it is enclothed within his or her will to receive, which reveals itself chiefly through the heart.

Consider this paragraph carefully. What does Rabbi Ashlag mean by 'the heart'? Rabbi Avraham Gottlieb, one of the foremost pupils of Rabbi Baruch Shalom haLevi Ashlag writes in his work *haSulam* ("The Ladder"—a biography of the Rabbis Ashlag) as follows:

> The will to receive is the basic constitution of a person and expresses itself in the person in two ways:
>
> 1) Via the mind: A person wants to know and understand the purpose for, and the logical consequence of, every act of his. For it is through the intelligent understanding of matters that the will to receive gets pleasure. This is not the case when a person performs an act whose purpose or use he does not understand. This causes him suffering.
>
> 2) Via the heart: This concerns the sensual will to receive, which is part of every person's make-up, which desires to sense and feel pleasure and delight in the different situations in this world, through the animal appetites of eating, drinking, sleep, desire for money, honor, power, and intelligence.
>
> These two aspects of the will to receive are two halves of the same nature, and they work in an integrated way within a person. ...
>
> Over and against these two aspects of the will to receive there are two modes of rectification (*tikkunim*):
> 1) for the mind—the work of faith,
> 2) for the heart—the work of serving God and one's fellow, not in order to receive a reward.[1]

Lesson thirteen

From this we can see that 'the heart' referred to above, in the *Introduction to the Zohar*, implies the sensual will to receive for oneself. This acts as a shell, within which lies the 'point of the soul', that is, the soul in potential. It is from this point that the desire to serve both God and one's fellow starts, and from which it can further develop, provided one pays attention and exerts oneself to that end.

Introduction to the Zohar

43. (*continued*) You may be familiar with the concept that whatever applies to the whole of reality applies equally in each individual world and to every particular particle in that world, however tiny it may be.

So, just as there are five worlds within the whole of reality which correspond to the five *Sephirot*: *Keter, Chochmah, Binah, Tiferet,* and *Malchut*, so there are five *Sephirot*: *Keter, Chochmah, Binah, Tiferet,* and *Malchut* within each world. Likewise, there are five *Sephirot* in every particle in every world.

As we have said, our world is divided up into the inanimate, plant, animal, and human aspects. These correspond to the four *Sephirot*: *Chochmah, Binah, Tiferet,* and *Malchut*; the light of the inanimate modality of the will to receive corresponding to the light of the *Malchut*, the light of the plant modality of the will to receive corresponding to the light of *Tiferet*, the light of the animal modality of the will to receive corresponding to the light of *Binah*, the speaking modality of the will to receive corresponding to *Chochmah* and the highest root of all of them corresponding to *Keter* (table 1, page 188).

However, as we have stated, one individual entity from any of the inanimate, plant, animal, or human species, also has within it all the four modalities pertaining to the inanimate, the plant, the animal, and the speaking. So, for example, within any person lie the inanimate, plant, animal, and speaking aspects which are the four modalities of his or her will to receive, that enclothe the point of his or her holy soul (table 2, page 197).

The inclusion of the worlds, one within the other, indicates that reality is arranged as a hologram. Each individual detail of reality is represented in every other detail, and therefore every detail exerts influence, both on every other detail, and on the whole. Rabbi Ashlag will enlarge on this further on.

Introduction to the Zohar

44. Before the age of thirteen, there is no outer manifestation of this point of the holy soul within the heart. After the age of thirteen, if a person begins to practise Torah and *mitzvot*, even if this is as yet without any inner intention, that is to say, without any degree of love or awareness of serving God, nevertheless, this practice causes the point of the soul within his or her heart to enlarge and to

show its action. **Even without positive intention,** the act of doing these *mitzvot* purifies the will to receive for oneself, but only at its first level, which is called the 'inanimate'.

It is important to clarify here just what Rabbi Ashlag means by "without positive intention." Does he mean that practising Torah and *mitzvot* in a mechanical fashion does something? Or does he mean that the practice of Torah and *mitzvot* for the sake of a reward, that is to say, in a manner that is self-serving is nonetheless useful?

Rabbi Baruch Shalom haLevi Ashlag clarifies the issue in his commentary, *Or Baruch* on the *Introduction to the Zohar*, as follows:

> The person sees that he is not able to practise Torah and *mitzvot* only with the intention of serving the Creator, because his will to receive only for himself does not let him. Therefore, he practises Torah and *mitzvot* in order that the practice itself should bring him to the purification of his will to receive. Then the practice of Torah and *mitzvot* **is** able to bring the person to purify his will to receive, in the first modality, which is the modality of the inanimate.
>
> However, if the person is practising Torah and *mitzvot* in order to receive a reward, then he does not desire his practice to lead to a purification of his will, but his practice is in fact an opposite action, that is to say, he **has** an intention in performing Torah and *mitzvot*—his intention is to receive a reward! [2]

In view of this, read paragraph 44 again from the beginning with a new understanding:

Introduction to the Zohar

> 44. Before the age of thirteen, there is no outer manifestation of this point of the holy soul within the heart. After the age of thirteen, if a person begins to practise Torah and *mitzvot*, even if this is as yet without any inner intention, that is to say, without any degree of love, or awareness of serving God, nevertheless, this causes the point of the soul within his or her heart to enlarge and to show its action. **Even without positive intention,** the act of doing these *mitzvot* purifies the will to receive for oneself, but only at its first level, which is called the inanimate.
>
> As he or she purifies the inanimate part of the will to receive, the person constructs the six hundred and thirteen limbs of the point of the soul within the heart, which is the inanimate modality of the holy *Nefesh*. When he or she has completed all the six hundred and thirteen commandments from the practical aspect, then all the six hundred and thirteen limbs of the point within the heart,

which comprise the inanimate modality of his or her holy *Nefesh*, are completed. The two hundred and forty-eight spiritual organs are built up by performing the two hundred and forty-eight positive commandments, and the three hundred and sixty-five spiritual sinews are built up by refraining from transgressing the three hundred and sixty-five negative commands. Then the inanimate modality of the holy *Nefesh* becomes a complete spiritual entity, and the *Nefesh* then ascends and enclothes the *Sephirah Malchut* that is in the spiritual world of *Assiyah*.

The question that arises from this paragraph is: What is the meaning of the numbers, six hundred and thirteen *mitzvot*, of which two hundred and forty-eight are positive ones and three hundred and sixty-five are negative ones? Surely one single person cannot fulfill them all!

Let us consider this question. First of all, here is an excerpt from the chapter "Keywords" from *In the Shadow of the Ladder*:[3]

> Six hundred and thirteen *mitzvot*
> Maimonides enumerated all the possible *mitzvot* as stated in the Torah. There are six hundred and thirteen.
>
> But, as he himself states, six hundred and thirteen cannot possibly apply to one person in their life-time. Some only apply to a man, others only to a woman. Some could only be carried out during the time that the temple stood in Jerusalem. Others only apply to people living in the land of Israel. For most people, the number of *mitzvot* they are ever likely to encounter in one lifetime is nearer sixty. Rabbi Ashlag uses the number six hundred and thirteen to imply the completion of a spiritual stage, which corresponds to the soul limbs of the spiritual entity. Basically, his meaning is that when the required work has been completed, the soul ascends.

However, the question still remains, how can we possibly complete any particular stage, if, as above, we are not capable of doing all the *mitzvot*?

The answer lies in that we may complete a spiritual stage in two ways:

1) Over many incarnations through which we have incarnated in different ways and different circumstances. In each incarnation we get the opportunity to fulfill different *mitzvot*.

2) By the fact that we are all interconnected, according to the phrase, *Kol Yisrael arevim zeh lazeh* (all Israel is a guarantor for each other). Thus, when a person does a particular *mitzvah*, the influence of doing that *mitzvah* helps

Lesson thirteen

everyone and is counted for everyone else also. That way we participate in the full stage of the six hundred and thirteen *mitzvot* together.

Here is a discussion on the meaning and potential of the *mitzvot*, which appears in a section of the *Perush haSulam* in which Rabbi Yehudah Lev Ashlag expounds on general concepts in the *Zohar*:

> In the language of the *Zohar*, the *mitzvot* of the Torah are called by the name *pikudin* (commandments). However, they are also called by the name of six hundred and thirteen *itin* (pieces of advice). The difference between these names stems from the fact that everything has a potential aspect to it and an actualized aspect to it. The potential aspect of any matter is its preparatory stage, whereas the achieving of the matter is its actualization.
>
> This also applies to Torah and *mitzvot*. According to the Scripture, "And he took the book of the covenant and he read it before all the people, and they said, 'All that the Lord has spoken, we shall do (*na'aseh*), and we shall understand (*nishmah*).'" (Exod. 24:7) [4] First we have the aspect of "*na'aseh*" (we shall do), which refers to the aspect of doing the *mitzvah* without understanding—potential; and then we have the aspect of "*nishmah*" (we shall understand), which refers to the aspect of performing the *mitzvah* with understanding—actual.
>
> As the Rabbis taught:
>
>> Rabbi Elazar said, "When Israel said, '*na'aseh*' (we shall do), before they said, '*nishmah*' (we shall understand), a heavenly voice came forth and said to them, 'Who revealed to My children the secret that the ministering angels use?' As it is written, 'Bless the Lord O angels, the heroes of power, who carry out His word, then understand the sound of His word' (Ps. 103:20). First comes the carrying out of His word, then comes understanding." [5]

When one fulfills Torah and *mitzvot* from the aspect of carrying out God's word before one has merited to attain the stage of understanding, then the *mitzvot* are called by the name of six hundred and thirteen *itin* (pieces of advice). They are in potential only, (that is to say that the light hidden within the *mitzvot* is potential only). However, when one merits the aspect of understanding the sound of His word, then the six hundred and thirteen *mitzvot* become *pikudim*, which comes from the term *pikadon*, meaning "a deposit." For there are six hundred and thirteen *mitzvot*, such that within each *mitzvah* there is a unique deposit of light that belongs to the specific spiritual level that corresponds to one particular organ of the six hundred and thirteen organs and sinews of the soul and of the body. Then we find that the performance of the *mitzvah*, in its actualized aspect, draws a specific level of light that is deposited in the *mitzvah* to the particular organ and sinew of the soul and of the body. This is the aspect of the actualization of the *mitzvot*, which are then called by the name *pikudim* (deposits).[6]

We may address the issue of the number of six hundred and thirteen from another aspect: We are taught that there is one *mitzvah* that includes all the Torah in it; that is, "Love your neighbor as yourself." If I can carry out that *mitzvah*, why do I need the others?

This is a question that Rabbi Baruch Shalom haLevi Ashlag addresses in his book *Bircat Shalom*:[7]

> The role of the other six hundred and twelve *mitzvot*
> Question: What does the general rule, "Love your neighbor as yourself" (Lev. 19:18) give us?
>
> Answer: It is through this general rule that we can come to the spiritual level of the Love of God.
>
> Since this is the case, what does fulfilling the other six hundred and twelve *mitzvot* give us?
>
> First of all, we have to know what the definition of a whole is: A whole is made up of many parts without which there cannot be a whole. For example: We may talk about a congregation, by which we mean a number of individuals who have joined together to make a group, one of whom the members appoint to be the head of the congregation, and so forth. This is called a '*minyan*' (prayer group) or 'congregation', which has to be made up of at least ten people. Then they can say certain prayers, such as the *kedushah*, which are only said in a *minyan*. Concerning this the Sages said, "The *Shechinah* rests on ten people."[8]
>
> Similarly, it follows, that the general principle of "Love your neighbor as yourself" is built up on the six hundred and twelve *mitzvot*. In other words, if we were to fulfill the six hundred and twelve individual *mitzvot*, then we could come to the general principle of "Love your neighbor as yourself." We conclude that the individual *mitzvot* allow us to reach the general principle, and then we would be able to arrive at the Love of God, as it is written, "My soul has yearned, indeed, it has pined for the courtyards of the Lord; my heart and my flesh will sing joyously to the living God" (Ps. 84:3).
>
> One person alone is not able fulfill all the *mitzvot*. For example, concerning the *mitzvah* of *pidyon haben* (redemption of the firstborn son), a father is not able to fulfill this particular *mitzvah* if a daughter was born first. Equally, a woman is exempt from *mitzvot* that are time dependent, such as *talit* and *tzitzit*. Nevertheless, due to the fact that all Israel are guarantors for each other, we find

that through the whole community, all the *mitzvot* are upheld. So we see that through the inclusion of everybody all the *mitzvot* are fulfilled.

Thus it really is the case that through the especial merit of the six hundred and twelve *mitzvot* we may arrive at the general principle of "Love your neighbor as yourself."

Many people have a somewhat distorted idea, or only a partial view, as to what 'Torah and *mitzvot*' actually consist of. This is true of both the secular and the religious Jew. Rabbi Ashlag, when he uses the term 'Torah and *mitzvot*', is referring to all the *mitzvot*: those that are practised between a person and God, and those that are carried out between a person and his or her fellow. Not always do we remember that the *mitzvot* of not gossiping, not hating, not taking revenge, are *mitzvot* of just as much importance as are the ritual *mitzvot* between the person and God. On the contrary, the *mitzvot* that are carried out between a person and his or her fellow have an additional value, as Rabbi Ashlag explains in his book, *Matan Torah* (The Gift of the Torah):

> There are two parts to the Torah: *a) mitzvot* that are practised between the One and the person, and *b) mitzvot* that are practised between a person and his fellow. They both have the same aim, which is to bring the created being to his final purpose of cleaving to the One, as we have explained.
>
> More than this, the practical aspect of both types of *mitzvot* is exactly the same. At the moment when a person performs an action for its own sake, without any admixture of selfish love, which is to say without getting any use out of it for himself, then he does not feel any difference in his action regardless of whether he is working for the love of his fellow or for the love of the One.
>
> This follows from the natural principle that applies to every created being, that everything that is beyond the normal boundaries of his self seems to him to be as something empty and completely unreal. Even every movement that a person makes in the direction of loving his fellow he does with some type of recompense, in the belief that any kindness he offers others will, in the end, come around and benefit himself. For this reason, such acts cannot be designated as "love of another" because they are judged according to the person's ultimate reason for performing them. This is similar to hiring something out and being paid only when the hired object is returned. An action for hire cannot be considered as love for one's fellow.
>
> However, to make any move or undergo any trouble only for the sake of the other, that is, without any sparks of light coming back or without any hope of recompense that may ultimately benefit oneself, is completely impossible from

Lesson thirteen

our nature. Therefore, only those who practise Torah and *mitzvot* are fitted for this. As the person trains himself to fulfill Torah and *mitzvot* just for the sake of giving pleasure to the Creator, he slowly and gradually removes himself from the lap of the natural creation and acquires a second nature, which is the aforementioned love of one's fellow.

We can see with our own eyes that a person who is really practising Torah and *mitzvot* for its own sake, even if only the practical *mitzvot*, does not feel any difference in carrying out the *mitzvah*, whether it is directed to one's fellow or to the Creator. This is because before he has reached perfection in this, it is necessarily the case that every action which is done for the other, whether this other is the Creator or his fellow, is felt by him as emptiness and is not apprehended. However, through great labor we see that a person ascends and is raised up gradually to this second nature, which is the desire to give benefit, and then he immediately merits the final purpose of the *tikkun*, which is *dvekut* with the One, as we have explained.

This being the case, logic leads us to think that the part of the Torah that is practised between a person and his fellow is more efficacious in bringing a person to the desired goal, because the work on the *mitzvot* between him and the Creator, may the One be blessed, is fixed and determined, and there is no one to complain about his performance of them, and a person becomes accustomed to them relatively easily. As we know, everything that a person does out of habit is not efficacious. This is not the case concerning the part of the Torah which pertains to the *mitzvot* between a person and his fellow. This is neither fixed nor determined, and complainants surround one wherever one turns. Thus, these *mitzvot* are more sure and more likely to achieve their purpose. [9]

Many people may not actually know just what is included in the term 'Torah and *mitzvot*'. As we have learned above, there are two main categories, those *mitzvot* which are practised between a person and the Creator, and those which are practised between a person and his or her fellow. Both the religious Jew and the secular Jew tend to look upon the world through the lens of habits of thought, and a tendency to limit the possibilities of life to known paths. A good exercise to open the eyes, is to glance every so often at the list of all six hundred and thirteen *mitzvot* as listed by the great sage Maimonides in his work *Sefer haMitzvot*, (The Book of the *Mitzvot*) and see what they include. [10] However, a note of caution: Don't get overwhelmed by seeing them all together, and especially don't get upset by the language. Remember that Maimonides lived and wrote in the medieval period, and his language reflects this. Nevertheless, it is quite

Lesson thirteen

an experience to look at the vast scope of the *mitzvot* and see how they relate to thought, feeling, expression, dealings with each other, ethical business practice, a fair court system, social justice, marital relationships, the cycle of the week and of the year, as well as *mitzvot* that are practised between a person and God.

Of course there may be *mitzvot* which don't speak to you, or which may even "press your buttons." What is important here, is to find which of the *mitzvot* are particularly yours. Remember what we have just learned, "all Israel are guarantors for each other." No one is expected to do them all!

We pray in the *Shabbat* morning service, "Give us our portion in your Torah." That is to say, give me my portion … . Which is my *mitzvah*? Which is the *mitzvah* I feel particularly close to, which I may take as far as I can? Write in your journal the meaning you find in a *mitzvah* you feel particularly drawn to and the different ways you find to practise it.

We return now to the *Introduction to the Zohar*. We shall start from the beginning of paragraph 44. Although we have read this before, through our intervening learning, we can now understand Rabbi Ashlag's work at a much deeper level:

Introduction to the Zohar

44. As he or she purifies the inanimate part of the will to receive, the person constructs the six hundred and thirteen limbs of the point of the soul within the heart, which is the inanimate modality of the holy *Nefesh*. When he or she has completed all the six hundred and thirteen commandments from the practical aspect, then all the six hundred and thirteen limbs of the point within the heart, which comprise the inanimate modality of his or her holy *Nefesh*, are completed. The two hundred and forty-eight spiritual organs are built up by performing the two hundred and forty-eight positive commandments, and the three hundred and sixty-five spiritual sinews are built up by refraining from transgressing the three hundred and sixty-five negative commands. Then the inanimate modality of the holy *Nefesh* becomes a complete spiritual entity, and the *Nefesh* then ascends and enclothes the *Sephirah Malchut* which is in the spiritual world of *Assiyah*.

All the spiritual units, the inanimate, plant, and animal, which are to be found in the world of *Assiyah* that relate to the *Sephirah Malchut* of *Assiyah*, help and assist that person's soul entity of *Nefesh* that ascends to the *Sephirah Malchut* of *Assiyah* according to the measure that the soul (*Nefesh*) is enlightened to receive them. This enlightenment becomes spiritual nourishment for the *Nefesh*, which gives it strength to grow and increase in capacity, until it can draw towards itself the light of the *Sephirah Malchut* of *Assiyah* in all its complete perfection, which then gives its light within the body of the person. This perfect light helps a person to increase his or her work in Torah and *mitzvot* so that he or she may go on to receive other levels.

You might like to consider the phrase, "according to the measure that the soul (*Nefesh*) is enlightened to receive them." How do we perceive the help we are given? Do we always see it as help? Are we open to it?

Write in your journal of two recent instances: One when you received help and perceived it as such, and one when you received help but did not recognize it as such at the time. You might even have felt the opposite.

Introduction to the Zohar

44. (*continued*) We have already stated that when a person is born, a point source of the light of *Nefesh* enclothes itself within his or her will to receive. Similarly here, when he or she has given birth to the spiritual entity which is the *Nefesh* of holiness, there is born together with it a point source which originates from the stage above. That is to say that there arises a point source from the inactive aspect of the light of *Ruach* of *Assiyah*, which enclothes itself within the inmost aspect of the entity of *Nefesh*, in a way similar to that above. The process proceeds in this way throughout all the stages. Whenever one stage is born, the point source of the inactive aspect of the next stage above it is born within it, making the connection between the higher stage and the stage below it. This process continues up to the very highest stages. Thus, through the assistance of the point of the higher level enclothing itself within the lower, the soul is enabled to ascend each time to a higher stage.

We are never alone, and help is always given to us that is appropriate to our level, and to help us progress from one stage to the next. Indeed, each stage has within it the seed of the next stage, making the connection from the very lowest level all the way up to the highest level, stage by stage.

1. HaSulam page 28
2. Or Baruch on the Hakdamah l'sefer haZohar paragraph 44, printed in the Hakdamot l'Chochmat haEmet, page 88
3. Keywords, page 214
4. Usually translated as "we shall hear" or "we shall obey." A better translation according to the Kabbalah interpretation is "we shall understand."
5. Talmud, Shabbat 88a

Lesson thirteen

6. *Marot haSulam (Perush haSulam at end of volume one.)*
7. *Bircat Shalom, volume one, year 5744, article five*
8. *Talmud, Sanhedrin 39a*
9. *Matan Torah, paragraphs 13–14, page 25 (edition Or Ganuz)*
10. Maimonides was not the only one to make a list of the commandments. There is also Sefer haChinuch. These lists may also be found on the Internet.

Ein Od Milvado!

"There is nothing other than the One!"

Lesson Fourteen

The lights of the *Sephirot*, the vessels and the worlds; the ascension of the soul through the worlds
Paragraphs 45–49 of the Introduction to the Zohar

In the previous lesson we considered how the soul starts to develop within the framework of holiness. Rabbi Ashlag continues by describing the light that the soul receives at the first level in the framework of holiness, *Nefesh*.

Introduction to the Zohar

45. The light of *Nefesh* is the light of the inanimate aspect of the holy world of *Assiyah*, and it corresponds to the purification of the inanimate modality of the will to receive as it exists within the body of the human being, as we have explained above. The action of its illumination in spiritual terms can be compared to that of the inanimate in the physical world, which does not manifest individuation of its particular parts but only a general movement of all its parts together. Similarly, the illumination which comes from the entity of *Nefesh* of *Assiyah* is a general illumination. Even though it contains within it 613 limbs, which are 613 different ways of receiving God's bounty, still, at this stage, they are not distinguishable from each other, but the light illuminates them all equally as a general illumination, so that individual parts are not recognizable as such.

At this level the *Nefesh* of a person still does not show an active will of its own but is enslaved to the will of the person. This is what Rabbi Ashlag means when he says that the spiritual entity of the soul of *Assiyah* does not manifest individuation of its particular parts, but only exhibits a general illumination. A person is still liable to err, and when he does, his soul is unable to oppose this, but is obliged to allow him to operate according to his choice.

Introduction to the Zohar

46. Know that the *Sephirot* are Divine. There is absolutely no difference between the *Keter* of *Adam Kadmon* (the very highest) and the *Malchut* of *Assiyah* (the very lowest) in the aspect of their light. Nonetheless, from the point of view of the receiver, there is a great difference. The *Sephirot* consist of lights and vessels. The light within the *Sephirot* is pure Divinity, but the vessels, which are called *Keter*, *Chochmah*, *Binah*, *Tiferet*, and *Malchut*, which exist in each of the three lower worlds, *Briyah*, *Yetzirah*, and *Assiyah*, are not Divine as such. Rather, they

Lesson fourteen

are covers that hide the light of the *Ein Sof*, blessed be the One, within them. They limit and put a measure on this light for those who receive it, in order that a person may only receive light according to the degree of his or her own purity. From this point of view, even though the light, in its essence, is one, nevertheless, when it enters the different vessels, we call it by different names according to the characteristics of these vessels. These names are *Nefesh, Ruach, Neshamah, Chayah,* and *Yechidah*.

Malchut consists of the thickest of the coverings that hide the light of the *Ein Sof*, blessed be the One. It only allows a very small amount of light from God through to the receiver, in a measure which is proportionate to the purification of the inanimate modality of the will to receive in the human, and thus it is called *Nefesh* (at rest).

The vessel of *Tiferet* is clearer than that of *Malchut*, and the light which it allows to pass through it from the *Ein Sof* relates to the purification of the plant modality of the will to receive for oneself. It is more active than that of the light of *Nefesh* and is called the light of *Ruach* (wind).

The vessel of *Binah* is clearer than that of *Tiferet* and the light that passes through it from the *Ein Sof* relates to the purification of the animal modality of the human being's will to receive for oneself and is called the light of *Neshamah* (breath).

The vessel of *Chochmah* is the clearest of all. The light which it allows to pass through it from the *Ein Sof*, may the One be blessed, is specifically related to the purification of the speaking part of the human being's will to receive for oneself and is called the light of *Chayah* (life). There is no limit to its action as we shall see below.

47. As we have already said, within the spiritual entity of *Nefesh*, which a person has acquired through the practice of Torah and *mitzvot*, even without proper intention, there is already to be found enclothed the point source belonging to the light of *Ruach*. As the person strengthens himself or herself through Torah and *mitzvot*, gradually refining his or her motivation, that part of the plant modality of the will to receive which is within him or her becomes purified and in like measure gradually builds up the point of *Ruach* into a spiritual entity. Through the person carrying out the 248 positive commandments **with intention**, the point expands into 248 spiritual organs. And by refraining from transgressing the 365 negative commands, the point of light expands into 365 spiritual sinews. When all the 613 spiritual limbs are complete, then the entity ascends and enclothes the *Sephirah Tiferet*, which pertains to the spiritual world of *Assiyah*. This transfers to the person a clearer light from the *Ein Sof*, the light

Lesson fourteen

of *Ruach*, corresponding to the purification of the plant modality of the will to receive within the body of the human being. All the particular items that relate to the inanimate, the plant, and the animal of the world of *Assiyah*, which are related to this stage of *Tiferet*, help the person's spiritual entity of *Ruach* to receive all the lights from the *Sephirah Tiferet* in all their entirety. The spiritual entity, the *Ruach*, is considered as the plant modality of holiness. And, indeed, the nature of its illumination is equivalent to that of a plant in the physical world, in that all individual elements have their own particular ability to move. **So the light of this spiritual entity already has great power and illuminates each specific pathway of each separate limb of the 613 limbs which are in the spiritual entity of *Ruach*, each one showing the different action related to that specific spiritual limb.**

As the spiritual entity of *Ruach* emerges, there is born within it a point source from the stage higher than itself, which is the point of the light of *Neshamah*, which it enclothes within its innermost part.

At this stage a person is already practising Torah and *mitzvot* for its own sake. He or she has already attained the requisite intention with which to serve the Creator. It is at this stage that the person is first designated as being a *Tzaddik*.

Introduction to the Zohar

48. **Through studying the innermost parts of Torah and practising the *mitzvot* with a deep understanding of their true nature and purpose**, a person purifies the animal part of the will to receive. To the degree that he or she does this, the point of *Neshamah*, which is enclothed within the person, develops into an entire soul-entity of 248 organs and 365 sinews and it then ascends and enclothes the *Sephirah Binah* of the spiritual world of *Assiyah*. This vessel is immeasurably purer than that of *Tiferet* or of *Malchut*. This vessel is fitted to receive a much greater light from the *Ein Sof*, which is called the light of *Neshamah*. All the aspects of inanimate, plant, and animal in the world of *Assiyah*, which are related to the level of *Binah*, function to assist the person in developing this soul-entity of *Neshamah* until he or she can fully receive the light emanating from the *Sephirah Binah*, in exactly the same way we described for the light of *Nefesh*. This soul entity is also referred to as the animal modality of holiness since it comes about through the purification of the animal modality of the will to receive for oneself.

The nature of its illumination is similar to that of the animal kingdom in the physical world. It gives an individual feeling to each and every limb of the 613 limbs of the spiritual entity. Each limb feels itself free and alive, independent of all the other limbs, without dependency on the entity as a whole, until the 613 limbs become 613 spiritual entities, each one illumined with its own

Lesson fourteen

spiritual light. The superiority of this light over that of *Ruach* in the spiritual world can be likened to the difference in consciousness of the animal kingdom over the plant and inanimate kingdoms in the physical world.

Likewise, a point source from the light of *Chayah* of holiness, which is the light pertaining to the *Sephirah Chochmah*, emanates together with the spiritual entity of *Neshamah* and is enclothed within its innermost aspect.

49. Once the person has merited this great light of *Neshamah* and each one of the 613 limbs of this spiritual entity is already giving forth a perfect and clear light, specific to each limb, as if each limb is a spiritual entity in its own right, **then a doorway is opened for him or for her to perform each and every *mitzvah* according to the true intention that is within it.** For every limb of the soul world of *Neshamah* illuminates for the person the inner wisdom of the particular *mitzvah* that is associated with that limb. With the great power of these lights, he or she is able to go on and purify the speaking modality of the will to receive for oneself alone, transforming it into the will to give. As the person does this, the point of the light of *Chayah* enclothed within his or her soul gradually acquires its 248 spiritual organs and 365 spiritual limbs until it becomes a complete soul entity. Then the soul ascends and enclothes the *Sephirah Chochmah* in the spiritual world of *Assiyah*.

There is no end to the purity of this vessel, and so it draws down to itself a great and mighty light from the *Ein Sof*, blessed be the One, which is called the light of *Chayah*. All the individual aspects of the world of *Assiyah*, the inanimate, the plant, and the animal aspects of the world of *Assiyah*, which are related to the *Sephirah Chochmah*, help the person to receive the light of the *Sephirah Chochmah* in its entirety. This is called the speaking modality of holiness, as it corresponds to the purification of the human being's speaking modality of the will to receive for oneself. The importance of this light over the previous lights within Divinity is comparable to the place of the human being with respect to the animal, plant, and inanimate modalities in the physical domain. The aspect of the light of the *Ein Sof* that is enclothed within this soul-entity is called the light of *Yechidah* (oneness).

This is a fascinating section in that it shows the wondrous levels at which the Torah and *mitzvot* may be carried out, when one has already achieved the practice of Torah and *mitzvot* for its own sake. Here follows a beautiful parable taken from the *Hakdamah l'Talmud Eser haSephirot* (Introduction to the Study of the Ten *Sephirot*) which illustrates this:

Lesson fourteen

The main work with Torah and *mitzvot* in the correct way begins only after a person has attained *teshuvah* through love for God. (The person has reached the stage of receiving with the intention of giving benefit.) Only then is it truly possible for him or for her to practise Torah and *mitzvot* with love of God and fear of sin, as we have been commanded. As it is written in the Talmud, "The world was created only for the sake of the complete *Tzaddik*."[1]

We can understand this better by analogy with the following story:

There was once a King who wanted to choose the most faithful subjects of his kingdom and bring them into his service in his innermost palace. So what did he do? He issued a public proclamation throughout his kingdom, that everyone who so desired, whether great or small, should come to him and work in his innermost palace. But he appointed many guards from amongst his servants whom he stationed at the entrance to the palace and along all the roads leading to it, commanding them to cunningly deceive all those approaching the palace and to lead them away from the road which led to the palace.

Naturally, all the citizens of the country began to run to the king's temple, but they were led astray by the cunning of the diligent guards. Still, many of them managed to overcome the guards, and succeeded in approaching the door of the palace. But those who guarded the doorway were the most diligent of all. If anyone actually arrived at the doorway, they deflected him with their great cunning until he went back the way he came. But these people would return more forcefully, stronger than ever and come back again and again and so it would go on for days, even years, until they would give up and not try any more. Only the most valiant of all, whose patience stood them in good stead, overcame those guards and opened the door. They immediately merited to see the face of the King who assigned each one to the duty most suited for him.

From then onwards, they no longer had any more dealings with those guards who had deflected them and embittered their lives for so many days and years, as they were going to and fro, for now they were worthy to work and serve facing the majestic light of the face of the King in his innermost palace.

The same is true of the work of the complete *Tzaddik*. The free will that functions at the time of concealment of God's face certainly no longer operates once he or she has opened the door to perception of the revealed Providence. However, he or she begins the main service of God at the moment of the revelation of God's face, when the *Tzaddik* begins to tread the many steps on the ladder whose base rests on the ground and whose head reaches up into heaven, as it is written, "And the *Tzaddikim* will go from strength to strength" (Ps. 94:8).

As the Sages explained: Each *Tzaddik* has his or her own unique task and one *Tzaddik* may not touch the work assigned to another. (Hebrew: Each *Tzaddik* is burned by the returned light of his fellow.[2]) Their service trains them to do God's desire, so that through the *Tzaddikim,* the purpose of creation, which is to give pleasure to the created beings according to His good and generous hand, may be fulfilled.[3]

1. Talmud, Berachot 61b
2. Zohar Bereishit II Perush haSulam, paragraph 22
3. Hakdamah l'Talmud Eser haSephirot, paragraph 133

Ein Od Milvado!

"There is nothing other than the One!"

Lesson Fifteen

The ascension of the soul (continued)
Paragraphs 50–55 of the Introduction to the Zohar

Introduction to the Zohar

50. However you should know that all these five aspects of light: *Nefesh*, *Ruach*, *Neshamah*, *Chayah*, and *Yechidah*, which are received from the world of *Assiyah*, are, however, only the *Nefesh*, *Ruach*, *Neshamah*, *Chayah*, and *Yechidah* of the light of *Nefesh* (which is the light associated with the world of *Assiyah*). (See table 3, page 227.) They do not yet have anything of the light of *Ruach*, which has its place in the world of *Yetzirah*. Similarly, the light of *Neshamah* has its home in the world of *Briyah*, the light of *Chayah* in the world of *Atzilut*, and that of *Yechidah* in the world of *Adam Kadmon*.

Much of this is difficult to relate to in view of our everyday experience. We are, as it were, only standing at the bottom of the ladder, whose foot is on the ground and whose top reaches the heavens.

One might ask then, is there any value in learning or teaching material which is outside our own range of experience or present attainment?

Rabbi Ashlag assures us that there is. The benefit is threefold. First of all by reading such work, even when we do not understand it, we wake up the surrounding light *(Or Makif)* which helps to awaken the vessel, that is, our desire to come closer to God and to the fulfillment of the purpose of creation. Secondly, we add to the field of holiness through which we are helping to bring all the souls, and the world, to the end of the *tikkun*, the transforming stage of the world's existence. Thirdly, when we read this material, even though we have not yet attained these lights in our worldly existence of state two, we **have** realized these stages and attained all these lights in our state three existence, and thus our souls connect with this material even when we have difficulty relating to it consciously through our intellect.

Let us look at the words of the *Zohar* and of Rabbi Ashlag in the *Perush ha-Sulam* in this context:

Zohar
[A person should] occupy himself with the Torah, to strive [to understand it] and to persevere with it every day, to correct his *Nefesh* and his *Ruach*.

Lesson fifteen

Perush haSulam

To occupy oneself with the study of the Torah: This implies meditating on the Torah by reading it aloud, even though one may not understand it. This is in accordance with the inner meaning of the Scripture, "It is Life to those that bring them forth" (Prov. 4:22), that is, to those who bring [the words] forth, through the mouth. Through this a person acquires a holy *Nefesh*.

To strive in the study of Torah: To strive and do all that one can in order to grasp it and to understand it. Through this means the person acquires a holy *Ruach*.

To persevere with the study of the Torah: After one has merited to correct the *Nefesh* and the *Ruach* one should not be satisfied with this, but one needs to work at it continually, according to the inner meaning of the phrase, "one goes up in holiness and not down," and thus merit a holy *Neshamah*.[1] And this is what the *Zohar* says, "and to persevere in it every day to correct one's *Nefesh* and one's *Ruach*." Through increasing the practice of Torah every day, the person adds to the *tikkun* of his or her *Nefesh* and *Ruach* and merits the holy *Neshamah*.[2]

Let us begin again from paragraph 50 of the *Introduction to the Zohar*:

Introduction to the Zohar

50. However, you should know that all these five aspects of light, *Nefesh*, *Ruach*, *Neshamah*, *Chayah*, and *Yechidah*, which are received from the world of *Assiyah*, are, however, only the *Nefesh*, *Ruach*, *Neshamah*, *Chayah*, and *Yechidah* of the light of *Nefesh* (which is the light associated with the world of *Assiyah*). (See table 3.) They do not yet have anything of the light of *Ruach*, which has its place in the world of *Yetzirah*. Similarly, the light of *Neshamah* has its home in the world of *Briyah*, the light of *Chayah* in the world of *Atzilut*, and that of *Yechidah* in the world of *Adam Kadmon*.

However, as we have already mentioned, every aspect of reality that exists in the macrocosm also manifests in the microcosm. This is true right down to the tiniest unit that it is possible to describe. Therefore, all five lights, *Nefesh*, *Ruach*, *Neshamah*, *Chayah*, and *Yechidah* are found in the world of *Assiyah* in the way we have described them, but here they are only the lights, *Nefesh*, *Ruach*, *Neshamah*, *Chayah* and *Yechidah* of *Nefesh*.

In exactly the same way, *Nefesh*, *Ruach*, *Neshamah*, *Chayah*, and *Yechidah* are found within the world of *Yetzirah* and they are the five lights within *Ruach*. Similarly, there are the five aspects, *Nefesh*, *Ruach*, *Neshamah*, *Chayah*, and *Yechidah* within the world of *Briyah*, and they constitute the five lights of *Neshamah*. Likewise in the world of *Atzilut*, the five lights, *Nefesh*, *Ruach*, *Neshamah*, *Chayah*, and *Yechidah*, constitute the five aspects of the light of *Chayah*. Indeed,

Table 3
The make-up of the worlds

The world of *Assiyah*		
Sephirah—*Malchut*		
The *tikkun* of the will to receive for oneself alone—modality: inanimate		
Light—*Nefesh*		
Rectified will to receive for oneself alone	*Sephirot*	Lights
	Keter of *Assiyah*	*Yechidah* of *Assiyah*
Speaking	*Chochmah* of *Assiyah*	*Chayah* of *Assiyah*
Animal	*Binah* of *Assiyah*	*Neshamah* of *Assiyah*
Plant	*Tiferet* of *Assiyah*	*Ruach* of *Assiyah*
Inanimate	*Malchut* of *Assiyah*	*Nefesh* of *Assiyah*

The world of *Yetzirah*		
Sephirah—*Tiferet*		
The *tikkun* of the will to receive for oneself alone—modality: plant		
Light—*Ruach*		
Rectified will to receive for oneself alone	*Sephirot*	Lights
	Keter of *Yetzirah*	*Yechidah* of *Yetzirah*
Speaking	*Chochmah* of *Yetzirah*	*Chayah* of *Yetzirah*
Animal	*Binah* of *Yetzirah*	*Neshamah* of *Yetzirah*
Plant	*Tiferet* of *Yetzirah*	*Ruach* of *Yetzirah*
Inanimate	*Malchut* of *Yetzirah*	*Nefesh* of *Yetzirah*

(table three continued)

(table three continued)

	The world of *Briyah*	
	Sephirah—*Binah*	
	The *tikkun* of the will to receive for oneself alone—modality: animal	
	Light—*Neshamah*	
Rectified will to receive for oneself alone	*Sephirot*	Lights
	Keter of *Briyah*	*Yechidah* of *Briyah*
Speaking	*Chochmah* of *Briyah*	*Chayah* of *Briyah*
Animal	*Binah* of *Briyah*	*Neshamah* of *Briyah*
Plant	*Tiferet* of *Briyah*	*Ruach* of *Briyah*
Inanimate	*Malchut* of *Briyah*	*Nefesh* of *Briyah*

	The world of *Atzilut*	
	Sephirah—*Chochmah*	
	The *tikkun* of the will to receive for oneself alone—modality: speaking	
	Light—*Chayah*	
Rectified will to receive for oneself alone	*Sephirot*	Lights
	Keter of *Atzilut*	*Yechidah* of *Atzilut*
Speaking	*Chochmah* of *Atzilut*	*Chayah* of *Atzilut*
Animal	*Binah* of *Atzilut*	*Neshamah* of *Atzilut*
Plant	*Tiferet* of *Atzilut*	*Ruach* of *Atzilut*
Inanimate	*Malchut* of *Atzilut*	*Nefesh* of *Atzilut*

it is the same for the world of *Adam Kadmon*, where they constitute the five parts of the light of *Yechidah*.

The way each world relates to the worlds that are higher or lower than it, is the same as the way the five levels of illumination, *Nefesh*, *Ruach*, *Neshamah*, *Chayah*, and *Yechidah*, relate to each other within the world of *Assiyah*.

Every aspect of every world includes within it all the different modalities, such that everything that is represented in the macrocosm of the worlds is also represented in every detail of every world.

Now Rabbi Ashlag will explain the transition from the stage of *Nefesh* to the stage of *Ruach*:

Introduction to the Zohar

51. You should know that the process of healing and purification of the will to receive for oneself alone only receives its full light when it is permanent and we no longer go back to our foolish ways. The Sages asked, "What constitutes the full healing (of the defective will to receive for oneself alone)?" and they answered, "When God Himself testifies that the person will never return to his foolishness."[3]

The transition from the spiritual stage of the inanimate in holiness, in which we receive the light of *Nefesh*, to the spiritual stage of the plant in holiness, in which we receive the light of *Ruach*, is as great as the difference between the inanimate and the plant in the physical world. At the inanimate stage we cannot apprehend the Divine Providence as being good and doing good as it really is. God's goodness is concealed from us. This means that all our spiritual work needs to stem from the power of faith and not from knowledge or experience. In this there is a tremendous labor. However, as we start to get closer to a higher level, progressing from the inanimate to the plant modality in holiness, we begin to move from the level in which we practise Torah and *mitzvot*, not for its own sake, to a level at which we practise Torah and *mitzvot* for its own sake. During this transition we experience many ups and downs until we are able to achieve the higher level permanently. The process progresses in a manner of two steps forwards, one step back. Rabbi Ashlag asks: Until when does this process continue? When do we achieve the higher level on a permanent basis? He answers in the language of Maimonides: Until the One testifies for us that we will not fall back to our old foolish ways any more. No longer will we use our will to receive for ourselves alone.

Lesson fifteen

Many of the writings of Rabbi Baruch Shalom haLevi Ashlag deal with the transition from the modality of the inanimate to the modality of the plant that we make when we are coming into affinity of form with the framework of holiness, and the difficulties and experiences on the way. Here is one of his articles from the *Bircat Shalom, Sefer haMa'amarim*. In it Rabbi Baruch Shalom haLevi Ashlag uses the word 'teshuvah' (repentance) as meaning achieving the higher modality of 'plant' in holiness in a permanent way.

What is the measure of *Teshuvah*?
The Scripture says, "Return, O Israel, unto the Lord your God, because you have stumbled in your sin (Hos. 14: 20)."

Firstly, we need to understand the meaning of "unto the Lord your God": The phrase, "unto the Lord Your God," seems to imply that if our *teshuvah* does not reach right up to God, then it is not designated as *teshuvah*. If this is so, how can we know if our *teshuvah* reaches right up to the Lord our God? Who could possibly go up to God to know whether it has arrived or not?

Secondly, we need to understand what the Scripture means when it writes, "because you have stumbled in your sin": "Because you have stumbled in your sin" seems to imply that this is the reason that our *teshuvah* needs to reach right up to God. What does one thing have to do with the other?

Furthermore, we need to understand the idea, "you have stumbled in your sin": What is meant by the term 'sin'? Could it be possible that stumbling may be caused by something other than a person's sin? Is this why the Scripture tells us that the stumbling comes from your sin and not from anything else? If this is so, what is the other thing that a person could think of that may be the cause of his stumbling?

Regarding the idea of stumbling: Stumbling means that a person intends to achieve something, but in the end he does not achieve his aim because some element causes him to stumble. Like a person who is walking on the road and does not see a stone lying there, so he falls. We need to understand what is the equivalent in spirituality: The person who fell spiritually, fell because of the equivalent in spirituality of a stone that was in the way. So we need to know, what is the equivalent of a stone that a person stumbles over and causes him to fall down when on his way? The Scripture tells us that the stumbling was from "your sin," that this is the stone through which we stumble and fall. We need this knowledge in order to take heed from stumbling blocks. We need to understand, Why does the sin of a person form the obstacle, which, if it were not for that, he could go on the way of God, and fulfill Torah and *mitzvot* for its own sake?

The issue is that the first transgression began with the sin of the Tree of Knowledge. The Sages teach that Adam, the first human, was born circumcised.[4] (This means that he was created according to the framework of holiness and that he acted only from the will to give benefit.) However, subsequently, by the sin of eating from the Tree of Knowledge, he pulled on his foreskin (he drew to himself the will to receive for oneself alone).[5] As it is explained in the *Hakdamah l'Panim Meirot uMasbirot*, the issue of 'pulling on his foreskin' refers to the three layers of uncleanness. When he was created he did not have this foreskin, because, as the Holy Ari tells us, Adam's physical body stems from the *Malchut* of the world of *Assiyah*, which ascended to *Binah* of the world of *Assiyah*. This is designated as the *Malchut* being sweetened by *Binah*, and this is what is meant by being born circumcised.[6]

The intention of Rabbi Baruch Shalom haLevi Ashlag is to emphasize that the first human, Adam, was created initially with the will to give benefit, which is the characteristic of the *Sephirah Binah*, and this overshadowed his will to receive.

(*Bircat Shalom* continued) Through the sin of the Tree of Knowledge Adam drew to himself the *Malchut* from the aspect of *din* (judgment). (That is to say, he drew on himself the will to receive for himself alone, which is the form of receiving that is subject to the rule of being forbidden for use, according to the framework of holiness.) The will to receive for oneself alone is the form of receiving that originated from the *Challal haPanui* (Hebrew: empty space) after the *Tzimtzum*. This is termed as 'pulling on the foreskin'; that is to say that Adam drew to himself the three unclean *klipot* (shells) from which come all the sins that a person is liable to do. This means the enormous receiving, which the first human drew to himself by his sin, is the cause of all sins and the root of all subsequent transgressions that come to the heart and to the mind.

Now we have asked, What is the explanation of "because you have stumbled in your sin"? We need to explain that these words refer to the sin of the Tree of Knowledge. That is to say that the stone over which all created beings stumble is that a person says, "I want to **understand** whether it is worthwhile for me to keep Torah and *mitzvot*, and what can I profit by it?" This question comes to him because of the form of receiving that Adam drew to himself through the sin of the Tree of Knowledge. This is similar to the situation that happens in the physical world. A person is walking along and does not notice a stone lying on the ground. He stumbles over it and falls down because of it.

Lesson fifteen

It is just the same with the service of God. When a person wants to walk the way of God, but he does not see the stone, which is the will to receive for oneself, then he stumbles and falls because of it. *Even* (Hebrew: a stone) is the same word as *avin* (Hebrew: I want to understand), that is, he desires to understand what pleasure or profit will ensue from his work that will satisfy the desire to receive for himself alone. Furthermore, when the person's teachers tell him that he needs to **believe,** as opposed to see, that the Divine Providence operates according to the Name of God, that the One is Good and does good, then he says, "I want to see that this is so. But to believe? That is against my understanding! For my understanding says, 'What I see is true, and what I do not see, how can I know whether it is true or not?'" Moreover, when the teachers tell him that he needs to believe, he maintains, "How do you know that what one believes is true?" This is the obstacle over which people stumble.

From all the above it follows that the stumbling block for everyone is our lack of faith. When a person begins to go on the path of service he complains to God, "Why do you hide Yourself to the extent that we cannot overcome this concealment and thus serve You with all our mind and all our heart?" This is indeed a good question. Why did God make it so that we need to believe, and why did He not act differently, so that whoever begins to work could immediately see the greatness of God? It seems to us that the way that the Creator laid down for us that we need to work from faith, forms a stumbling block for all those who falter, and causes many people to actually distance themselves from this work.

Why does God do it like this? Concerning this, my father, of blessed memory, said that we need to believe that the *way itself* that the Creator laid down for us, which is that our work needs to be through the modality of faith, in the sense of, "And they believed in God and in Moses His servant" (Exod. 14:31), is the most successful way to reach the complete goal of the creation, which is to give pleasure to the created beings. It is precisely through faith that the created beings can arrive at their goal, which is to receive the good and delight that the Creator thought to give the created beings. But we may not say that the Creator could not have prepared for us a different way through the medium of knowledge. It is certainly the case that the Holy Blessed One is omnipotent and can do whatever He wants. However, just as we need to believe in the purpose of creation, which is to give benefit to the created beings, so we have to believe that the pathway to reach the goal, through the medium of faith, is the best and most successful way. The Creator chose the way of faith, because only through the way of faith can a person reach the complete goal.

We have said that the explanation of the verse, "For you have stumbled in your sin," relates to the huge vessel of receiving that Adam, the first human being, attracted to himself through the sin of the Tree of Knowledge. However, we still need to explain the answer to the question that we asked: "What is the connection between, "for you have stumbled in your sin," and "Return, O Israel, unto the Lord your God," as if a person could go up to see if his *teshuvah* had reached the Lord God!?

From all the above we can explain: All our failures that cause a person not to reach perfection, but to fall down in the middle, are due entirely to the first sin, which is the stumbling block over which a person falls. The person wants to make *teshuvah*, but he does not know what *teshuvah* is. Then the prophet says to him, "Return, O Israel, unto the Lord your God." This means that all the deeds a person does should be for the Lord God. "Unto," that is, until you know clearly that all that you do is for the Lord your God. That is to say, you reach the stage in which you feel that it is simply not worth living just for yourself and that your being alive at all is only for God to have use of you. This is designated as *teshuvah*. If a person has not yet reached this stage then he has not reached the stage of *teshuvah*. The reason is as above, "for you have stumbled in your sin," which is receiving for oneself alone. This alone is the obstacle which prevents a person from coming to *dvekut* with God. A person may be said to have done his *tikkun* when he has reached "unto the Lord your God," at which stage all his deeds are only for the purpose of giving benefit. This is designated as *teshuvah*. We see that a person does not need to ascend up to God to see if his *teshuvah* reaches "unto the Lord your God"; a person can see and feel for himself if he has any intention in his life other than that which is for the use of God. For his own self-use he himself says it is not worthwhile to live. However, even here a person could deceive himself, that is to say, he agrees to work for the sake of God because he thinks that from this he will get great pleasure for himself.

Still, even in this case, it is yet possible for a person to see the truth, that if he really wants to cleave to God, and he already has affinity of form with the Creator, then he should merit the stage of having his eyes opened in the Torah, according to the principle: One who learns Torah for its own sake merits that they reveal to him the secrets of the Torah.[7] If he has not yet merited the secrets of the Torah, this is the sign that he is still far from the situation that his intention is directed only for the sake of God.

It is written in the *Introduction to the Zohar*, paragraph 32:

> This part (of a person's life) applies to the work with Torah and *mitzvot* which is done for its own sake, that is, in order to give pleasure to God and not for the sake of a reward. This work purifies the will to receive for oneself alone and transforms it into the will to give, whereby, according to the

measure of purification of the will to receive, it now becomes a suitable and fitting vessel to receive the five parts of the soul, which are called: *Nefesh*, *Ruach*, *Neshamah*, *Chayah*, and *Yechidah*.

These lights, which belong to the will to give, cannot be enclothed within a person's body so long as the will to receive for oneself alone dominates it, as the soul is in opposition of form to the body. Even if it is in some difference of form, the soul still cannot be enclothed within the body. For the light to be enclothed within a vessel, there must be affinity of form between them, for enclothing of the light within the vessel and affinity of form go hand in hand with each other.

At the very moment when the person merits to be wholly concerned only with the will to give and has no aspect left of the will to receive for oneself, then the person is in complete affinity of form with the five parts of the soul, the *Nefesh*, *Ruach*, *Neshamah*, *Chayah*, and *Yechidah*. These originate in their source in the *Ein Sof* in state one, come through the worlds of holiness, and are immediately drawn to the person who enclothes them, one by one.

From the above we see that if a person walks the pathway of giving benefit, then he should merit the level of the secrets of the Torah. If he did not merit this level it is a sign that he is still in the consciousness of selfish love, even though he feels that he would like to be able to act only for the sake of giving benefit. Therefore, the person needs once more to consider ideas and tactics of how to merit the stage of loving God instead of being in the consciousness of selfish love. But we need to remember that to merit the ability to love God and to leave the consciousness of selfish love is not actually in our hands; it is a grace from God.

So we need to know that when a person wants to move onwards from practising the Torah and *mitzvot* in their practical aspects only, which is without intention, and they want to begin the practical work of the *mitzvot* with the intention of giving benefit, they are taking upon themselves a great labor. The moment the will to receive begins to hear about the intention of giving benefit, it immediately starts to raise up objections; it does not let a person do this work, but shows him this work as painted in dark colors.

In this situation a person needs to believe that only God can help him; here is a situation in which a person can give a true prayer. This is called a true prayer because it really is true that the Creator has organized things such that a person cannot help himself. This is for the well-known reason that no light may be apprehended without a vessel suitable for it, as we have stated many times. My father, of blessed memory, said that the reason that God made it so that a person cannot get out of his selfish love on his own was in order that a person should need God to help him. Otherwise, a person does not need to receive the light of the Torah but would be content with fulfilling Torah and *mitzvot* not for its own sake. Then the person would not feel the need to receive the *Nefesh, Ruach, Neshamah, Chayah,* and *Yechidah* of the soul that have been prepared for him. When he sees that he cannot get out of his selfish love and merit affinity of form, then he knows he needs the help of God.

How does God give this help? Through the holy soul, which is the *Or Elyon*, which reveals to a person that he should feel that he has within him a soul that is part of God above. We see that according to the measure of the person's endeavor, so there is a corresponding increase in the revelation of the light of God. For this reason God made the hardening of the heart, in order that it would not be within the power of the person to overcome his own evil, but he will need the Creator. So, therefore, a person would need to merit the *Nefesh, Ruach, Neshamah, Chayah,* and *Yechidah* of his soul.

However, this arrangement of the hardening of the heart comes just at the time when the person really wants to work for the sake of giving benefit and he is really putting forth all his strength to come to the practice of Torah for its own sake. Then the whole matter of the hardening of the heart begins. This is similar to a mother who wants to teach her child that he can walk on his own. She sits on her knees and allows the child to get close to her, but when she sees the child is close she moves away from him, so that the child will get used to walking on his own to a greater degree than he did. But the child begins to cry. After all, he has just made the effort to get to his mother! So he cries, "Why does my mother move away from me?" He thinks, "Perhaps she does not love me, and that is why she moves away from me?" He cannot see the true reason and understand that her moving away is for his good. Before the child has started to walk on his own the mother does not move away from the child, but he sees that wherever he goes his mother holds his hand and leads him.

The case is similar in our inner work. Before a person begins to walk on his own, he is still at the stage in which he does not want to leave the general mode of people who practice Torah and *mitzvot* from the practical aspect only, without their having any intention of giving benefit. This stage is designated as 'the mother leading the child by the hand'. At this stage he does not feel that the Creator is distancing Himself from him—on the contrary, he cannot see any lack in his work and does not feel himself as being pushed away; after all he feels close to God. The reason for this feeling is that since the person is working according to the mode of the general population, he receives a reward for his work, as it is for his own benefit. This is acceptable to the will to receive for himself alone, which therefore does not object to this work. In consequence, the person feels

Lesson fifteen

himself as being perfect. We see that the person is in the same situation as that of the child whom the mother is holding by the hand and leading.

When the person leaves the mode of the general population and wants to work for the sake of giving benefit, it is designated as analogous to a child who is beginning to walk by himself. Like the mother who distances herself from the child, every time the person thinks he is getting close to the work of giving benefit they show him from Above that he is still far away from this work. How do they show him that he is far away? By showing him each time what the meaning of having a real intention of giving benefit is. This brings the person harsh thoughts, until sometimes he just wants to run away from the whole battlefield. After that they allow him to come close once more, and so again he begins to feel that now he is close, like a child is close to the mother, and then again he sees that he is pushed away.

This is what we say in the book of Psalms, "Do not go far from me" (Ps. 22:12). Likewise it is written, "Do not hide Your face from me" (Ps. 27:9). These verses have two explanations: 1) That You distance Yourself from us makes us want to run away from the whole battlefield (and we do not in fact want to do that). 2) "Do not go far from me," meaning, let us understand that this is not an estrangement, but that You are doing it solely for our benefit, so we may we know that all that You do is for our benefit. [8]

So we see that the transition from the inanimate in holiness, wherein a person still has mixed motives, but he wants to come to affinity of form, to the plant in holiness, wherein a person's sole intention is to give benefit, is accompanied by many ups and downs.

Can you remember a time in your life which was accompanied by many ups and downs? What got you through? Are you going through such a period now? Sometimes these times can be very intense. What helps you keep your balance? Remember, despite whatever it feels like, it is progress. Prayer and a good friend on the path can both be of great help.

Let us continue with the *Introduction to the Zohar*, beginning again with paragraph 51:

Introduction to the Zohar

51. You should know that the process of healing and purification of the will to receive for oneself alone only receives its full light when it is permanent and we no longer go back to our foolish ways. The Sages asked, "What constitutes the full healing (of the defective will to receive for oneself alone)?" and they

answered, "When God Himself testifies that the person will never return to his foolishness."

We said that when a person purifies the inanimate part of the will to receive for oneself alone, he merits the soul entity of *Nefesh*, which then ascends and enclothes the *Sephirah Malchut* of *Assiyah*. This implies that the purification of the inanimate modality is completely permanent and he will never return to his foolishness again. Now he can ascend to the level of the spiritual world of *Assiyah*, as he enjoys purity and complete similarity of form with that world. However, the other stages that we mentioned, namely, *Ruach, Neshamah, Chayah,* and *Yechidah* of *Assiyah* require purification of the corresponding parts of the will to receive for oneself, namely the plant, animal, and speaking aspects of the will to receive for oneself, in order that they may enclothe and receive these lights. Here, however, the purification does not need to be completely permanent to the extent that "God Himself testifies that he will never return to his foolish ways." The reason is that the whole world of *Assiyah*, with its five component *Sephirot*: *Keter, Chochmah, Binah, Tiferet,* and *Malchut*, really only constitutes the *Sephirah Malchut*, which relates solely to the purification of the inanimate modality alone; the five *Sephirot* here being merely the five components of *Malchut*. Thus, since the person has already merited to purify at least the inanimate modality of his will to receive on a permanent basis, he has already attained affinity of form with the whole world of *Assiyah*.

However, every *Sephirah* in the world of *Assiyah* draws its sustenance from that modality in the higher worlds that corresponds to it. For example, the *Sephirah Tiferet* in *Assiyah* receives its sustenance from the world of *Yetzirah*, which, in its essence, is entirely *Tiferet* and whose light is that of *Ruach*. The *Sephirah Binah* in the world of *Assiyah* receives its sustenance from the world of *Briyah*, whose light is *Neshamah*. Likewise, the *Sephirah Chochmah* of *Assiyah* receives its sustenance from the world of *Atzilut*, whose essence is *Chochmah* and whose light is *Chayah*.

Therefore, even though a person has only purified the inanimate modality of the will to receive for oneself in an irreversible way, and has worked on the plant, animal, and human aspects of the will to receive, but has not completely and irreversibly transformed them, nonetheless, he can still receive the *Ruach, Neshamah,* and *Chayah* from *Tiferet, Binah,* and *Chochmah* of the world of *Assiyah*, but not on a permanent basis. The moment one of these three levels of will to receive for oneself alone wakes up again, these lights are immediately lost.

52. Once a person has purified the plant modality of the will to receive for himself alone in an immutable way, he may then ascend to the world of *Yetzirah*.

Lesson fifteen

There he receives the light of *Ruach* permanently. He is able, at that level, to attain the lights of *Neshamah* and *Chayah* associated with the *Sephirot*, *Binah* and *Chochmah* in the world of *Yetzirah*, which are *Neshamah* of *Ruach*, and *Chayah* of *Ruach*, respectively. The person attains these lights in an intermittent way, even before he has transformed the animal and human aspects on a permanent basis, in the same way as we explained for the world of *Assiyah*. Once he has completely purified the plant modality of the will to receive for oneself alone on an enduring basis, then he is in affinity of form with the whole world of *Yetzirah*, even with its highest aspects, in the same way as we learned for the world of *Assiyah*.

When a person arrives at the stage of the plant modality in the framework of holiness he is in affinity of form with the world of *Yetzirah*. He has already achieved *dvekut* with the Creator in his intention of performing the *mitzvot*. This affinity of form is designated as the reward of the *mitzvah*. He also apprehends the dreadful separation that occurs as an accompaniment to the transgression. This separation from the Creator is in fact the punishment of the transgression. This is contrary to the generally held opinion that punishment is the suffering we receive in this life. Suffering is one of the means of rectification and does not constitute punishment.

Here are the words of Rabbi Yehudah Lev Ashlag as brought in the *Hakdamah l'Talmud Eser haSephirot* (Introduction to the Study of the Ten *Sephirot*):

> However, once God sees that a person has put in the required amount of effort, and has done all he could to manifest his choice and has strengthened himself in his faith in God, then God helps him attain the perception of the Divine Providence in its open manifestation, so that the face of God is revealed to him. Through this perception he comes to be completely transformed, and he cleaves to Him with all his heart, soul and might, inspired by his perception of the revelation of God's true role in a person's life.
>
> This perception of the Divine Providence, and the *teshuvah* that goes together with it, comes to a person in two stages. The first stage is the clear awareness of a definite cause and effect. Not only does the person clearly perceive the good consequences that result from a *mitzvah*, which he receives in the world to come, but he also experiences wondrous pleasure at the moment of performing a *mitzvah* in this world. In the same way, not only does the person perceive that there

is a bitter consequence following each sin after one's death, but he also merits to experience the bitter taste of a sin while still in this life.

It is obvious that one who has merited such direct perception of God's Providence can be quite sure of himself that he will not sin any more, in just the same way that a person would not contemplate cutting off one of his own limbs and thus causing terrible suffering to himself. It is equally certain that the person would not let the opportunity of a *mitzvah* go by if it presented itself to him in the same way that he would be sure not to forego any pleasure of this world or great profit that might come his way.

By this you may understand what the Sages implied when they asked, "What constitutes *teshuvah* (transformation)?" and answered, "when God Himself testifies that the person will never again return to his foolishness." This is a surprising definition, as who is going to go up to heaven to hear God's testimony? What is more, to whom is God expected to give this testimony? Is it not enough that God Himself knows that the person has made *teshuvah* with all his heart and will not sin anymore?

Yet from what we have already clarified, the matter is quite simple. In truth, a person can never be completely certain that he will not sin again unless he has already merited the perception of God's Providence, which is that He acts with cause and effect. This is the revelation of God's face. This direct revelation of God's face, coming as it does as a grace from God, is termed 'testimony', as it is God's grace itself that enables a person to attain this perception of cause and effect, which ensures that he will not sin again. Thus we can say that it is God Himself who testifies for the person.

So when the Sages asked what constitutes *teshuvah*, they meant, "When can a person be sure that he has reached perfect *teshuvah*?" The answer comes as a clear sign, when God Himself testifies that the person will no longer return to his foolish ways. In other words, the person merits the direct revelation of God's face, when God's grace itself testifies for him that he will not return to his foolish ways.

At this level of spiritual attainment, designated as being the level of consciousness of the plant in holiness, a person is already termed 'a *Tzaddik*' because he or she is able to justify (*lehatzdik*) the way that the Divine Providence manifests in the world.

Rabbi Ashlag continues in the *Introduction to the Zohar* by describing the ascent of the soul from the stage of the plant level in holiness to the higher

Lesson fifteen

levels of consciousness, namely the modalities termed 'animal' and 'speaking' in the framework of holiness.

Introduction to the Zohar

53. Then the person purifies the animal modality of the will to receive for oneself alone and transforms it into the will to give to such an extent that "God testifies that he will never again return to his foolishness." The person is now in affinity of form with the world of *Briyah*. Here one can receive all the lights up to and including the light of *Neshamah* permanently. Now, through working on the speaking modality of the will to receive, a person is able to ascend to the *Sephirah Chochmah* and receive its light of *Chayah*. This is so even if the person has not purified the speaking modality of the will to receive in a permanent way. However, as long as the process is incomplete, the light that illuminates him is similarly not permanent.

54. When the person has merited to purify the speaking component of the will to receive for himself alone irreversibly, he comes into affinity of form with the world of *Atzilut* and then he receives its light of *Chayah* for good. When the person becomes even more purified, he merits to receive the light of the *Ein Sof* and the light of *Yechidah*, which is enclothed within the light of *Chayah*. There is nothing more to add here.

Here is a beautiful passage from the *Zohar* and from Rabbi Ashlag's commentary on the *Zohar*, the *Perush haSulam*, that illustrates all we have just learned:

Zohar
As it is written, "Bless God, O His angels" (Ps. 103:20). This refers to the people who practise the Torah. They are called "God's angels on earth." And this is in accordance with the Scripture, "and birds will fly over the earth" (Genesis 1:20), which is so for this world. And for the next world we have learned that in the future the Holy Blessed One will give them wings, like the wings of eagles, to fly throughout the world; as it is written, "and those who hope for the Lord will renew their strength, receiving wings like eagles" (Isa. 40:31).[9]

Perush haSulam
Explanation: "Bless God, O His angels, His mighty warriors who do His word and then understand His word" (Ps. 103:20). The Sages have explained this verse as meaning, first carry out [God's command] and then understand [God's command].[10]

Normally a person is not capable of carrying out any mission unless he understands what the one sending him on the mission is telling him to do. However, this is not so regarding the angels: they perform their missions before they understand or comprehend what it is that the One, may He be blessed, has commanded them. The reason is that God's will governs them, and they do not have anything that forms a barrier between themselves and the will of God, and therefore they are drawn after God, just as a shadow is drawn after a person. Thus we find that the angels perform their mission before they understand it.

The *Zohar* states that the people who occupy themselves with Torah for its own sake draw to themselves a *Nefesh* from the framework of holiness. Thus we find that their substance, even though they are of this world, transforms to be like that of the angels on high, with the carrying out of God's work preceding their understanding. They carry through God's commandments with all perfection before they grasp what it is they are doing, as they are drawn after God as a shadow is drawn after a human being.

This is similar to what happens when the wind blows dust into someone's eyes. He shuts his eyelids quickly, as a reflex, before it registers in thought. One finds that the action, that is, the shutting of the eyes, always precedes the awareness in thought of the approaching dust. This is what the *Zohar* is saying regarding those people who are practising the Torah for its own sake: they are called, 'His angels on earth'. Even though they are of this earth, their body (their will to receive) has become like that of the angels on high, and their doing precedes their understanding. They are not ruled by their intelligence in carrying out God's *mitzvot* perfectly, but they do the *mitzvah* completely before they have managed to become aware with their thought of what they are doing, just like the closing of eyelids against the dust that precedes the thought. Therefore, these people are designated as being God's angels on earth. This is what the *Zohar* says: "In the future, the Holy Blessed One will make them wings like eagles, to roam throughout the world, as it is written, 'and those who hope for the Lord will renew their strength, receiving wings like eagles' (Isa. 40:31)."

While a human being has not yet merited a holy *Nefesh*, the *sitra achra* governs him or her, according to the inner meaning of the verse, "and He shall throw out the soul of your enemies, as from the hollow of a sling" (I Sam. 25:29). The explanation of this verse is given in the *Zohar*: "The souls of the wicked go and wander throughout the world but they do not find any place to rest where they can connect with God. They become contaminated from the framework of uncleanness, as they do not enter the framework of holiness and cannot be included within it."[11]

Explanation: It is impossible to cleave to the Blessed One and to fulfill His *mitzvot*, as is fitting, unless one first has faith in the Names of God, that the One is Good and does good to all; that the One is merciful and is gracious. Those

Lesson fifteen

people who did not yet merit to draw to themselves the *Nefesh* of holiness, are still ruled by the *sitra achra*, and they go and wander throughout the world but do not find a place to rest. That is to say, when their thoughts wander through the world and they see the conduct of the One with the people of the world as being, in their opinion, not as good as it should be, according to God's holy Names, then this causes a defect in their belief in the holy Names of God, and they cannot find a place to rest, that is, they cannot find a place of rest wherein they can believe in the holy Names of God, to remain connected with Him. Thus they become contaminated from the framework of uncleanness, that is to say, they deny God. This is all because they did not enter into the framework of holiness and are not included within it, as they did not merit a holy *Nefesh* and do no actions that would help themselves become included in the framework of holiness.

However, those who practise the Torah for its own sake, and draw to themselves a *Nefesh* of holiness, change their body to be like that of the angels. They merit to perform God's word even before they understand it, just like the angels do. Therefore, about them it is written in the Scripture, "and birds shall fly through the earth," and then God gives them wings like eagles and they wander throughout all the world. That is to say, they wander in their thoughts throughout the entire world and they see God's management with His created beings. Yet, not only do they not stumble into the *sitra achra*, but they even gain further strength to do good deeds and offer up prayers, increasing the power of their belief, as it is written, "and those who hope for the Lord will renew their strength, receiving wings like eagles" (Isa. 40:31). Through their receiving wings like eagles, they can wander through all the happenings of the children of the world, continually renewing their strength, offering up prayers through the power of their faith in the unity of the One, and drawing to themselves a holy *Ruach* from Above.

We shall continue with our study of the *Introduction to the Zohar*:

Introduction to the Zohar

55. Now we have given a full and complete answer to the question, "Why does a person require all the higher worlds that God created for him? What need does he have of them?" (paragraph 41). We see now that it would be completely impossible for a person to perform any acts in order to give pleasure to the Creator, were it not for the help of all these worlds. For according to the degree to which he has purified his will to receive for himself alone, he attains the lights and ascensions of the soul which are called *Nefesh*, *Ruach*, *Neshamah*, *Chayah*, and *Yechidah*. At every level that he attains, the lights of that level help him in

Lesson fifteen

the process of purification. The person ascends up the levels until he merits and attains all the delights that constitute the ultimate purpose of the thought of creation (as above paragraph 33).

The *Zohar* discusses the expression of the Sages, "When someone tries to purify himself, he gets help." And asks, "How does he get help?" The *Zohar* answers, "Through the holy soul" (*Zohar, Parshat Noach*). For it is impossible to arrive at the purification that is required for the purpose of creation to be carried out, except through the help of all the stages of the soul, which are *Nefesh*, *Ruach*, *Neshamah*, *Chayah*, and *Yechidah* of the soul, as we have described above.

Here is the full quotation from the *Zohar* that is mentioned in the above paragraph:

> If a person comes to purify himself, they help him via his holy soul (*Neshamah*), and they purify him and sanctify him and he is designated as being "holy." But if the person does not merit and does not want to get purified, then only two levels are open to him—those of *Nefesh* and *Ruach*. But he does not have the holy *Neshamah*.
>
> Not only that, but if he wants to defile himself, they will defile him and help from Above is removed from him. From here onwards everyone goes according to the path he has chosen.
>
> That is to say if he returns (repents) and again wants to purify himself again they help him.
>
> And there is no need to ask, "Since a person is born only with the *Nefesh* (of *Assiyah*), how can he be helped?" The answer is that *Ruach* is always included with the *Nefesh* at the time he is born, as stated here, so the person has *Nefesh* and *Ruach* at the time he is born, but *Neshamah* of *Assiyah* is acquired only according to his deeds.
>
> This is so at every level.[12]

We shall now read a further excerpt taken from the *Zohar* that contains terms we have not learned, and which defy translation. However, through this piece it is possible to see the incredible potential hidden within every human being and to wonder at the high level of holiness a person may achieve. (Please be careful not to pronounce the Holy Names of God that are printed here; one reads them with the eyes only.)

> Come and see: When a person is born they give him or her a *Nefesh* from the level of the animal, but on the side of purity, from the level called *Ofanei*

Lesson fifteen

haKodesh from the world of *Assiyah*. They give him or her *Ruach* from the level of *Chayot Kodesh* from the world of *Yetzirah*. If the person merits, they give him or her *Neshamah* from the level of *Kisai* from the world of *Briyah*. These three are the maidservant, *(amah)* the servant *(eved)*, and the handmaiden *(shifchah)* of the daughter of the King.

The person merits further, they give him or her *Nefesh* from the level of *Atzilut* from the level of the daughter of *Yechidah*, who is called "the daughter of the King." That is the *Malchut* of the world of *Atzilut*. He or she merits further, they give him or her *Ruach* of *Atzilut*, that is from the middle line, which is *Tiferet*, called "the son of the Holy Blessed One." As it is written, "You are sons to the Lord Your God" (Deut. 14:1). He or she merits further, they give him or her *Neshamah* from the level of *Binah*, as it is written, "And He breathed in his nostrils the breath of life *(Nishmat Chaim)*"(Gen. 2:7). What is life *(Chaim)*? It is the letters י'ה' *(Yud-Hay)* of which it is written, "The whole soul *(Neshamah)* shall praise Y-H" (Ps. 150:6) and so the Name י'ה'ו'ה' (Y-H-V-H) is completed by them. For *Ruach* and *Nefesh* of *Atzilut* are ו'ה' (V-H) and *Neshamah* of *Atzilut* is י'ה' (Y-H) which together make י'ה'ו'ה' (Y-H-V-H).

He or she merits further, they give him י'ה'ו'ה' furnished with letters as follows, י'ו'ד' ה'א' ו'א'ו' ה'א' that has the inner meaning of אדם (*Adam*) in *Atzilut* above. This is in the form of "Master," of whom it is written, "And you shall have dominion over the fish of the sea and over the bird of the heaven and over every creature that creeps on the earth" (Gen. 1:28). This is Adam who has governance over the firmaments, over all the *Ofanim*, over the *Seraphim*, over the *Chayot*, over all the *Tzvaot*, and has the powers of Above and below. For this reason, when a person merits *Nefesh* at the level of the daughter of the King it is written, "You shall not go out in the manner that servants go out" (Ex. 21:7). [13]

Now let us reread paragraph 33 from the *Introduction to the Zohar* as Rabbi Ashlag suggests we do in paragraph 55, and see how its meaning deepens and becomes more focused in the context of our learning, and see how it also gives life to the learning we have just been doing.

Introduction to the Zohar

33. Now all that is left for us to explain is the sixth inquiry. Its subject was the statement of the Sages that all the worlds—the higher worlds as well as the lower worlds—were only created for the sake of the human. On the surface, it seems to be rather astonishing that for the sake of this little human, the Creator, blessed be the One, should create all this! When one compares the value of a man or a woman with the whole of the reality of this world, not to mention the

Lesson fifteen

> higher spiritual worlds, one cannot say that he has the value of even a tiny hair! Yet God created all this for us.
>
> An even more astonishing question is: What need does the human have for all these many and splendid spiritual worlds?
>
> Now you need to know that all the satisfaction God has in giving pleasure to His created beings depends upon the measure to which the created beings can feel that it is God who is their benefactor and it is God who gives them their enjoyment. Then God takes great delight in them, like a father who delights in playing with his dear child. His pleasure increases according to the degree that the child can feel and recognize the greatness and the noble qualities of the father. Then the child's father shows the child all the treasure houses that he has prepared for him. Just as Scripture says, "'What a dear son Ephraim is! He is my darling child! For whenever I speak of him, I earnestly remember him. My compassion is stirred for him. I shall surely have mercy on him,' says the Lord" (Jer. 31:19). Look carefully at this sentence and you will understand and know the great delight that God enjoys with those people who have reached their wholeness. They have merited to sense His presence and to recognize His greatness in all the ways that He has prepared for them. God relates to them as a father relates to his dear child, as a father with the child of his delight.
>
> As we meditate on this description, we can understand that for the sake of the pleasure and delight God takes in these people who have come to their wholeness, it was worth it to God to create all these worlds, the upper as well as the lower, as we shall further explain.

The person who has reached his wholeness is the one who has transformed his vessels of receiving into those of giving benefit according to all the levels enumerated above and thus is now able to receive all that God wants to give him.

Here follows a lovely article taken from Rabbi Baruch Shalom HaLevi Ashlag's *Bircat Shalom*. It deals with inner work based on the material we have just learned. This is an excerpt from it.

> Why is the soul sometimes referred to as 'Neshamah' and sometimes as 'Nefesh'? We would like to understand why the Torah refers to the soul sometimes by the term 'Neshamah', as the Sages say, "the body and *Neshamah* (soul)," [14] and sometimes our spiritual nature is referred to as 'Nefesh', as in the Scripture, "And you shall love the Lord your God with all your heart and with all your *Nefesh* (soul)" (Deut. 6:5).
>
> Generally speaking, when we are discussing the soul we refer to it according to the highest level that it has, which is *Neshamah*, so that a person may know

that there is a great level of holiness ready for him, which is that of *Neshamah*. This should awaken within his heart the desire to achieve this level, and he may start to consider, "Why haven't I achieved this level already?" Then he may come to realize that all that is lacking within us, which prevents us from achieving this level of spirituality, is affinity of form with our Creator. However, a person is born with an inborn nature of selfish love that is in antipathy of form with respect to the Creator, whose only desire is to give goodness, as the Sages who attained this perception have taught.

Consequently, a person needs to purify his will to receive for himself alone in order to come into affinity of form with the Creator, which means that he needs to yearn to be able to do deeds that have the sole motive of benefiting others. Then he will be able to arrive at the great level of soul which is called '*Neshamah*'. Thus the Sages speak in terms of the body and the *Neshamah* (soul).

However, this is not the case when we speak about the order in which we come to serve God. After the stage of the body, which constitutes the will to receive for oneself alone, comes the stage of the *Nefesh*. Therefore, the Scripture states, "And you shall love the Lord your God with all your heart and with all your *Nefesh*, (soul) and with all your might," (Deut. 6:5) as this is the second stage which follows that of the body (the will to receive for oneself alone). Therefore it is written "with all your heart," and after that "with all your *Nefesh*." What this implies is that whatever level the person has achieved, he has to be prepared to give it to God. If after *Nefesh* the person achieves a higher level, *Ruach*, and subsequently *Neshamah*, he has to be prepared to give also these levels to God. It is only that the Scripture is beginning at the first level following that of the body. All that a person has, he needs to give to God. This implies that the person does not do anything for his own benefit but everything he does is only for God, such that all his deeds are carried out only in order to benefit. He does not work to benefit himself at all, but everything he does is for God.

Now we can understand what is written in the *Zohar* concerning the phrase, "with all your *Nefesh*."

> Rabbi Yitschak asks, "The Scripture could simply have written, 'and you shall love the Lord your God with your *Nefesh*.' What is the force of 'with **all** your *Nefesh*'? What do the words 'with all' have to add to the meaning here?"
>
> Rabbi Elazar replies, "The words 'with all' imply the inclusion of all the levels of soul, that is all the levels of *Nefesh*, *Ruach*, and *Neshamah*. 'With all your *Nefesh*,' means with all that your *Nefesh* has achieved." [15]

From here we see that the *Zohar* explains that the words "with all" as they are written in the Scripture, are present, in order to teach us that *Ruach* and

Neshamah are included within the concept of *Nefesh;* but we start from the aspect of *Nefesh,* as after the body comes the *Nefesh.*

This is not the case when we are speaking of spirituality in general. Then we use the name "*Neshamah,*" as it is written, "And God blew into his nostrils *Nishmat Chayim* (the living *Neshamah*)" (Gen. 2:7). [16]

1. Talmud, Shabbat 21b
2. Hakdamat Sefer haZohar, Perush haSulam, paragraph 215
3. Maimonides Hilchot Teshuvah, chapter two, no. 2
4. Avot d'Rabbi Natan chapter two, verse five
5. Talmud, Sanhedrin 38b
6. Hakdamah l'Panim Me'irot uMasbirot paragraph 19
7. Avot chapter six, mishnah one
8. Sefer haMa'amarim, volume three, part two, article one
9. Hakdamat Sefer haZohar volume one, Perush haSulam paragraph 217
10. Talmud, Shabbat 88a
11. Zohar, Parshat Vayikra, Perush haSulam, paragraph 425
12. Zohar, Parshat Noach, Perush haSulam, paragraph 63
13. Zohar, Parshat Mishpatim, Perush haSulam, paragraphs 11–13
14. See for example Rashi on Bereishit, chapter two, verse seven
15. Zohar, Parshat Terumah, Perush haSulam, paragraph 670
16. Bircat Shalom, Sefer haMa'amarim, volume one, year 5744, article thirteen

Ein Od Milvado!

"There is nothing other than the One!"

Lesson Sixteen

The holographic nature of reality and its relationship to Torah; the nature of the book of the *Zohar* and its authorship
Paragraphs 56–60 of the Introduction to the Zohar

Introduction to the Zohar

56. Now, one needs to know that these five aspects, *Nefesh*, *Ruach*, *Neshamah*, *Chayah*, and *Yechidah*, of which we have spoken, are five parts into which the whole of reality may be subdivided. Everything that is present in the macrocosm behaves in the same way in even the smallest possible subdivision of reality.

That reality is holographic in nature, and that every part of reality is represented in every part, is not just a theoretical intellectualization, it has practical implications for our lives. It implies the interconnection between the souls, thus changing our perspective on how we look at each other and at society as whole. It also changes the way we perceive the rest of God's creation.

Consider the fact that the interconnection between the souls implies that acts we do affect the whole community of souls. Describe ways in which you feel encouraged and empowered by this fact.

Introduction to the Zohar

56. (continued) So, for example, even within the inanimate modality of the spiritual world of *Assiyah*, one needs to attain the five aspects of *Nefesh*, *Ruach*, *Neshamah*, *Chayah*, and *Yechidah* of that level, which are related to the macroscopic divisions of *Nefesh*, *Ruach*, *Neshamah*, *Chayah*, and *Yechidah*. This implies that it is impossible to attain even the light of *Nefesh* of *Assiyah* except through working on all of the four parts of the will to receive, as we mentioned above (in paragraphs 47–49).

These four parts of the will to receive are worked on as follows: 1) fulfilling the Torah and *mitzvot* from the practical aspect (the inanimate level); 2) fulfilling the Torah and *mitzvot* with the required intention (plant level); 3) occupying oneself with the innermost parts of the Torah and the reasons for the *mitzvot* (animal level); 4) occupying oneself with each and every *mitzvah* according to its true intention (speaking level).

Lesson sixteen

Introduction to the Zohar

56. *(continued)* It follows that no one can exempt themselves from dealing with all of the four parts of the will to receive, according to their capacity. It is necessary for a person to involve himself or herself in Torah and *mitzvot* with the intention of giving benefit, in order to receive the light of *Ruach* according to one's capacity. Likewise, it is necessary for the person to deal with the innermost aspect of Torah according to his or her capacity so that they may receive the light of *Neshamah* at their level. The same follows as regards the reasons of the *mitzvot*. Even the smallest light in the reality of holiness cannot be completed without the involvement of all the modalities.

57. From here you will understand the nature of the dryness and the darkness which is to be found in the Judaism of our generation. **There was nothing like it at all in previous generations.** This is because even those people who take their religious life seriously, have abandoned the study of the secrets of the Torah, that is to say, the Kabbalah. Maimonides gives a true example of this: He asks us to imagine a line of a thousand blind people going on a journey, who are led at the head of the line by at least one person who can see. They can still be sure that they are going in the right direction. They will not fall into any snares or traps in their path since they are following the one who can see. But if the one person who can see is missing, they will undoubtedly stumble over every obstacle laid in their path and they will all fall into a dark pit. This is exactly our situation. If at least the people who are the spiritual leaders of our generation would occupy themselves with the innermost aspect of Torah that is the Kabbalah, they would draw to themselves a complete light from the *Ein Sof*, blessed be the One. As a consequence, the whole generation would be able to follow after them; everyone would be sure of their way and would not stumble. But if the spiritual leaders of our generation have removed themselves from this wisdom, then it is little wonder that the whole generation stumbles on account of them. From the great sorrow that I feel, I cannot write any more on this.

Take time to feel the truth of this paragraph and to feel the pain that Rabbi Ashlag is expressing. How would society be different if the educators in both formal and informal education, the spiritual leaders and other leaders of the community would know and act according to this material?

If you feel that you personally have suffered from this deficit, write about it in your journal.

Introduction to the Zohar

58. I know that the reason that this has arisen is mainly due to a lessening of faith in general and, in particular, a weakening of faith in the great *Tzaddikim*

Lesson sixteen

and Masters of previous generations. The books of Kabbalah and the *Zohar* are full of images drawn from the physical world, and so people became afraid that they might not understand this imagery in the correct way and fall into a form of idolatry.

The second of the ten commandments states, "You shall not have other gods before Me. You shall not make any sculpture or picture of anything that is in the heavens above or on the earth beneath or in the waters beneath the earth" (Exod. 20:3). From here follows the prohibition of making material imagery out of spiritual concepts.

Introduction to the Zohar

58. *(continued)* This is what has inspired me to undertake the task of properly explaining the work of the Ari and of the holy *Zohar*. I have completely removed this fear because I have explained and clearly demonstrated the spiritual analogue that exists for every entity, stripped of any material image, not connected to space and time. Those who are interested can see this for themselves. I have made it possible for everyone in the House of Israel to study the holy *Zohar* and warm themselves by its holy light. I have called my commentary, "The Ladder" (the *Perush haSulam*), to illustrate the fact that the purpose of my explanation is the same as that of any other ladder. If you have an attic full of bounty, all you need is a ladder to go up, and then all the good of the world is within your reach.

However, the ladder is not a goal in itself. If you were to rest on the steps of the ladder and not enter the attic, then you would not have fulfilled your intention.

Consider this statement very carefully. What would making a goal out of the ladder look like? What is Rabbi Ashlag warning us against doing here?

Introduction to the Zohar

58. *(continued)* So it is with my explanation of the *Zohar*. Its words are unfathomably deep. The means by which to express its depth have yet to be created. However, my explanation, at any rate, constitutes a path and an introduction which any person can use to ascend and to look deeply into the book of the *Zohar* itself. Only then would my intention in writing this explanation be fulfilled.

59. All serious students who have studied the holy *Zohar*—that is, those who understand its contents—universally agree that its author is the holy Sage, Rabbi Shimon Bar Yochai. Only those who are far from a true understanding of this wisdom have doubts about its authorship. On the basis of external evidence

Lesson sixteen

they claim that its author was the noted Kabbalist, Rabbi Moshe De Leon or one of his period.[1]

60. As for myself, from the day that I merited through the light of God to understand a little in this holy book, it never occurred to me to question its authorship for the simple reason that from the content of the book, there came to my heart a sense of the holiness of the *Tanna* Rabbi Shimon Bar Yochai, which was immeasurably greater than that of the other holy *Tannaim*.[2] If it was completely clear to me that the author was someone else, such as Rabbi Moshe De Leon, then I would think of him as having attained a level far beyond that of the *Tannaim* and even greater than that of Rabbi Shimon Bar Yochai. Actually, the book reaches such a depth of wisdom that if it turned out that its author was one of the ancient prophets of the Bible, I would find that even more reasonable than ascribing its authorship to one of the *Tannaim*. Even were it to be proved that Moses, our Teacher, received it straight from God at Mount Sinai, I would have no difficulty accepting this fact, so deep is the wisdom I see in it.

Therefore, since I have been privileged to write an explanation of this book in such a way that anyone who is interested can understand something of it, I feel myself discharged from the need to research the identity of its author. When the reader begins to appreciate the depth of this work, he or she will themselves feel satisfied that it must have been written by someone who has attained, at the very least, the spiritual level of the Holy Rabbi Shimon Bar Yochai.

---

1. *A thirteenth century Kabbalist who lived in Spain.*
2. *Tanna means a Rabbi who taught at the time of the Mishnah.*

Ein Od Milvado!

"There is nothing other than the One!"

Lesson Seventeen

The revelation of the Kabbalah in our generation and the nature of our generation compared to previous generations
Paragraphs 61–64 of the Introduction to the Zohar

Introduction to the Zohar

61. We both can, and should, ask at this point why the *Zohar* was not revealed to earlier generations. They were, undoubtedly, higher souls than the later generations and more suited to it. We can also ask why the explanation of the *Zohar* was only revealed at the time of the Ari and not to the Kabbalists who preceded him. The most astonishing puzzle of all, however, is why has the explanation of the words of the Ari and of the *Zohar* only been openly revealed in this generation and not prior to it?

The answer to these questions is that the world is one spiritual entity, which divides up into three parts within the time period of its existence. There is a head part, a body part, and a tail part, which divides in accordance with the *Sephirot* as follows: *Chochmah*, *Binah*, and *Da'at*[1] being the head; *Chesed*, *Gevurah*, and *Tiferet* being the body; *Netzach*, *Hod*, and *Yesod* being the tail part. According to the Sages, the head part of the spiritual entity corresponds to the stage of chaos; the body part corresponds to the stage of Torah, and the tail part corresponds to the days of the Messiah.[2]

In any spiritual entity, the growth of the vessels of that entity always occurs in the opposite order compared to the incarnation of the lights in the entity; the general rule being that the highest vessels grow first, whereas, for the lights, the opposite applies. The lowest lights enter the spiritual entity initially.

In the first time period of the world's existence, namely the head part, the lights were few and considered only as potential lights. They were of the quality of *Nefesh*. Thus, so long as only the highest vessels are present—that is those related to the *Sephirot*, *Chochmah*, *Binah*, and *Da'at*, only the lights of *Nefesh*—the lowest lights—can come down to be enclothed within these vessels. Thus the first time period of the world is designated by the Sages as the stage of chaos.

Then came the second time period of the world. The vessels that evolved at that time relate to the *Sephirot*, *Chesed*, *Gevurah*, and *Tiferet*. The vessels enclothed the light of *Ruach*, which is the Torah, in the world. Thus the Sages designated this time period as the stage of Torah.

Lesson seventeen

In the final period of the world's existence, the last vessels of *Netzach*, *Hod*, *Yesod*, and *Malchut* come in and then the light of *Neshamah* is enclothed in the world. *Neshamah* is a greater light and thus this period is called the days of the Messiah.

This process applies for any spiritual entity: When the highest vessels, *Chochmah*, *Binah*, *Da'at*, together with *Chesed*, *Gevurah*, and *Tiferet*, are in the entity, that is from the head until the level of the chest, then the lights are still covered and they do not begin to shine with the revealed illumination of the light of God until the lower vessels are ready. These are *Netzach*, *Hod*, *Yesod*, and *Malchut*, which belong in the spiritual entity from the level of the chest and downwards.

So, therefore, concerning the spiritual entity that constitutes the world, before its vessels of *Netzach*, *Hod*, *Yesod*, and *Malchut* began to emerge—which is to say in the last period of its existence—the wisdom of the Kabbalah in general, and of the *Zohar* in particular, was hidden from the world. However, during the time of the Ari, in which the lower vessels were forming, the higher light became revealed through the Divine soul of Rabbi Yitschak Luria (the Ari), who was able to receive this great light. He was able to reveal the underlying principles of the book of the *Zohar* and of the wisdom of the Kabbalah to the extent that he superseded all those who had preceded him.

Since, however, the vessels were not yet completed in his time, the world was still not ready for his words and thus his teachings remained available only to a few very special individuals of great attainment who did not have permission (from Above) to reveal their understanding to the world.

However in this, our generation, we are close to the completion of the last period of the world. Therefore, we have been permitted to reveal the teachings of the Ari and of the *Zohar* in a most significant measure to the world. From our generation onwards, the words of the *Zohar* will begin to be revealed more and more until their whole measure is revealed according to the will of God.

62. Now we can see in actual fact that the souls of the earlier generations were immeasurably higher than those of the later generations. The rule for all spiritual entities, both pertaining to worlds and to souls, is that the purest vessels always incarnate first in the spiritual entity. Thus, the vessels pertaining to *Chochmah*, *Binah*, and *Da'at*, both of the world and of the souls, incarnated first, making the souls that incarnated during the head period of the world incomparably higher than those who came after them.

Despite their tremendous elevation, they could not receive the full amount of light due both to the lack of lower souls in the world and to the lack of their own lower components which are the *Sephirot, Chesed, Gevurah, Tiferet, Netzach, Hod, Yesod*, and *Malchut*.

Even during the middle period, when the vessels of the world and of the souls that emerged were of the *Sephirot, Chesed, Gevurah*, and *Tiferet*, the souls were still extremely pure, seeing that the vessels of *Chesed, Gevurah*, and *Tiferet* are close to the vessels of *Chochmah, Binah*, and *Da'at*. At this stage, the higher lights were still concealed from the world due to the lack of incarnation of vessels from the level of the chest and below, both in the world and in the souls themselves.

In our generation, the souls that are incarnating are from the very lowest *Sephirot*. However, they complete both the spiritual entity that consists of the world, and the spiritual entity that consists of all the souls. They are the last of the vessels to incarnate. The work, therefore, from the aspect of the vessels, is only completed through these souls. Now that the vessels of *Netzach, Hod*, and *Yesod* are complete, all the vessels of the head, middle, and tail of the spiritual entity can draw on the full measure of the lights in the head, middle, and tail, for all who are worthy of them. These are *Nefesh, Ruach*, and *Neshamah* in their entirety. So only with the perfection of the lowest souls could the highest lights be revealed, and not prior to this.

63. This was a problem that also preoccupied the Sages of the Talmud. They raised it in their characteristically metaphorical way:[3]

> Rav Papa said to Abaya (of the fourth and fifth generation), "How is it that for the former generations miracles were performed, but for us miracles do not seem to happen? It cannot be because they were better at studying, because in the time of Rav Yehudah (of the second generation, which was earlier), all they learned was the one tractate, *Nezikin*, whereas we study all six tractates of the *Mishnah*! And when Rav Yehudah was learning the law in the section *Uzkin*: 'If a woman presses vegetables in a pot …,'[4] he used to say, 'I see all the difficulties of Rav and Shmuel (of the first generation) here.' (That is to say, this passage presents as many difficulties as all the rest of the Talmud.) Yet we (of the fourth and fifth generation) have thirteen versions of this section, *Uzkin*! Nevertheless, when Rav Yehudah merely took off one shoe (in preparation for fasting to pray for rain), the rain used to arrive instantly, whereas we torment ourselves and cry loudly and no notice is taken of us!"
>
> Abaya replied, "The former generations used to be ready to sacrifice their lives for the sanctity of God's Name. We do not sacrifice our lives for the sanctity of God's Name."

Lesson seventeen

So, even though the later teachers were more skilled in answering difficult questions of law than were the earlier generations, it was clear to them that the former generations were of a holier essence than they were. Rav Papa and Abaya may have been considerably more skilled in Torah and its wisdom than were the earlier generations, but the former generations were closer to the level of the *Ein Sof* in the essence of their souls. The reason is that the purer vessels incarnate first whereas the wisdom of Torah (being the light) is revealed more and more to the later generations. As we have stated, it is precisely through its lowest vessels that the spiritual entity becomes completed. Then the more complete lights are drawn to the entity, even though the essence of the lowest vessels is furthest from the *Ein Sof*.

64. One need not ask then that if this is the case, why do we always follow the earlier generations in issues concerning the revealed Torah?

The matter, however, is as follows: With regard to the practical aspects of the *mitzvot*, the earlier generations had a more complete practice than the later generations. This is because practice and practical matters are drawn from the holiest vessels of the *Sephirot*, whereas the innermost aspects of Torah (the wisdom of Torah) and the reasons for the *mitzvot* come from the lights within the *Sephirot*. We have already seen that vessels follow an opposite rule to that of lights. With regard to vessels, the highest ones develop first. Therefore, the earlier generations had a greater understanding of practical Torah than the later ones. The opposite is true as regards lights, the lowest ones entering first. Thus, the later generations have a more complete understanding of the wisdom of Torah than the former generations had.

From here we learn that the interest in the wisdom of the Kabbalah, which is so prevalent today, and is expressed in so many ways, is a true expression of the need of our souls at this time. This is the reason that it is so important for all of us to learn the Kabbalah in a serious and deep way from an authentic source. Through our learning we complete the vessels and bring in the lights not only for ourselves, but for all the souls of the generations that preceded us, and for all who, accompanying us together, constitute the entire spiritual entity of the created world.

1. *Da'at is a Sephirah which is actually a duplication of Tiferet in the head part of the entity.*
2. *Talmud, Sanhedrin 97a*
3. *Talmud, Berachot 20a*
4. *Uzkin 2.*

Ein Od Milvado!

"There is nothing other than the One!"

Lesson Eighteen

The innermost aspect of the Torah and its relationship to Israel and the world

Paragraphs 65–70 (end) of the Introduction to the Zohar

Introduction to the Zohar

65. Now you must know that everything has an inner aspect and an outer aspect. In the world as a whole, Israel, the seed of Abraham, Isaac and Jacob, is considered to be the innermost aspect. The seventy nations are considered to be the outer aspect of the world. Within Israel itself, there is an inner aspect which consists of those people who are seriously committed to their spiritual work of serving God, and there is an outer aspect consisting of those who are not involved in spirituality. Likewise, amongst the nations of the world, there is an inner aspect which consists of the saints of the world, and an outer aspect which consists of those who are destructive and coarse.

Even amongst those of Israel who serve God, there is an inner aspect and an outer aspect. The inner aspect is those people who are privileged to understand the soul of the innermost aspects of Torah and its secrets, and the outer part consists of people who only deal with the practical aspects of Torah.

All this can also be considered likewise in one individual person. The individual has, within him or her, the innermost aspect which is the aspect of "Israel" within the person. This is the point of Divine light within his or her heart. He or she also has an outer aspect which corresponds to the seventy nations of the world and relates to the will to receive. These internal "nations of the world" have the capacity for *teshuvah*. They can cleave to the innermost divine part of the person's soul, and they then become like the righteous converts who join with the community of Israel.

66. A person may reinforce and respect his or her innermost aspect, which is the aspect of Israel within the person, over his or her external aspect, which is the aspect of the nations of the world within the person. He or she then strives to put most of his or her energy and labor into increasing and enhancing his or her innermost aspect for the soul's sake. To those aspects of himself or herself, which correspond to the internal nations of the world within that person, he or she gives only the minimum required. That is to say that the person only gives the minimum to his or her wills to receive for oneself, according to what is written in *Pirkei Avot* (The Ethics of the Fathers), "Make your Torah your main

Lesson eighteen

occupation and your work secondary to it." The person's deeds affect both the inner aspect and the external aspect of the world as a whole. He or she causes the spiritual level of Israel to go up, and then the nations of the world, which comprise the external aspect of humanity, recognize and value Israel.

But if, God forbid, the opposite occurs, that an individual of Israel reinforces and values his or her outer aspects, which is the aspect of the nations of the world within him or her, over and above his or her inner aspect of Israel, then, according to the prophecy of Deuteronomy, chapter 28, "The stranger that is within you," which refers to the external aspects of the person, "will prevail over you higher and higher," "and you,"—as you are in yourself, in your innermost aspect, in your aspect of Israel within you—"will go down further and further" (Deut. 28:43). Then the person causes by his or her deeds that the externality of the world, which is the nations of the world, ascends higher and higher and has power over Israel and humiliates it to the dust, and they, that are the innermost aspect of the world, go down further and further, God forbid.

67. Do not be surprised by the fact that an individual person, through his or her deeds, can cause an elevation or degradation of the whole world. There is an unalterable law that the macrocosm (the totality) and the microcosm (the individual) are as like to each other as two drops of water. The same procedures that occur with respect to the macrocosm occur with regard to the individual and vice versa. Furthermore, it is the individual components themselves which make up the macrocosm, and thus the macrocosm is only revealed through the manifestation of its individual components according to their measure and their quality. So certainly, the act of a single person, according to his or her capacity, may lower or elevate humanity as a whole.

This is how we can understand what is stated in the *Zohar*, that through the study of the *Zohar* and the practice of the true wisdom we can bring about an end to our state of exile and a complete redemption.

We could ask what studying the *Zohar* could have to do with redeeming Israel from among the nations?

> *Zohar*
> And so many people in this world will benefit from this book, the book of the *Zohar*, which will be revealed in this world, in the last generation, at the end of days, for the sake of that generation. It is through the merit of the book of the *Zohar* that the redemption will come, as it is written, "And you shall proclaim freedom throughout the land for all its inhabitants, a jubilee it should be for you, and each one shall return to his ancestral home and to his family" (Lev. 25:10).[1]

68. From what we have already seen, it is easy to understand that the Torah, like the world itself, has an inner and an outer aspect. Likewise, the one who occupies himself or herself with Torah has these two levels. So, to the degree that a person, when practising Torah, strengthens and focuses on the innermost aspects of Torah and its secrets, he or she gives strength in this measure to the innermost aspect of the world, which is Israel. Then Israel begins to fulfill its true function with respect to the nations who then value Israel's role amongst them. Then shall the words of the prophet be fulfilled, "And the people shall take them and bring them to their place. And the House of Israel will settle in the Land of the Lord" (Isa. 14:2). Similarly, "Thus says the Lord God, 'Behold I shall lift up My hand to the nations and set up My standard to the peoples. And they shall bring your sons in their arms and your daughters shall be carried on their shoulders. And kings shall be your foster fathers and their queens your nursing mothers'" (Isa. 49:22). (In other words, Israel, that is to say, the will to receive in order to give benefit, will triumph over the will to receive for oneself alone, which will then act as support and handmaiden to the will to receive in order to give benefit.)

But, God forbid, the opposite could happen. A person of Israel might devalue the most intimate part of Torah with its secrets, which deal with the ways of our souls and their levels, devaluing also the intellectual considerations and reasons of the Torah, emphasizing instead the outermost aspect of Torah that deals with practical issues alone. If such a person ever concerns himself or herself with the innermost aspect of the Torah, he or she sets aside only a small portion of his time to it, not giving to it the attention it deserves but treating it as if it were superfluous material. By behaving in this way, he or she lowers and degrades the innermost aspect of the world, the Children of Israel, reinforcing the externality of the world over them, who are the nations of the world.

Then they, the nations of the world, cast Israel down and despise the children of Israel and consider Israel to be a superfluous entity in the world of which there is no need, God forbid. Not only this, but these people further cause the outer aspects of the nations of the world, who are coarse people who damage and destroy the world, to prevail over the inner aspects of the nations of the world, who are the righteous amongst the nations. They then cause terrible destruction, slaughter, and holocausts, such as our generation has been a witness to, God preserve us from here onwards.

Therefore we can see that the redemption of Israel and all the worth of Israel is dependent on the learning of the *Zohar* and the innermost aspect of the Torah. The opposite is true also. All the afflictions and degradations that have come upon the Children of Israel are on account of their neglecting the most intimate

Lesson eighteen

part of Torah, and not having valued it but having related to it as something superfluous, God forbid.

69. This is what is said in the *Tikkunei haZohar*: [2]

> Come and wake up, for the sake of the Holy *Shechinah*. Your heart is empty and you lack the understanding to know and comprehend her, even though she is in your midst.
>
> The inner meaning of the Scripture, "A voice says, 'Call out!'" (Isa. 40:3) is that a voice is knocking in the heart of each and every person to encounter and to pray for the raising up of the holy *Shechinah*, which encompasses the souls of all Israel. The *Zohar* brings a proof that 'calling out' means prayer, by quoting from the book of Job, "Call out now! Is there any that will answer you? And to which of the holy ones will you turn?" (Job 5:1)
>
> The *Shechinah* herself says, "But what shall I call out? I have no strength to raise myself from the dust because all flesh is as grass. Everyone is behaving like animals, eating grass and clover."
>
> "When they perform *mitzvot*, they do so in the way that animals would, without any inner understanding. Even all the kindness that they do, they really do primarily for their own benefit. They do not have the intention of carrying out the *mitzvot* in order to give pleasure to their Creator, but even the *mitzvot* they do perform are only done out of their own self-interest. Even the best amongst them, who give of their time to the study of Torah, only do this to serve their wills to receive for themselves alone and without true intention of giving pleasure to God.
>
> "It is said about such a generation that a spirit goes and does not return to the world. That is the spirit of the Messiah, who is needed to redeem Israel from all their sufferings, and bring them to the final redemption, when the Scripture, 'The world will be full of the knowledge of God, just as the water covers the sea' (Isa. 11:9), will be fulfilled. It is this spirit that departs from the world and does not give light to the world.
>
> "Woe to those people who cause the spirit of the Messiah to depart and leave the world, unable to return to it. They make the Torah a dry desert without any moisture of inner understanding and knowledge. They confine themselves to the practical aspects of Torah and they do not make any effort to try and understand the wisdom of the Kabbalah. They will not contemplate the innermost principles of the Torah and the deeper reasons for the *mitzvot*.
>
> "Woe to them! They cause by their actions poverty, war, violence, pillage, killings, and destructions in the world."

70. These words, as we have explained, concern those people who study Torah but disparage their own innerness and the intimate part of the Torah, leaving both aside. They treat them as if they are something unnecessary in the world and do not set aside the required time for them. In relation to their own innermost aspects, they are like blind men groping along a wall. They strengthen the outermost aspects of themselves, that is their will to receive for themselves alone. They act similarly with regard to the Torah, emphasizing the outermost aspect of Torah over the innermost aspect of Torah. Thus they cause by their deeds that all the outer aspects of the world are strengthened over the innermost aspects of the world, each aspect according to its essence. In this case, the outer aspects of Israel prevail and neutralize the innermost aspects of the community, who are the great Masters of the Torah. Likewise, the outermost aspects of the nations of the world, which are the warlords amongst them, prevail and hold sway over the innermost aspects, which are the saints and pious ones of the nations of the world. Then the external aspect of the whole world, which is the nations of the world, prevail over and negate the children of Israel who are the innermost aspect of the world. In a generation such as this, all the warlords of the nations of the world raise up their heads and want primarily to destroy and kill the people of Israel. As it is written in the Talmud, "Sufferings only come to the world on account of Israel." This is exactly what we see written in the above passage in the *Zohar*. This is what causes poverty, violence, robbery, killing, and destruction in the whole world.

To our great sorrow, we ourselves have born witness to everything that has been said in the above passage. The finest of us were destroyed in the Holocaust. As the Talmud tells us, "The Righteous are the first to suffer."[3] All that remains of the community of Israel that was destroyed in Europe is a remnant in the Holy Land and it is incumbent upon us, the remnant, to heal this grave error. Every one of us from now on should take upon himself or herself with all our soul and strength, the work of enhancing the innermost aspect of Torah to give it its true place as being more important than the Torah's outward aspect. In this way, each of us will strengthen our own innermost aspect, which is the aspect of Israel within us. This is the need of our soul, as opposed to our external aspects, which are our wills to receive for ourselves alone. This power will then touch all the community of Israel until the other nations, which are aspects within us, will recognize the value of the Sages of Israel and they will then want to listen to them and obey them. Likewise, the innermost aspects of the nations of the world—the righteous ones amongst them—will prevail and subdue the outer aspect of the nations of the world—the violent and destructive elements. Then the innermost aspect of the world, Israel, will fulfill its true function with respect

Lesson eighteen

to the other nations who will recognize, appreciate it, and value it. Then will the prophecies of Isaiah be fulfilled, "and the people shall take them and bring them to their place and Israel will settle in the land of the Lord" (Isa. 14:2).

This is why the *Zohar* states that through studying this book of the *Zohar*, the redemption of the world will come about in love.

Amen, may this be His will.

Finished and Complete
Praise be to the Creator of the World

May your learning, your study, your contemplation and your sharing of this work with others contribute to the peace, healing and stability of each one of us and of the world, and bring the long awaited redemption to us all, Amen.

1. *Tikkunei haZohar, Ma'alot haSulam paragraph 71*
2. *Tikkunei haZohar 30, column 2*
3. *Talmud, Bava Kamma 60a*

Ein Od Milvado!

"There is nothing other than the One!"

Rabbi Yehudah Lev Ashlag

Biography

Rabbi Yehudah Lev Ashlag was born in Warsaw into a Chassidic family in 1886. Even at an early age his interest in the Kabbalah was awakened. The story is told that a book fell off the shelf hitting him on the head; it was a book of the Kabbalah. Picking it up, his father remarked that is was a book intended for angels, not for humans, but the young boy decided that if it was written, it was certainly intended for humans. His interest awakened, he began to try to understand the work of the Ari whilst pursuing his regular studies in the Yeshivah, slipping pages inside those of his Talmud. His teachers were the Prosover Rebbe and the Belzer Rebbe. At the age of nineteen he became ordained as a Rabbi in Warsaw, where he served the community for the next sixteen years.

All this time Rabbi Ashlag's yearning for the wisdom for the Kabbalah continued unabated and the story of its first transmission to him is told below in the section *The Revelation of the Hidden*.

In 1922 Rabbi Ashlag left Poland and came to Israel where he first tried to remain in obscurity. But with his immense learning he soon attracted to himself a small band of devoted students. All his life he had the habit of arising at one o'clock in the morning to study the Kabbalah, and his students joined him. In 1924 he left the Old City of Jerusalem where he had first lodged and moved to the suburb Givat Shaul where he served as Rabbi. His students made their way every night, over the then very dangerous terrain, to meet with him. He chose his students with exceptional care, each of them a Torah giant in their own right, mature and willing to work on themselves. At first the material was so unfamiliar to them that they had to work much harder over it than over a page of Talmud.

In 1926 Rabbi Ashlag commenced writing his works; the first work, *Panim Meirot u'Masbirot* was a commentary on the *Etz Chayim* of the Ari, written in two volumes. He wrote more than eighteen hours a day. But it was very difficult to print and publish the work, because ink and paper were so expensive, and both he and his students lived in dire poverty. Rabbi Ashlag then published a short collection of articles collected into the volume entitled *Matan Torah*, intended to open up and explain the essence of the Kabbalah for the secular Jew. In 1933 he started his monumental work, the *Talmud Eser haSephirot*, and in 1943 he started to compose his great commentary on the *Zohar*, the *Perush haSulam*.

Although Rabbi Ashlag came from the very strict orthodox Hareidi world, it is fair to say that he held opinions that differed widely from many of those around him. He believed that the students should not depend upon charity for their livelihood but every one should endeavor to earn his own living. His son, Rabbi Baruch Shalom haLevi Ashlag became a building laborer. Earning the livelihoods for their families as well as getting up every night to study in the early hours of the morning was a strain on all. But the students were devoted to their Rabbi whom they regarded as a true man of God.

Rabbi Ashlag taught the way of the individual, that each person must learn to think for himself and not just follow the general crowd. Examining one's motives and asking, "who am I serving?" helped turn his students' thoughts to the presence of God, and the importance of unconditional service without thought of reward.

His work opened up the language, the thought and the principles of the Kabbalah to a generation, which now, more than ever, is thirsty for his work. He passed away in 1955. Rabbi Abraham Brandwein, and Rabbi Baruch Shalom haLevi Ashlag were the two main disciples who carried on his teaching.

The Revelation of the Hidden

We do not have the capability to understand or apprehend reality the way the *Tzaddik* sees it. In this generation the way that Torah is learned has become extremely confused. Most teachers are teaching from their intellect alone without any true enlightenment. Therefore it is incumbent upon us to try with all our might to learn directly from the teaching of the *Tzaddik*.

In our generation we have merited the revelation of a great light to illumine our path and to help us correct the distortions and blindness we have been prone to, namely, the manifestation of the holy soul of Rabbi Yehudah Lev Ashlag, may his memory be for a blessing. Through the light of his learning and his teaching, the One has given us a lifeline to save us from drowning in the sea of materialism and separation, so we may find our way back to the Source of our life.

In the letter that follows, Rabbi Ashlag, uncharacteristically, speaks of how this wisdom was initially revealed to him.

> A letter written by Rabbi Yehudah Lev Ashlag to Rabbi Abraham Mendel Bronstein:
> 10th Tevet 5688
> … I shall describe to you everything that happened from beginning to end through which I merited this wisdom by virtue of the great mercy of God.
>
> On the twelfth day of the month of *MarCheshvan*, on a Friday morning, a certain man came and introduced himself to me. It became clear to me that he was wondrously wise in Kabbalah and also in many other disciplines. As soon as he started to speak, I began to sense his Divine wisdom. All his words had a wondrous quality to them, a sort of glory. I really trusted my feelings in this regard. He promised to reveal to me the true wisdom. I studied with him for three months, meeting him every night after midnight in his home. Mostly we talked about matters of holiness and purity. However, each time I would implore

him to reveal to me a secret from the wisdom of Kabbalah. He began to tell me chapter headings but he never explained any concept fully. So I was left with tremendous yearnings. Then one time, after I had greatly implored him to do so, he fully explained a concept to me and my happiness knew no limits.

However, from that time I began to acquire a little ego, and as my self-assertion increased, so my holy teacher began to distance himself from me. But I did not notice this happening. This continued for around three months, at the last days of which I could no longer find him in his home at all. I searched for him but I could not find him anywhere.

Then I truly became aware of how he had become distanced from me. I was extremely sorry and began to mend my ways. Then in the morning of the ninth day of the month of *Nisan*, I found him and apologized profusely for my behavior. He forgave me and related to me as before. He revealed to me a great and deep teaching on the subject of a ritual bath that is measured and found to be too small. I once more experienced tremendous joy.

However, I saw that my teacher had become weak. I stayed at his house and the next morning, the tenth day of *Nisan*, in the year 5679 (1919), he passed away, may his memory shield us and all Israel. There are no words to describe the greatness of my sorrow, for my heart had been full of hope to merit this great wisdom of Kabbalah, and now I was left naked and with nothing. I even forgot at that time all that he had taught me on account of my extreme sorrow.

From then on, I prayed with all my heart and soul with untold longing, I did not rest a single moment of the day until I found favor in the eyes of my Creator, may the One be blessed. Then, the merit of my holy teacher and his Torah stood by me and my heart was opened to the higher wisdom ever increasingly, like a flowing spring. Through the mercy of the One, I also remembered all the deep teachings that I had received from my late teacher, may his memory be for a blessing. Blessed be the One who has kept me alive and sustained me! How can I, poor in deeds as I am, have any way to thank the One? From the beginning God knows my poverty that I have neither intelligence or wisdom to thank and praise Him for His mighty goodness. However, who can say to Him what He should do, or how He should act?

My holy teacher was a very successful businessman and known throughout town as an honest trader, but no one at all knew that he was a Master Kabbalist. He did not give me permission to reveal his name.[1]

Letter written by Rabbi Ashlag in 1947
And you should surely know, that since the time of the Ari, may his memory be for a blessing, until this day, there has been no one who has understood the system of the Ari to its root. ... And now by the Highest Grace, may the One be blessed, I have merited to receive the soul of the Ari within me. Not because

of my good deeds, but because of the Highest will that it should be so. I do not understand why I should have been chosen to receive this wonderful soul, which no man has merited to receive since the passing of the Ari until this day.

I cannot talk further on this subject as it is not my way to speak of miracles.[2]

1. Letter printed in Perush haSulam edition of Zohar, also in haSulam by Rabbi Avraham Mordecai Gottlieb
2. Excerpt from letter printed in Pri Chacham (Letters)

Original Kabbalah Art by Avraham Loewenthal

Front Cover:
Light and Vessels

This picture is divided into ten squares that represent the ten *Sephirot*.

Within each square we see that each *Sephirah* is itself composed of ten *Sephirot*, some of which appear as *Or Yashar*, direct light (the goodness that comes directly from the Creator), and some appear as *Or Chozer*, returning light (light given back from the created being to the One). The *Or Yashar* appears as triangles pointing downwards, and the *Or Chozer* appears as triangles pointing upwards.

The *Sephirah Keter*, for example, has nine *Sephirot* of *Or Yashar* and one *Sephirah* of *Or Chozer*. The *Sephirah Chochmah* has eight *Sephirot* of *Or Yashar* and two *Sephirot* of *Or Chozer*. All the main *Sephirot* are represented in similar fashion according to their composition. The *Sephirah Malchut* is represented entirely by *Or Chozer*, as ten triangles pointing upwards.

Frontispiece:
(Literal Translation)

> ***Lamnatzeach!* Psalm 67**
>
> *Lamnatzeach* on tunes, a Psalm of song:
> May God favor us and bless us, may the One shine the light of His countenance on us, *Selah*. That Your way shall be known on the earth and Your salvation throughout all nations. The peoples will thank You, O God, all the peoples will thank You. The nations will rejoice and sing, for You judge the peoples rightly and You will guide the nations in the land, *Selah*. The peoples will thank You, O God, the peoples will thank You, all of them. The land will give of its produce; God, who is our God, will bless us. God will bless us, and the ends of the earth will have awe of Him.

(Translation according to the language of the branches)

> ***Lamnatzeach!* Psalm 67**
>
> *Lamnatzeach* on tunes, a Psalm of song:
> May we be in affinity of form with God; may the emanation of the goodness of the One be revealed to us, *Selah*. That Your way will be known by the will to receive for the sake of giving, and all the wills to receive for themselves alone will know Your salvation. All parts of the vessel will acknowledge You, O God; all the parts of the will to receive will thank You. Even the ego will be happy and rejoice, as You guide it into affinity of form and lead all the wills to receive into the path of giving benefit, *Selah*. All parts of the vessel will acknowledge You, O God; all the

parts of the will to receive will thank You. The will to receive in order to give benefit will flourish and produce fruit. God will bless us, O our God! God will bless us, and all the wills to receive will refrain from receiving for themselves alone.

The tradition of including this psalm in the morning prayer stems from the Ari. The Hebrew text is composed of forty-nine words, which represent the seven lower *Sephirot*: *Chesed, Gevurah, Tiferet, Nezach, Hod, Yesod,* and *Malchut* respectively.

According to *Sephardi* custom this psalm is printed in the *siddur* (prayer book) in the form of a *Menorah* of seven branches and is intended to awaken the soul to prayer. This is a modern rendering of an ancient tradition.

Between each chapter:
Ein Od Milvado! "There is nothing other than the One!"
"You have shown us, that we may know, that 'ה'ו'ה'י (Y-H-V-H) is God; there is nothing other than the One" (Deut. 4:35).

This is a profound meditation which expresses one of the deepest principles of the learning. All is an expression of the One. This artistic expression of a phrase from the Torah is inserted between chapters to remind the reader to pause for reflection, to breathe, and to connect the learning with the deepest part of himself or herself.

Avraham Loewenthal studied art at the School of the Art Institute of Chicago, following a degree in Psychology at the University of Michigan. He divides his time between studying Kabbalah and working at his art, which he creates and displays in his gallery in Safed, Israel. The form of the psalm *Lamnazeach!* (the frontispiece), and the form of *Ein Od Milvado* (between chapters), are influenced by the ancient calligraphic art of the Jewish scribe *(sopher)*. Other works of his, as for example, the *Light and the Vessels* (front cover), draw their inspiration from the writings of the Ari and the teachings of Rabbi Ashlag.

Further examples of Avraham's work may be seen in his gallery in Safed where he lives and works, or on his web site at www.kabbalahart.com.

Glossary

This glossary includes both Hebrew words and Kabbalah terms according to the language of the branches.

Adam Kadmon—the highest of the spiritual worlds; the first to emerge following the *Tzimtzum*.

affinity of form—God is giving; so when the vessel is giving, it has the same form or desire. This is affinity of form.

angels—This is the term in the Kabbalah for the animal modality of the spiritual worlds. Angels are messengers; they do the bidding of the Creator, but have no free will of their own.

animal modality—This is the third modality of the will to receive. As the will to receive for oneself alone it is expressed by the will for power over others, the desire for glory and appreciation. In its rectified form it is a very advanced stage that has the light of *Neshamah* and every limb of the soul and of the body exhibits an individual consciousness.

Ari—Rabbi Yitschak Luria, sixteenth century Kabbalist, author of the *Etz Chayim* (Tree of Life).

Assiyah—the lowest of the created spiritual worlds. Our world is connected with the spiritual world of *Assiyah*.

Atzilut—the highest of the created spiritual worlds. *Adam Kadmon* is higher, but works on a different principle. *Atzilut* is the highest one that we, as created beings in this world, can relate to.

Atzmut—the essence of God; Unknowable.

Bar mitzvah/Bat mitzvah—This is the age at which the spiritual will to receive starts to develop. (Thirteen years for a boy, twelve for a girl.)

barah—to create. In the Kabbalah the word relates specifically to the creation of a vessel.

before and after—*see* cause and effect

bet—the second letter of the Hebrew alphabet; the letter that opens the whole Torah.

Binah—This is the *Sephirah* that comes after *Chochmah*. The light it attracts is the light of *Chassadim*, as its vessel is that of giving.

Bircat Shalom—books of articles and letters on the inner work written by Rabbi Baruch Shalom haLevi Ashlag.

Brachah—blessing. The one light that emanates from the *Ein Sof* all the way to this world without undergoing any diminution whatsoever.

Glossary

Briyah—the next created world after *Atzilut*. Known as the quarry of the souls, it is in *Briyah* that the soul is first individuated. The light of *Briyah* is *Neshamah*.

body—the term used in Kabbalah to refer to the will to receive in actual practice. In this world it refers to the will to receive for oneself alone. It implies the mental, emotional, and spiritual will to receive, as well as the physical will to receive. In the higher worlds it refers to that aspect of the spiritual entity that receives the light in practice.

cause and effect—It is a basic premise in Kabbalah that everything has a cause, and there is an effect. Thus we find many terms in the language of the branches that describe the concept of cause and effect; as for example, before and after, reward and punishment.

Challal Panui—lit., 'empty space'. The vessel of the *Ein Sof* that is left empty of light after the *Tzimtzum*. It is the precursor for the will to receive for oneself alone and the origin of the framework of uncleanness.

Chayah—the light of the *Sephirah Chochmah*.

Chesed—one of the ten *Sephirot*.

chesed—loving-kindness.

Chochmah—one of the ten *Sephirot*; its vessel is that of receiving.

cohen—a man descended from the priestly family of Aaron. The cohanim serve in the Temple and have other ritual functions and privileges.

creation—the bringing into being of the vessel, which is the will to receive all the Good that the Creator wants to give to the created beings.

created beings—The *Zohar* relates primarily to the souls of humankind as being the most important of the created beings.

Da'at—The *Sephirah Tiferet*, in her capacity of uniting the *Sephirot Chochmah* with *Binah*, or *Chesed* with *Gevurah*, is called *Da'at*. This role of *Tiferet* only applies in the created worlds, that is from *Atzilut* downwards.

death—separation from the Life of all Lives; the wicked who use their will to receive for themselves alone are called 'dead' even in their lifetimes.

difference of form—occurs when two spiritual entities are not in exact agreement in their desire to give or to receive.

d'mut—lit., 'likeness' as in Gen. 1:26, "and God said 'Let us make Man in our image, like us.'" According to the Kabbalah Rabbi Ashlag understands the word as being derived from the word *mavet*, thus its meaning is "appertaining to death."

dvekut—affinity of form; unity.

Echad—one.

ego—the will to receive for oneself alone.

Ein Sof—the Infinite. It is the first level below the *Atzmut* (God's essence). It consists of the light of God, which emanates from the *Atzmut*. It has within it the vessel that receives all the light, both as a potential, and as a finished vessel in all its completion. It is not given to any created being to understand the paradox of the *Ein Sof*. All

Glossary

begins and finishes at the *Ein Sof* and all is included within it, in the inner meaning of He and His Name are One.

enclothe—A lesser modality enclothes a higher modality providing it with support and a framework. The souls of the human enclothe the *Sephirot* and they themselves are enclothed by the animal modality of the will to receive.

enclothing—The outermost part of the higher modality is in affinity of form with the innermost part of the lower modality, allowing enclothing to occur.

enosh—man.

essence (*Atzmut*)—Unknowable. We also do not know our own essence.

Etz Chayim—the Tree of Life. It is the term in Kabbalah for faith. It is also the name of the major book of the Kabbalah composed by the Ari.

evil—whatever creates separation between ourselves and the Creator is termed 'evil'; the will to receive for oneself alone.

faith—what we believe; not what we know or experience, or know through someone else's knowledge. Faith feels shaky, uncertain, with no logical grounds for believing in it. Faith is not provable. Faith is a choice that we make. It needs renewing constantly. Nevertheless, despite all this, it is the way to *dvekut* as it opposes the will to receive for oneself alone, which wants to know and understand everything.

female—aspect of receiving.

four aspects of the vessel—The vessel develops through four aspects or modalities; these are the inanimate, plant, animal, and speaking.

four modalities of the spiritual will to receive—These are equivalent to the inanimate, plant, animal, and speaking modalities within the framework of holiness.

garments—This is the term for the plant modality of the spiritual will to receive.

gever—man.

Gevurah—one of the ten *Sephirot*.

giving—Giving unconditionally is an action that does not come naturally. As we are created with the built-in will to receive for oneself alone, most giving has the intention for us to receive benefit by our giving. Nevertheless, as we practice doing it we get closer to being able to give unconditionally.

haca'ah—lit., 'hitting'. This term refers to the presence of two opposing ideas or desires. For example, the desire of the *Or Yashar* when it comes to the vessel is to enter the vessel. This is opposed by the *Masach*, which denies it entry to the vessel but 'hits' it back towards the Creator. The desire of the light is to give to the vessel, while the desire of the vessel is to stay in *dvekut* and not to receive.

haHakdamah l'Talmud Eser haSephirot—"The Introduction to the Study of the Ten Sephirot."

haHakdamah l'Panim Meirot uMasbirot—"The Introduction to the Welcoming and Explaining Revelations."

haHakdamah l'Sefer haZohar—"The Introduction to the Book of the *Zohar*."

halachah—lit., 'the way of walking; the system of *mitzvot* also known as Jewish law.

Glossary

haPetichah l'Chochmat haKabbalah—"The Gateway to the Wisdom of the Kabbalah."

haShem—lit., the Name; used as a term for God.

hashgachah pratit—Divine Providence; the idea that our lives are not random or meaningless, but all that happens to us comes from the Creator.

haSulam—The Ladder"—the commentary written by Rabbi Yehudah Lev Ashlag on the *Zohar*. A different book entitled *haSulam*, comprising the biographies of the Rabbis Ashlag, was compiled by Rabbi Avraham Mordecai Gottlieb.

Histaclut Pnimit—"Inner Look"—one of Rabbi Ashlag's commentaries on the *Etz Chayim* in the *Talmud Eser haSephirot*.

Hod—one of the ten *Sephirot*.

holiness—whatever is in affinity of form with the light of the Creator is in holiness.

higher—that which is closer to the act of giving is called 'higher'. Thus the term also applies to a vessel that refrains from receiving. *See also* pure.

houses—the inanimate modality of the spiritual will to receive.

illumination—a small amount of light given from afar, not the full amount of light.

inanimate—the lowest aspect of the will to receive. In the will to receive for oneself alone the inanimate is characterized by the will to survive. In its rectified form it is the stage in which there is a general illumination of the spiritual entity, but no individual movement of its parts. It is the stage of Torah 'not for its own sake'. Its light is *Nefesh*.

innermost—purest.

ish—man.

Israel—lit., 'straight to God' (*Yashar-El*). The name 'Israel' also refers to the soul.

kedushah—holiness.

Keter—the highest of the ten *Sephirot*.

klipot—lit., 'shells'. These are the lights given over to the framework of uncleanness that entice a person to receive for oneself alone and yet at the same time keep the innermost part of a person untouched until he or she is ready and mature enough to receive the lights of holiness.

life—connection with the Creator.

light—goodness; bounty. The light is not created but emanates from the *Atzmut*. It is called *yesh m'yesh*. It has the desire of giving unconditionally.

light of Chassadim—light of loving-kindness; joy of giving.

light of Chochmah—The light which comes straight from the Creator; the goodness He wants to give us.

lower—In the Kabbalah this refers to receiving. Whatever is closest to the fourth and final level of the will to receive is considered as lower.

mahut—essence.

Glossary

Malchut—The last of the ten *Sephirot*. The *Malchut* in its rectified state is also referred to as the *Shechinah*. There are many expressions in the Kabbalah for the Malchut. It is the vessel that receives the light.

Malchut of the Ein Sof—The vessel of the *Ein Sof*.

male—In the language of the Kabbalah 'male' relates to the attribute of giving.

Masach—The vessel prevails over its will to receive and rejects the light even though it has a lack for the light, the spiritual entity preferring to stay in affinity of form with the light.

Matan Torah—collected articles by Rabbi Ashlag called "The Gift of the Torah."

material—refers to the consciousness of the will to receive for oneself alone.

mavet—lit., 'death'; separation from the Creator by using the will to receive for oneself alone.

Mavo l'Zohar—"Prologue to the *Zohar*."

Meyuchad—Unity. At this stage we see that all that God does unites into the one desire to do good to His creatures.

mind—The will to receive knowledge and to do everything from rationality and with understanding. The antidote is faith.

minyan—prayer quorum.

mitzvah, pl. mitzvot—The unique actions that the Creator prescribed via Moses our Teacher to correct the endemic will to receive for oneself alone.

Name of God—All Names of God refer to the light of God as viewed from different vessels. None of the Names of God refer to God as He is in Himself since the One is Unknowable. Even the four-letter Name of God Y-H-V-H is a term for the light of God.

nations—Those aspects of the personality that are concerned with receiving for oneself alone.

Nefesh—lit., 'resting' or 'passive'; the lowest light of the soul. The light that *Nefesh* gives is passive; at this level the soul has no independent movement of its own but is subject to the desire of the person. If the person wants to do good the *Nefesh* is happy. If the person wants to do evil, the *Nefesh* has no choice but to allow him to so do.

Neshamah—The highest light of the soul that we may ordinarily reach before the end of the *tikkun*. It is the light found in the world of *Briyah* and is associated with the *Sephirah Binah*.

Netzach—one of the ten *Sephirot*.

Nisan—the first of the Hebrew months of the year.

Or Chozer—lit., 'returning light'; light that is returned by the created being back to the Creator.

Or d'Chassadim b'ha'arat Chochmah—The main part of this light is the light of loving-kindness with an illumination (not the full quality) of the light of *Chochmah* included with it.

Or d'Chochmah—the light of *Chochmah*; synonymous with the *Or Elyon*.

Glossary

Or Elyon—the highest light; the light that comes from the Creator.

Or Makif—the light that surrounds the vessel. It affects the vessel from afar by influencing it to desire it and thus to strive to transform, so that it will be able to accept it in holiness. It is the light that will be accepted by the vessel in the future.

Or Pnimi—the light that enters the vessel. It is the light that the vessel receives in the present. It views the *Masach* as a good thing as it was the action of the *Masach* which permitted it to enter. This is in contradistinction to the *Or Makif*, which takes the opposite view of the *Masach*, as it is the *Masach* that prevents the *Or Makif* from entering the vessel.

Or Shalom—oral commentary by Rabbi Baruch Shalom haLevi Ashlag on his father's works, subsequently transcribed by his pupils and printed in published editions of the *Talmud Eser haSephirot* and the *Petichah l'Chochmat haKabbalah*.

Or Yashar—direct light; synonymous with *Or Elyon*.

one—God is one. All that seems opposite to us as opposite attributes such as bitter/sweet are united in Him in one simple unity.

partzuf—A complete spiritual entity that contains within it all ten *Sephirot*. It consists of a head part, a body part, and an end part.

parzufei kedushah—spiritual entities in the framework of holiness. They are in affinity of form with the Creator.

perfect rest—The *Or Elyon* is said to be in perfect rest. In the language of the branches, this means that it has one desire and that is, to give good to all His creatures. It does not imply passivity.

Perush haSulam—the commentary written by Rabbi Yehudah Lev Ashlag on the *Zohar* entitled *HaSulam* (The Ladder).

physical—the forms that the inanimate, plant, animal, and speaking take in this world. Their state of holiness depends on the consciousness of the human. Contrast this definition with the definition of *material*.

plant—the second of the modalities of the will to receive, after the inanimate. In the will to receive for oneself alone it is expressed by the desire for luxuries beyond that needed for survival. In the rectified form of the will to receive, it is the stage at which a person keeps Torah and practises *mitzvot* with the intention of giving. Its light is *Ruach*, which has the ability to feel and act by itself, unlike that of *Nefesh*.

point of the heart—the potential soul. The *Nefesh* of the framework of holiness which is still in potential. Each stage of the soul has a point source within it of the stage above it, which steadily grows as the person works and grows in holiness. These points act as connections between a lower stage and the next stage above.

pure—giving; in affinity of form.

purification—becoming closer to affinity of form.

purpose of creation—The purpose of creation is to give joy to the created beings, it is also called 'the thought of creation'.

reward and punishment—*see* cause and effect.

Glossary

Rosh haShanah—Jewish New Year.

Ruach—the light of the soul that comes after *Nefesh*. When a person achieves the light of *Ruach* on a permanent basis he or she is considered as being in affinity of form with the Creator. It is the light associated with the world of *Yetzirah*.

Sefer haMa'amarim—articles on the inner work written by Rabbi Baruch Shalom haLevi Ashlag; also called *Bircat Shalom*.

Sefer haYetzirah—one of the earliest books of the Kabbalah.

Sephirah, pl. Sephirot—lit., 'shining ones'. These are the most subtle vessels that carry the Divine light. They originate in the *Ein Sof* and are enclothed in each of the worlds by the souls of the human being.

separation—difference of form.

Shechinah—lit., 'Divine dwelling'. The rectified will to receive as it manifests within the souls of the human. Also called *Malchut* or *Knesset Yisrael*.

shells—see *klipot*.

sin—any action that leads a person into opposition of form and therefore separation from the Creator.

sitra achra—lit., 'the other side'. The framework of uncleanness.

613—the full complement of the *mitzvot*, which, when fulfilled, makes up a stage in holiness.

soul—a vessel created in the *Ein Sof*, but only uses the will to give and is therefore always in the framework of holiness, unlike the body. It is in *dvekut* with the Creator. The lights it receives are: *Nefesh, Ruach, Neshamah, Chayah,* and *Yechidah* according to its development.

speaking—the largest will to receive; the most complete modality. It can be either the largest vessel for the light of the Creator, or it can be the furthest away in terms of opposition of form from the Creator. This depends on whether it is rectified or not. In the will to receive for oneself alone it is expressed by the desire for knowledge. In the rectified form of the will to receive its vessel is the highest light the soul of the human can receive. Its light is that of *Chayah*.

spiritual—in affinity of form. The adjective 'spiritual' also applies to physical objects or acts. The wearing of a *talit* (prayer shawl) may be either a material or a spiritual act depending on the intention of the wearer.

tav—last letter of the Hebrew alphabet.

teshuvah—lit., 'turning back'; also translated as repentance. *Teshuvah* occurs when a person moves from the consciousness of having his or her own self-interest as the focus, and moves to the consciousness of the benefit of the other as being the focus.

Tiferet—one of the ten *Sephirot*. Its desire is that of giving benefit with just enough receiving of the light of *Chochmah* to survive. Its light is that of loving-kindness with an illumination of wisdom. See *Or d'Chassadim b'ha'arat Chochmah*.

tikkun—lit., 'rectification'. The rectification of creation implies that instead of using our will to receive that which God wants to give us, as in the purpose of creation, we

Glossary

use the will to give. At the final *tikkun* the entire world will be using the will to give, leading to the fulfillment of the purpose of creation, in which we will all be able to receive that which the Creator wants to give us, with the intention of giving benefit.

Tikkunei haZohar—a part of the *Zohar*.

transforming—see *teshuvah*.

Tzaddik—lit., 'a righteous one', or 'one who justifies'; the one who has reached the stage of using his will to give benefit in a permanent way. His or her eyes are opened to receive the innermost secrets of the Torah.

tzelem—lit., 'the image'; the light of God within us.

Tzimtzum—the contraction of the will to receive for the sake of receiving. At the level of the *Ein Sof*, the initial *Tzimtzum* enabled the creation of the worlds. In the framework of holiness, *tzimtzum* applies to any situation in which the vessel simply stops receiving in order to stay in holiness.

tzitzit—fringes on a four-cornered garment.

unity—affinity of form; *dvekut*.

upper—more giving, closer to the desire of the Creator, further away from the fourth modality of the vessel when receiving. *See also pure, also higher.*

vessel—the will to receive; it is desire, lack. A vessel is not simply an absence of something. For example, I don't own a car. Since, however, I don't desire to have one, the lack of a car does not constitute a vessel. The measure of the vessel determines the amount of light that can enter. Light cannot be apprehended without a vessel.

will to give benefit—the will to give in order to benefit the other without any self-interest. This is surprisingly hard to achieve. One's self-interest intervenes all the time. Nevertheless, one must persevere in giving and believe that one day we will be able to give unconditionally.

will to receive—the vessel that the light of the Creator created and stamped in every created being to enable it to receive all the good He wants to give. This is the entire material of creation. *See also yesh m'yesh.*

will to receive for oneself alone—the default consciousness of this world. It is the consciousness that we have inherently in our nature. It is also known as the ego, or as selfish love.

world—a collection of five *partzufim* (complete spiritual entities) that have all the modalities of inanimate, plant, animal, speaking, and divine for that level.

Yachid—single. Even though we see God as doing good acts and bad acts in our reality, we need to know that one single motivation underlies them all and that is to give good to all the created beings.

Yashar-El—lit., straight to God. *Yashar-El* is a name for Israel. It also refers to the soul.

Yechidah—one of the lights of the soul. It is the light that is related to the *Sephirah Keter*.

yesh m'yesh—"is-ness." The light emanates. It is not created but always is.

Glossary

yesh m'ayin—new creation; the vessel.

Yesod—one of the ten *Sephirot*.

Yetzirah—the spiritual world above the world of *Assiyah*. Its light is *Ruach*. The world of *Yetzirah* relates to the plant modality of the spiritual will to receive.

Yirat Shamayim—lit., 'the fear of Heaven'. The fear of doing something that will bring us into separation from the Creator.

Yom Kippur—the Day of Atonement.

Yud-Hay-Vav-Hay—the four letter Name of God. It represents the ten *Sephirot*. See also Name of God.

zachut—lit., having purity or merit. These two definitions are intimately connected. The term 'purity' relates to not receiving; if a person strives to give, instead of receiving for himself or herself alone, that is meritorious.

zivug—describes the light entering the vessel once the process of compromise with the action of the *Masach* has taken place. The term *zivug* implies that the vessel has achieved affinity of form with the amount of light it allows to enter.

zivug d'haca'ah—letting the light (*Or Elyon*) into the vessel, after initially opposing it. The *haca'ah* first opposes the desire of the light to enter and gives the light back as *Or Chozer*. This *Or Chozer* then enclothes the light, allowing *zivug* to take place.

Zohar—the main book of the *Kabbalah*.

Zohar Chadash—one of the parts of the *Zohar*.

Bibliography and Resources

Writings by Rabbi Yehudah Lev Ashlag:

Petichah l'Chochmat haKabbalah (The Gateway to the Wisdom of the Kabbalah): This work is both a summary and an introduction to the *Talmud Eser haSephirot* (The Study of the Ten *Sephirot*). Well-named, it truly is a gateway to all further learning of the Kabbalah. It is however a technical work, difficult for the beginner, but immensely rewarding.

Talmud Eser haSephirot (The Study of the Ten *Sephirot*): This is the major commentary Rabbi Ashlag wrote on the *Etz Chayim* of the Ari. It comprises sixteen parts, on each of which Rabbi Ashlag wrote two commentaries: 1) the *Or Pnimi* (Inner Light), which consists of a spiritual dictionary, explaining the definition of each spiritual term used, and 2) the *Histaclut Pnimit* (Inner View), which deals with the main ideas expressed by the Ari.

Perush haSulam on the *Zohar* (The commentary "The Ladder" on the *Zohar*): This is Rabbi Ashlag's seminal work on the *Zohar*; beautiful, technical, moving. It is all of these.

Mavo l'Zohar (Prologue to the *Zohar*): A short philosophical work which examines some of the ideas in the *Zohar*. It complements the "Introduction to the *Zohar*."

The *Hakdamah l'Panim Meirot uMasbirot* (The Introduction to the Illuminating and Welcoming Revelations): This introduction was written for an earlier commentary on the work of the Ari, which was later replaced by the *Talmud Eser HaSephirot*. The introduction contains a brilliant exposition on the beginnings of humankind and the makeup of this world.

The *Hakdamah l'Talmud Eser haSephirot* (Introduction to the Study of the Ten *Sephirot*): This introduction deals with the purpose of learning Kabbalah, the ways we practice Torah and *mitzvot* and the perception of Divine Providence.

Matan Torah (The Gift of the Torah), a collection of short articles written by Rabbi Ashlag, originally for secular Jews, explaining the main thought of the Kabbalah.

Writings by Rabbi Baruch Shalom haLevi Ashlag:

Or Shalom (The Light of Peace): This comprises extensive commentaries on the *Talmud Eser Sephirot* compiled from oral discourses that Rabbi Baruch Shalom haLevi Ashlag gave on the writings of his father.

Bircat Shalom, Sefer haMa'amarim, (the Book of Articles): This four-volumed work comprises essays Rabbi Baruch Shalom haLevi Ashlag wrote on the inner work, based on oral discourses he heard from his father.

Bibliography and Resources

Other writers:

Rabbi Avraham Mordecai Gottlieb: *haSulam* (The Ladder), a biographical work of the Rabbis Ashlag, their lives, their work, and their students.

Mark and Yedidah Cohen: *In the Shadow of the Ladder—Introductions to the Kabbalah*, comprising translations from the Hebrew of the *Introduction to the Zohar* and the *Introduction to the Ten Sephirot* by Rabbi Yehudah Lev Ashlag with added explanatory chapters *(Nehora Press)*.

Resources:

Please visit the web-site of Nehora Press at **www.nehorapress.com** where Yedidah posts short audio talks to further the connection between the work of Rabbi Ashlag and the inner work. She also posts essays and translations of articles written by Rabbi Ashlag on the web-site in both Hebrew and English. You may contact Yedidah through the web-site.

Books may be obtained from Nehora press web-site:

A Tapestry for the Soul is also available in its original Hebrew (*Ma'arag l'Neshamah*) through Nehora Press.

Other Hebrew books mentioned above may be obtained may be obtained from the organization Or Baruch Shalom at www.kabbalah-sefer.co.il

Index

Symbols
248
    positive commandments, 208, 213
    spiritual organs, 213
288 sparks of light, 148, 151–152
365
    negative commandments, 208
365 spiritual sinews, 213
612 *mitzvot*, 210
613
    limbs of the soul, 213, 217–220
    mitzvot, 207–211, 213
ב, *bet*, 60–63
ת, *tav*, 60

A
Abaye, Rav, 257
above to below. *See Or Elyon*
action, 163–164
acts, 59
actualization, 209
Adam
    name, 31
    perfect human being, 31, 231
Adam and Eve
    eating from Tree of Knowledge, 148, 233
    soul of, 19, 148
Adam Kadmon, 187
affinity of form
    as cause for *dvekut*, 96, 122–123, 123, 167
    as cause of tranquility, 92
    as holiness, 115, 128
    as *tikkun*, 75–79
    between light and vessel, 172, 193, 234
    definition of, 51–52
    with respect to Creator, 65, 80, 112, 130
alphabet, Hebrew, letters of, 59, 61
angels, 196, 200, 240
animal lusts, 131–132, 199
animal modality, 179, 182, 196–200, 240
    level of Torah, 219, 249
    light of, 206, 218, 219
    of holiness, 219
    purification of, 219

Ari
    and revelation of the Kabbalah to, 255, 256
ascent
    definition of, 68–69
Ashlag, Rabbi Yehudah Lev, 13
    and the Ari, 270
    early life, 268
    method of teaching, 15, 269
    students of, 269
    teachers of, 268, 269
    writings of, 268
Assiyah, 64–66, 194
    and fourth modality of the will to receive, 191, 195
    and *Sephirah Malchut*, 187, 213, 237
    and this world, 61, 66, 180, 181, 192
    components of, 220, 249
Atzilut, 187, 194, 240
Atzmut. *See God: essence of*

B
Bar or Bat mitzvah, 153
battle (inner), 172–173
belief. *See faith*
below to above. *See Or Chozer*
bet. *See* ב
Binah, 63, 187–190, 194, 206, 218
    of *Assiyah*, 219, 237
blessing, 61–63. *See brachah*
body. *See also will to receive for oneself alone*
    and framework of uncleanness, 76, 141
    and will to receive, 64–66, 79, 131, 133, 180, 191–192, 246
    as enclothing soul, 76, 195
    as opposing altruistic giving, 173
    nature of, 31
    need for, 80
    nullification of, 101, 105, 106, 111, 133
    revival of, 142–143
    transient, 101, 105, 134, 142
    true, 101
bounty, 49. *See also light*
    for world, 152
    within body, 180
brachah, 60–63
Briyah, 187, 194, 195, 237, 240
Briyah, Yetzirah, and *Assiyah*, 217

C
cause and effect, 166, 238
    perception of, 239

Index

Challal haPanui, 19, 49, 123, 128, 148, 231. *See also receiving for oneself alone*; *See also will to receive*
Chananiah ben Akashia, Rabbi, 72, 190, 196
Chayah, 187, 193, 218
    as complete soul entity, 220
    point source of, 220
    receiving by the soul, 240
chesed, 160
Chesed, Gevurah, and *Tiferet*, 255, 257
Chochmah, 187–190, 193–194, 206, 220
    light of, 193, 218
    of *Assiyah*, 220, 237
    receiving the light of, 240
Chochmah, Binah, and *Da'at*, 201, 255, 257
choice, 243
circumcision, meaning of, 231
clarification of good from evil, 61–63, 103
community, 115, 203
    inner aspects of, 265
consciousness, 128
consciousness, states of, 112
    of this world, 70
created beings, 42, 181
    as measures of will to receive, 42, 49, 53, 96, 121, 123, 183, 190, 192
    as originating from *Ein Sof*, 192
    as receiving, 75
    as separate from the Creator, 49, 52, 183
    giving to the Creator, 74, 75
    perfection of, 96, 104
    worth of, 39–40, 101
Creation, 29, 48
    acts of, 27, 43, 94, 103
    as included within God, 28
    as new, 28, 42–43, 48. *See also yesh m'ayin*; *See also will to receive*
    completion of, 63, 83. *See also tikkun*, end of
    for humankind, 33
    nature of. *See will to receive*
    paradox of, 53, 58
    prior to, 42
    process of, 37–40
    source of, 28, 29. *See also Ein Sof*
Creator
    affinity of form with, 80, 92
    as all-inclusive, 93
    as cause of all our deeds, 173–177
    as eternal, 83
    as giving, 53, 58, 75, 123, 172–173. *See also purpose of creation*

Creator *(continued)*
    as not lacking anything, 51, 52, 58, 75, 183, 191
    as omnipotent, 28, 232
    as perfect, 20, 38, 57, 141, 151
    as responsible for creation, 38–39
    as root, 28, 173
    as single. *See Echad*
    as unknowable, 22
    knowledge of, 94
    loving-kindness of, 173
    need of, 234
    recognition of, 172, 177
    separation from, 51, 53, 58
    serving the, 164, 173–175

D

daily review, 198
dead
    and wills to receive for oneself alone, 143
    klipot as, 58, 140
    revival of. *See resurrection of the dead*
death, 19, 150
descent, 68
    definition of, 68–69
desire, 114. *See also lack*
    for *dvekut*, 246
difference of form
    as cause of shame, 74
    definition, 53, 78, 122
    in spiritual entities, 51–53
differences between people, 131–132
distance, spiritual. *See difference of form*
dog, 160
dvekut
    achievement of, 75–76, 79, 158, 238
    as choice of vessel, 128
    as *tikkun*, 212
    definition of, 96, 193
    desire for, 128, 160, 233

E

Echad, 93–94
economic systems, 59, 106–107, 180
ego, 102, 104, 198, 211
egoism, 91, 203. *See also evil*; *See also will to receive for oneself alone*; *See also selfish love*
Ein Sof, 144
    and will to receive, 84
    as all-inclusive, 93
    as source for both body and soul, 121
    as source of Creation, 29, 192

Ein Sof (continued)
  light of, 29
Elazar, Rabbi, 38, 209
Eliezer, Rabbi, 88
enclothing, 124–130, 158, 196–198, 234
endeavor, 235
environment, 201–202
essence, 17–18, 51, 93, 111, 120. *See also God, essence*
ethics, 91
evil, 58, 152. *See also framework of uncleanness*
  as cause of pain, 91
  as sterile, 61
  recognition of, 89, 91–92
  transformation of, 97, 104, 177
excess, 151
exile, 89, 115
existence
  confused nature of, 61, 152
  maintenance of, 151–152

F

faith
  as a path, 229, 232
  as neccesity, 241
  as *tikkun* for the mind, 205, 232
  definition of, 111–112, 113
  in the future, 117, 119
  lack of, 232
  lessening of, 250
  measure of, 113
fear of God. *See Yirat Shamayim*
feelings, 59
  consonant with holiness, 173–174
  of being perfect, 235
  of despair, 114, 118, 174, 236
  of each other, 182
  of jealousy and envy, 180
  of self-pity, 152, 176
first modality of the vessel, 193
  and the soul, 194
four aspects of the vessel, 121, 178, 192, 193
four categories of work, 163–167
four-letter Name of God, 181, 187, 192, 193
four modalities, 178, 193
four modalities of the spiritual will to receive, 196
four modalities of the will to receive for oneself alone, 199–200, 206
fourth modality of the vessel, 68, 123–130, 178, 179, 194–195, 201
four worlds, 181, 187, 192

framework of holiness, 58–59
  and *Masach*, 123
  and souls, 80, 120, 153
  and spiritual entities of, 124
  as giving benefit, 76
  as source of blessing, 61
  in opposition of form to vessels of receiving, 148, 151
  prevailing over the framework of uncleanness, 62
  stages in, 236–238
framework of uncleanness, 30, 57–59, 80, 123. *See also worlds of uncleanness*
  and body, 64, 76, 111
  and *klipot*, 148–149
  and souls of the wicked, 241
  and will to receive for oneself alone, 58
  as separated from the Creator, 58
  maintaining existence, 151
free will, 88
fulfillment, 113
future. *See also Or Makif*
  as present, 83, 86, 116–119
  faith in the, 113, 117–119, 119
  of the world, 105

G

garments, 196, 200
gender in Kabbalah, 22, 32
general population, 235
generation, this, 255
  and revelation of the Kabbalah, 256, 258, 262
  darkness in, 250
generations
  earlier versus later, 258
giving, 69–70
  and framework of holiness, 76
  definition of, 47, 77
  difficulty in, 161–162
  intention in, 74–75. *See intentions*
  to God, 246
  with the intention of receiving, 164
God. *See also Creator*
  and framework of evil, 30, 59, 242
  as Good, 23, 97, 105, 112, 241, 246
  concealment of, 221, 232, 236
  delight of in creation, 245
  essence of, 27, 51
  Names of, 22, 28, 166, 181, 190–191
God's providence, 166, 175–177, 221–222
  concealment of, 229
  denial of, 176

287

Index

God's providence *(continued)*
   perception of, 92–93, 238–239, 242
   revealed, 238–239
godliness, 196
good, 97. *See light*
grace, 234, 239
group, 203

H
habits, 212
haca'ah, 123–130
Haman, 88
Hamnuna Saba, Rav
   Letters of, 59–63
happiness, 67
hashgaha pratit. *See God's providence*
hate
   and opposition of form, 122
heart, 205
   hardening of, 235
help, 213, 219, 243
help of God, 235
higher
   as innermost, 196
   definition of, 69
holiness, 128. *See also kedushah*
holocaust, 265
holographic nature of reality, 196, 206, 249–250
houses, 196, 200
human
   and purpose of creation, 182
   as center of creation, 104, 105, 199, 244–245
   as whole, 244
   creation of, 104
   in framework of holiness, 151
   in framework of uncleanness, 151
   nature of, 51, 96, 103–104, 160, 199, 246
   potential, 243
   sustenance of, 199
   work of, 182
human appetites, 131, 199
humanity, 262

I
imagery, 251
inanimate modality, 178–179, 181, 196–200, 249
   level of Torah, 207, 218, 249
   light of, 206, 217, 218
   of will to receive, 213, 229
   purification of, 237

individual, 115
   affecting the world, 261–265
   innermost part of, 261, 265
   nations of the world within, 261
inner aspect, 261
inner work, 14, 113–118, 114
   stages in, 235, 245–246
intellectual knowledge, 132
intention, 69–70, 163, 211
   achievement of, 219
   clarification of, 164
   of giving benefit, 74
   practising without, 206
   purifying of, 154, 157, 164
intentions and hidden Torah, 70
Israel, 161, 173, 261–266, 263
   elevation or degradation of, 262–264

J
jealousy, 180
Joshua, Rabbi 88
joy, 112, 182
   a necessity of life, 118

K
Kabbalah
   accessiblity of, 15
   as inner wisdom of Judaism, 13
   language of, 137–139. *See also language of the branches*
   learning of, 15, 72, 250, 258
   revelation of, 256
kedushah, 128. *See also holiness*
Keter, 187, 206
klipot
   and fourth modality of the will to receive, 126
   and lack, 63
   as sustained by God, 57
   dead, 58
   definition of, 149
   lights of, 30, 149
knowledge, thirst for, 199–200, 231

L
lack, 112–114
   necessity of, 113
language of the branches, 29, 137–139
learning the Kabbalah, 131
learning Torah, 225–226
left-hand side, 88, 117, 155
   (also left-hand line), 112

life, human
    part four, 158, 159
    part one, 147–153
    parts of, 147
    part three, 158
    part two, 153–158
    work of, 160
light. *See also Ein Sof*; *See also Or Pnimi, Or Makif, Or Elyon*
    and pleasure, 41, 190
    as emanation, 41–42, 49, 54, 121, 122, 191, 192. *See also yesh m'yesh*
    as unity, 189
    definition of, 41, 47, 64, 65, 121, 180, 191
    flow of, 172
    has desire of giving, 79, 122, 192
    highest, 29
    measure of, 176, 182
    received within will to receive, 42, 49, 172, 176, 191
    relationship with vessel, 217, 234
light of *Chassadim* (loving-kindness), 62, 193
    with the illumination of *Chochmah*, 194
light of *Chochmah* (wisdom), 62
lights in spiritual entity, 255
love
    and affinity of form, 122
    for one's fellow, 107, 210–212
    for the Creator, 107, 155–156, 210–211, 221, 234
lower, 69

M
macrocosm and microcosm, 226, 249, 262
Maimonides (Rambam), 94, 208, 212
Malchut, 187–190, 194, 206
    as allowing good and evil, 175
    as *Yirat Shamayim*, 113
    light of, 218
    of *Assiyah*, 208, 237
    of spiritual entities, 123–130
    rectification of, 104
    sweetend by *Binah*, 231
Malchut of the *Ein Sof*, 121, 127
    and *tzimtzum*, 128
    as origin of the *Challal Panui*, 128
    desiring affinity of form, 144–145
male, 22
Masach, 123–130
material, 64, 68
materialization, 71
Meir, Rabbi, 116

Messiah
    period of, 255
    spirit of, 264
    waiting for, 115–118
Meyuchad, 93–95
middle line, 89
mind, 205, 231
mitzvah
    light within, 210, 220
    love your neighbor, 210
mitzvot
    as actual, 209, 238
    as path, 71
    as potential, 209
    between person and fellow, 73, 107–108, 211–212
    between person and God, 73, 211
    content of, 73, 213
    number of, 74, 208–209
    performed for oneself alone, 264
    practical aspect of, 211, 258, 261
    practised with intention of giving, 75, 166
    purpose of, 74–75, 190, 211
    reasons for, 219
    reward of, 238
Moses
    and faith, 113, 232
    our Teacher, 74–75
    song of, 113

N
Nachmanides (Ramban), 94
Name of God, 181. *See also God, Names of*
    belief in, 242
nations, or nations of the world, 159, 173, 261–265
    innermost aspects of, 265
    outer aspects of, 263
nature of humans, 160, 161, 164. *See will to receive*
    and Creator, 40
    and giving unconditionally, 75, 161, 174–175, 212
needs, 131–132
Nefesh
    as referring to the soul, 245
    enclothes *Malchut*, 205, 213
    enclothes point source of *Ruach*, 218, 243
    help for, 213
    meaning of, 218
    nature of light, 195, 217
    of *Assiyah*, 195, 217, 227, 243
    of holiness, 226, 241
    point source of, 153, 205–206, 208, 213–214

Index

Nefesh (continued)
    stage after body, 246
Nefesh, Ruach, Neshamah, Chayah, and *Yechidah*
    and will to give, 234
    need for, 235
    of *Assiyah,* 225
    of each world, 226–228
    of reality, 249
    of the *Sephirot,* 196, 218
    of the soul, 142, 182, 242
    of the worlds, 187
    originate in *Ein Sof,* 234
negativity, 114
Neshamah
    and *Sephirah* of *Binah,* 218
    as referring to the soul, 195, 245
    complete entity, 219
    light of *Briyah,* 187, 195
    of holiness, 226
    point source of, 219
    receiving by the soul, 240, 243, 246
New Age, 154

O

Olam haZeh. See world (this)
One, 84. See also *Echad*
opposition of form, 52–53, 57–59, 75, 148, 173, 192. See also *difference of form*
    definition of, 78
Or Chozer, 123–130
Or d'Chassadim, 193
Or Elyon, 123–130, 235
Or Makif, 116–118, 129, 225
Or Pnimi, 116–118, 129
ourselves
    as perfect, 20, 38–40
outer aspect, 261

P

pain. *See suffering*
Papa, Rav, 257
parable of the animal with the ulcer, 150
parable of the blind men, 250
parable of the father and the child, 171
parable of the garden, 90
parable of the host and the guest, 77–78, 124–125
parable of the King and his subjects, 221
parable of the maidservant, 154–155
parable of the man with a knife, 94–95
parable of the merchant, 116–117
parable of the mother teaching the child to walk, 235
parable of travel to Jerusalem, 165
parallel reality, 112
parts of life. *See life, human: parts of*
partzufei kedushah, 123. See also *spiritual entities*
    body aspect, 124
    head aspect, 124
path of consciousness, 90–91. See also *Torah and mitzvot*
path of suffering, 91
patience, 221
Perush haSulam, 13, 34, 251
phenomenon of the lion and the dog, 159
physicality, 71
physical needs, 66
plant modality, 179, 182, 196–200
    level of Torah, 218, 249
    light of, 206, 218, 219
    of the framework of holiness, 238
    purification of, 219, 237
pleasure
    and purpose of creation, 40–43, 47–48
    and will to receive, 43, 48
    as consequence of light, 43
    as father of life, 149–150
    experience of, 40, 42–43, 150
    of separation, 150
point source, 205, 206, 214
    613 limbs of, 207–208, 213
    of every stage, 214
positivity, 114, 119
potential aspect, 209
prayer, 112, 234, 236, 242, 264
pride, 148
punishment, 238
purification of the vessel, 196. See also *will to receive for oneself alone, purification of*
purpose of creation, 27, 47–48
    and will to receive, 41, 57, 64, 141, 180
    consequence of, 40, 42, 74, 113
    definition of, 40, 47, 80, 190, 192. See also *pleasure*
    fulfillment of, 142, 159, 167, 171–172, 181, 196
    importance of knowing, 37, 40, 119
purpose of life, 115, 118

R

Rav, 88, 257
reality
    as branches from higher root, 149
    new, 28

Index

reality, chain of, 18–20
receiving, 69–70
    at end of *tikkun*, 85
    definition of, 47
    intention in. *See intentions*
receiving for oneself alone, 19, 164
receiving with the intention of giving, 74, 77–79, 111
rectification. *See tikkun*
redemption, 115, 262, 266
reincarnation, 208
relationships, 49, 52–53, 59, 63, 106–107
religious Jew, 73–74, 107
resurrection of the dead, 31, 140–142, 159
revival of the dead. *See resurrection of the dead*
reward, 164, 175
reward and punishment, 173, 175–176
right-hand side, 88, 118
    (also right-hand line), 112, 155
    necessity of, 114–115, 119
righteous one. *See Tzaddik*
Ruach, 219
    613 spiritual limbs of, 218, 219
    and world of *Yetzirah*, 187
    enclothes point source of *Neshamah*, 219
    light of, 218–219, 238, 255
    of holiness, 226
    point source of, 214
    stage of soul, 195, 246

S

second modality of the vessel, 193, 195
second nature, 212. *See also will to give benefit*
secrets of the Torah, 116, 233–234
secular Jew, 72–73, 107
Sefer ha Yetzirah, 94
self-esteem, 186
self deception, 165, 233
selfish love. *See also ego, egoism, will to receive for oneself alone*
    acting from, 115, 118, 160
    as evil, 58
    as inborn nature, 164, 203, 234
    consciousness of, 234
    light of, 91, 152
    practising Torah and *mitzvot* from, 165
    releasing of, 75, 90
sensual will to receive, 205
separation. *See also materialization*
    caused by pleasure, 150
    definition of, 51, 64–65, 79, 123

separation *(continued)*
    from God, 51, 58, 148, 177, 238
    growth of, 150
Sephirah
    as divine vessel, 217
    light of, 217
Sephirot, the ten, 186–189
    and the four modalities, 194
    correspondence with four-letter Name of God, 181, 192
    definition, 123, 130
    found at every level of reality, 206
    lights of, 196, 258
    vessels of, 258
service, 205
serving God, 173, 233
    as cause of pleasantness, 91
shame, 74–75
shattering of the vessels, 148
Shechinah, 154–155, 210, 264
Shimon Bar Yochai, 251–252
Shmuel, 88, 257
similarity of form. *See affinity of form*
sin, 97
    bitterness of, 239
    consequence of, 166, 238
    definition of, 230, 233
sitra achra. *See framework of uncleanness*
society, 59, 106–107
soul
    acquisitions of, 133–134
    and completion of *tikkun*, 84, 85
    and framework of holiness, 76, 80, 120, 217
    and God's light, 54
    and happiness, 67, 83
    and will to give benefit, 85, 120, 131, 234
    and will to receive, 41, 48, 52, 190
    as center of every world, 200
    as eternal, 133
    as part of God, 29–30, 30, 51, 54
    as separated from God, 51, 52–54, 58
    associated with body, 76, 80, 158, 195, 234
    as spiritual entity, 133
    awareness of, 13
    degrees of, 142, 158, 182, 195, 245. *See also Nefesh, Ruach, Neshamah, Chayah, and Yechidah*
    expression of, 131–133
    nourishment of, 200
    originates from *Ein Sof*, 194

291

Index

soul *(continued)*
   potential, 205, 206. *See also point source*
   states of, 83, 85–87, 142. *See also state one, state two and state three*
   tikkun of, 80, 141, 145
souls
   community of, 19, 208, 249
   incarnation of, 256–257
speaking modality, 179, 196–200
   level of Torah, 249
   light of, 218, 220
   purification of, 220, 240
   spiritual, 65, 66–68
spiritual entities, 255. *See also partzufei kedushah*
   body part of, 128, 255
   definition of, 128
   development of, 256
   differences between, 133
   head part of, 128, 255
   lights of, 255
   of the framework of holiness, 124
   tail of, 255
   vessels of, 255
spirituality, 68
   no compulsion in, 127, 183
   not having time or space, 87
spiritual stage, 246
   completion of, 208
spoiling, 64
state one, 85–86, 101, 111, 120, 142
state three, 85–86, 102. *See also tikkun, end of*
   as already attained, 111, 225
   inevitability of, 89, 105, 120, 142
state two, 85–87, 101
stumbling blocks, 230
suffering
   and separation, 51
   as path, 88–92
   come to the world, 265
   from lack of bounty, 152
   from not understanding, 205
   purpose of, 90, 94, 105, 106
   source of, 92–93, 96
survival, 199
sustenance, 113, 199

T

Talmud Eser haSephirot, 50
tav. *See* ת

teshuvah
   as a stage, 233, 238–239
   definition of, 166, 230, 233
   for love for God, 96, 221
   measure of, 230
third modality of the vessel, 193–194, 195, 201
thirteen, age, 71, 76, 141, 153, 206
thought of creation. *See purpose of creation*
thoughts, 59, 131
Tiferet, 187–190, 194, 206, 218
   of *Assiyah*, 218, 237
tikkun, 74–75
   of Creation, 61–62, 79, 80, 103–104, 167
   of individual, 104, 162, 205
tikkun, end of, 62
   as already existing, 83–85
   time required for, 88–92
   what it will be like, 105, 141, 177
Torah
   as hidden, 70, 261, 263
   as revealed, 70, 258
   essence of, 72
   eyes opened in, 233
   for its own sake. *See Torah, for its own sake*
   innermost part of, 265
   learning of, 72–73, 226
   not for its own sake. *See Torah, not for its own sake*
   transforming power of, 72, 97
   wisdom of, 258
Torah, for its own sake
   as stage, 219
   as truth, 165–166
   definition of, 154–155
   experience as path, 235
   leading to affinity of form, 75–76
   practice of, 212
   reward of, 116, 241–242
Torah, not for its own sake
   as a lie, 165, 264
   as leading to Torah for its own sake, 163–165, 229, 234
   as stage, 163–165
   definition, 79, 154
   importance of, 154–157
Torah and *mitzvot*
   as path of conciousness, 88–92
   content of, 71
   healing spice of, 185, 190, 212
   intention in, 206

Torah and *mitzvot* (continued)
  practice of, 80, 96, 153, 154, 162, 207, 218, 221. *See also Torah, for its own sake, and Torah, not for its own sake*
  reward of, 160
transition from *Nefesh* to *Ruach*, 229
Tree of Knowledge
  as first sin, 231
  as *Malchut*, 175
  consequence of, 19, 148–152
truth, 112, 165. *See also left-hand side*
Tzaddik
  as opposed to evil one, 61, 63
  definition of, 239
  first stage of, 79, 158, 219
  perception of, 13, 21
  relationship of student with, 13
  work of, 221–222
Tzimtzum, 123–130, 145

U

understanding, 63, 92–93, 116, 186
  and will to receive, 205
  as opposed to faith, 232
  of Divine Providence, 175
  of *mitzvot*, 209–210, 219
  the language of Kabbalah, 138
union, 126–130
unity. *See affinity of form; d'vekut; Echad; Creator as single*
ups and downs, 112, 173, 229, 236–237

V

vessel. *See also will to receive*
  as defining light, 189
  as empty of light, 122
  completed, 124, 142, 145, 194. *See also zivug d'haca'ah*
  definition of, 41, 47, 49, 64–65, 65, 113, 180, 182, 191
  development of, 180, 192–194
  has desire of receiving, 79, 121–122, 192
  nullified by the light, 193
  of giving benefit. *See will to give benefit*
vessels in spiritual entity, 255

W

whole entity, 150, 210
  revealed by its individual parts, 262
wicked
  and framework of uncleanness, 241
  as dead, 58

will to give benefit, 193, 195
  and framework of holiness, 58, 79
  and light of *Chassadim*, 62, 193
  and soul, 85, 246
  as second nature, 212
  as spiritual, 66
  as vessel for lights of the soul, 234
  attainment of, 186
  definition of, 79
  difficulty of, 234
  for the sake of giving benefit, 79, 167
  obtaining the, 160, 233
  to one's fellow, 106
will to give with the intention of receiving, 79, 164
will to receive
  and commensurate pleasure, 41–43, 48, 49, 57, 142, 182, 190
  as cause of separation from the Creator, 53, 54, 58, 123
  as consequence of purpose of creation, 41–42, 42, 48, 53, 57, 64, 141, 180.
  as evil, 57. *See also will to receive for oneself alone*
  as nature of humans, 42–43
  as root of all created beings, 41, 49, 53, 190, 193
  as sole material of creation, 42, 44, 48, 49, 142, 191
  as vessel, 41, 43, 47, 53, 121
  as vessel for the light, 54, 57, 143, 191
  complete, 121, 154, 162, 181, 192–193, 195. *See also fourth modality of the vessel*
  contraction of. *See Tzimtzum*
  development of, 180, 192, 192–194
  emotional, 67
  included within the light, 121, 180, 190–191
  manifestation of, 49, 131
  materialization of, 64–68, 180, 191
  mental, 67
  not found in essence of Creator, 48, 52
  physical, 66, 147, 153
  spiritual, 67, 153, 157
  tikkun of, 80, 83, 141, 159, 196, 207. *See also tikkun*
will to receive for oneself alone. *See also framework of uncleanness; See also opposition of form*
  and framework of uncleanness, 58, 74, 76, 141, 150
  and state two, 142
  as body, 66, 101, 105, 133, 148
  as cause of separation, 74, 151, 176
  as cause of suffering, 95, 97, 105
  as contracted, 69, 176, 185–186
  as evil, 74, 203
  as forbidden, 231

293

Index

will to receive for oneself alone *(continued)*
    as innate nature of created beings, 96
    as root of all sin, 231
    as root of low self-esteem, 186
    as stumbling block, 232, 233
    as transient, 101, 105, 133
    consequences of, 106, 160
    definition, 79
    for material things, 147
    four modalities of, 199, 249. *See also four modalities*
    giving to, 261
    growth of, 147, 150, 152–153, 161–163, 178, 180
    in spirituality, 153–154, 161–163
    necessity of, 101–102, 162
    objects to the will to give benefit, 234
    purification of. *See also teshuvah*
        and affinity of form, 246
        as complete stage, 229
        as process, 236–238
        at the end of the *tikkun*, 141–143
        causing attraction of holy soul, 76, 80–81
        difficulty of, 162, 174
        help with, 203
        through suffering, 88. *See also suffering, as path*
        through Torah and *mitzvot*, 71, 76, 158, 233. *See also Torah and mitzvot as path of consciousness*
will to receive in order to give pleasure to the Creator, 167
    and affinity of form, 83, 142
    and the redemption, 263
    as complete measure, 176
    as desired by the vessel of the *Ein Sof*, 145
    as fulfillment of the purpose of creation, 80
    as perfection of the human being, 96, 159
world(s)
    as parallel, 87, 112
    creation of, 145, 171–172, 176, 182
    evolvement of, 84, 127
    make-up of, 186, 200
    need for, 186, 242, 244
    of holiness and uncleanness, 58
    of uncleanness, 61
    relationship to each other, 149, 178, 196, 200
    spiritual, 181
world (this), 76
    as physical, 149, 198
    as spiritual entity, 256
    as whole, 97, 105, 255
    completion of, 257

world (this) *(continued)*
    consciousness of, 65–70, 164
    difference from upper worlds, 180, 191
    elevation or degradation of, 262
    klipot in, 148
    outer aspect of, 265
    stages of, 255

Y

Yachid, 93–95
Yechidah
    light of, 187, 220
Yehudah, Rav, 257
yesh m'ayin, 42–43, 65, 161, 191–192
yesh m'yesh, 41–42, 65, 191–192
Yetzirah, 187, 194, 195, 237
    ascension to, 237
Yirat Shamayim, 113, 155–156, 173, 221

Z

zachut, 159–160, 190
zivug, 129. *See also union*
zivug d'haca'ah, 129
Zohar, 34
    as central text of Kabbalah, 13
    author of, 251
    commentary on. *See Perush haSulam*
    focus on soul, 199
    Introductions to, 13
    revelation of, 255
    study of, 251, 262, 266

Index of Excerpts

Bircat Shalom (Sefer haMa'amarim), 74–75, 113–120, 159–167, 172–173, 173–175, 203, 210–211, 230–236, 245–247

Hakdamah l'Panim Meirot u'Masbirot, 19–20, 148–152

HaSulam, 90–91, 205

In the Shadow of the Ladder, 21, 23, 23–24, 31–32, 47, 78–79, 102–103, 208

Mavo l'Zohar, 17–18, 18, 187–188, 199–201

Matan Torah, 27, 58, 73, 91–92, 202, 211–212

Petichah l'Chochmat haKabbalah 28, 41–42, 53, 64–65, 68, 77–78, 122–127, 180–181, 190–196

   Or Shalom on the *Petichah l'Chochmat haKabbalah*, 42–43, 65–66, 68–70, 71–72

Siddur, 30

Talmud, 33, 38, 88, 257

Talmud Eser haSephirot,
   Hakdamah l'Talmud Eser haSephirot, 92, 156–157, 221–222, 238–239
   Etz Chayim, 21–22, 27, 29, 84, 144
     Or Pnimi on the *Etz Chayim*, 49, 84, 87, 121–122, 144–145, 182–183
    Histaclut Pnimit, 93–94, 137–139
     Or Shalom on the *Histaclut Pnimit*, 94–95

Zohar, 28, 32, 32, 60, 62, 83, 83, 96, 140, 155–156, 225, 240, 243, 243–244
   Perush haSulam on the *Zohar*, 60–62, 62–63, 88–89, 96–97, 103–104, 175–177, 209–210, 225, 240–242, 264
   Petichah l'Perush haSulam, 189–190
   Or Baruch on the *Hakdamah l'Sefer haZohar*, 72, 207

Yedidah Cohen

Yedidah Cohen, together with her late husband Mark, studied the work of Rabbi Ashlag with a pupil of Rabbi Baruch Shalom Halevi Ashlag. For the last ten years she has been leading study groups on the work of Rabbi Ashlag, in both Hebrew and English. The members of her groups come from all parts of the Jewish spectrum, and she has introduced this work to young people as well. For a long time she broadcast talks on the Kabbalah of Rabbi Ashlag on Israel National Radio and she has also given seminars at the Gifted Children's College in the School for Science and Technology at Tel Hai, Kiryat Shmoneh in northern Israel.

"I see the healing within ourselves and the healing in relationships that takes place as the learning progresses. I admire the efforts made by the students as they strive to put their understanding into their daily lives, and I am filled with awe and happiness."

Yedidah may be reached via the web-site **www.nehorapress.com** which is fast developing into a resource center for those who are interested in the work of Rabbi Ashlag. You can find ten-minute talks on the application of the learning of Kabbalah to specific aspects of our lives, and you can find support for establishing study groups. The web-site is constantly evolving.